Innovation Economy

True Stories of Start-Ups, Flame-Outs, and Inventing the Future in New England

By Scott Kirsner

Cover design by Anne-Margaux Drew
Photos throughout are republished courtesy of their owners.
© 2021 Scott Kirsner. All Rights Reserved.

For a map of key places mentioned in this book, visit
http://bit.ly/innoeco-map

Table of Contents

Introduction	1
1. How Things Work Here	
The Secret to Boston's Innovation Economy	4
A Cambridge Courtyard at the Center of the Action	7
The Story of an Acquisition, in a Fishbowl	10
Kendall Square's Transition from Building Railroad Cars to Discovering New Drugs	13
Singing the Praises of a No-Frills Building on Kingston Street	17
A Microcosm of the Biotech Industry in One Building	21
Turning the Lights Back on in a Chelsea Factory	25
Gifts of Invention and Ingenuity	28
2. Links Between Today and the Past	
How Cambridge Became the Life Sciences Capital	32
The Wizards of '78	35
From a Factory in Peabody to the Surface of the Moon	39
The Incredible Endurance of the Shoe Biz	42
The Mystery of the Last Candy Factory	46
In Boston, the Keynote to Apple's Turnaround	50
YankeeIngenuity.com	53
What Happened to the Real Animal House	61

3. Failures, Conflicts & Challenges

What Happens When Startups Go South	66
A Bold Attempt to Reinvent Solar Power	69
On Founders, Venture Capitalists, and Competition	72
The Intern Who Started a $9 Billion Company	76
Y Combinator, WebInno, and Support for Fledgling Ventures	79
Two Duffel Bags, a Shovel, and the Hunt for a Breakthrough Cancer Drug	83
Getting a License Plate for a Flying Car	86
Waking Up from a Biofuel Dream	90
The Columnist and His Critic Hash Things Out	93

4. The Valley

Over 36 Hours, a Glimpse of What Fuels the Silicon Valley Simulation Machine	98
Why Facebook Went West	103

5. Profiles & Interviews

Tim Berners-Lee, the Web's Creator	108
Dean Kamen, Inventor & Cultural Commando	114
Ray Kurzweil, Immortal	126
Joe Caruso, Angel Investor	129

6. True Crime

Catch Me if You Can	133
Murder by Internet	145

7. Robotics

Making Robots, with Dreams of Henry Ford	162
Before Robots Rise, They Have to Master the Stairs	167
Can the World's Most Successful Maker of Robot Videos Go Mass Market?	170
Betting a Quarter-Billion Dollars on More Efficient Warehouses	173

8. Looking Ahead

I Chucked It All and Became a Turker	177
Microbes that Can Do the Dirty Work	180
Printing the Future	184
The Hottest Class at MIT	187

9. The Pandemic Year

How One Layoff Played Out, from Two Perspectives	191
She Bought an RV and Hit the Road to Raise Money	195
Will COVID Kill Cities?	198
A Tweet That Paved a New Path for Blacks in Tech	201
Moderna: 'When the Spotlight Found Them, They Were Ready'	204

10. Fun Stuff

Tin Toy	208
DNA-Testing Louie, the Mystery Mutt	211
Four Centuries of Massachusetts Innovation: The Quiz	214
A Freedom Trail for Innovators	217

About the Author   222

Introduction

My career as a journalist started the day I quit the Boston *Globe*, in the spring of 1997.

I had been building websites and developing online strategy for the newspaper; I also sold the first ad for the *Globe*'s first website, after being sent to knock on doors along Newbury Street. But I couldn't figure out a way to move from the digital division into a writing job in the newsroom. I started to line up freelance assignments and gave my notice, hoping that checks would start showing up in the mail fast enough. My first goal was to earn enough to cover the $900 monthly rent on my North End apartment.

I managed to do that, and then spent the next 23-plus years writing about the challenges of entrepreneurship, and of shepherding new discoveries out of the lab and into the real world, in publications like *Wired, Fast Company*, the New York *Times, Newsweek*, the San Jose *Mercury News, Variety, The Hollywood Reporter, CIO* magazine, and *Boston* magazine. The work felt to me like an extended grad school program that I was getting paid to participate in. I traveled to the White House, the Google-plex, the Summer Olympics in Athens, Hollywood backlots, Amazon's headquarters, and the underground lair beneath Walt Disney World. It was always fun, whether I was exchanging holiday gifts with Jeff Bezos (for a story; we're not pals) or shooting the breeze in Morgan Freeman's trailer between takes of a movie.

But my steadiest gig started in 2000, when I went to lunch with Peter Mancusi, then the *Globe*'s business editor, and he asked me whether I'd consider writing a weekly column covering Boston's dot-com boom. Initially it was called "@large." As the internet boom fizzled out, I expanded my scope to medical devices, biotech, robotics, and every other sector I found interesting, from toymaking to snowmaking.

When I moved to California for a few years, the column downshifted from weekly to monthly. But when I returned to Cambridge in 2007, we changed the name to "Innovation Economy," to reflect my broadened focus, and it began running in the Sunday paper. By my estimate, I've written more than 1000 columns for the *Globe*.

A few principles have guided me. First, try to explain new technology or science the way that you would if you wanted a neighbor to understand it at a backyard barbecue. Second, whenever you can, dig like an archaeologist to understand the things that came before. Finally, respect the entrepreneur, even when you're pointing out potential potholes, because starting a new venture and keeping it alive is incredibly tough work.

I'm grateful for my readers, my sources, and great editors and mentors like Mark Pothier, Shirley Leung, Rob Weisman, Larry Edelman, Caleb Solomon, Ande Zellman, Bill Taylor, Alan Webber, Lew McCreary, Katrina Heron, Greg Huang, and Rob Gavin. Thanks to Dan Bricklin for the idea of creating a map to highlight all of the key places I mention in the book (at http://bit.ly/innoeco-map). My family, especially Amy and Max, has provided endless support, love, and laughter.

These are a few of my favorite stories about the founders, the innovators, the investors, the criminals, and what Henri Termeer, the late CEO of Genzyme, once described to me as the incredibly innovative soil here in New England. It's like no other place on earth.

Scott Kirsner
January 1, 2021
Brookline, Mass.

1. How Things Work Here

The Secret to Boston's Innovation Economy

Published in the Boston Globe, June 1, 2018

This week, Boston plays host to two major gatherings: more than 16,000 biotech and pharma executives attending the annual BIO International Convention, and approximately 250 US city mayors, who are taking part in the US Conference of Mayors.

What might I tell a biotech entrepreneur from Berlin, or a mayor from Missouri, about the things that make Boston's innovation economy work — and some of the things that could still use improvement?

We like our history in Boston, and you need to go back to the 1630s to understand the foundation of what exists today — when the first public school in America was founded here, and when the state Legislature appropriated the first 400 pounds sterling for a "schoale or colledge." The former institution, Boston Latin School, is regularly ranked as one of the top 50 high schools in the country, and has produced several presidents of the latter institution: Harvard University.

A few centuries later, we can lay claim to the most educated workforce in the United States, and a cluster of universities — including newbies like Tufts (1852) and MIT (1861) — that pull in hundreds of millions of dollars of philanthropic donations and federal grants annually to support their research.

But even by burning that cash to fuel scientific breakthroughs in university labs, you don't automatically get job creation or economic value. Plenty of universities have file cabinets full of patents that do nothing. You need entrepreneurially minded students and professors, and investors willing to give them money to transform a breakthrough research paper into a real business. Alexander Graham Bell was a professor at Boston University when he invented the telephone in 1876.

Georges Doriot was a professor at Harvard Business School in 1946, the year he founded American Research and Development, one of the earliest venture capital firms in the United States. Its biggest home run was a computer maker called Digital Equipment Corp., founded by MIT alumni. Digital's success helped create the Route 128 technology corridor in Boston's suburbs. At one point, it was the second biggest technology company in the world, after IBM.

From the 1970s on, university researchers here began unraveling the secrets of DNA and RNA — racking up a few

Nobel Prizes in the process. That led to another wave of innovation and spinout companies. Biogen, Genzyme (now Sanofi Genzyme), and Alnylam Pharmaceuticals all trace their roots to academic research. They employ thousands of people, generate billions of dollars in revenue, and are clustered a short walk from the Kendall Square T stop.

In the 1980s, the neighborhood was known as "AI Alley" for all of the MIT-spawned startups that were making artificial intelligence software. The name "Genetown" was floated but never stuck.

Today, there are biotech companies everywhere — they even fill the old brick building on Cambridge's Main Street, right, where Alexander Graham Bell's assistant, Thomas A. Watson, set up a telephone for the first demonstration of a long-distance, two-way phone call.

Much of the enthusiasm in the 'hood in 2018 is about being able to "edit out" disease-causing errors in our genetic code, adjusting the microbial colony that lives on us and in our guts to treat diseases, or stimulating the body's immune system to fight cancer, says Pearl Freier, founder of the advisory firm Cambridge BioPartners.

Joost Bonsen, a lecturer at MIT's Media Lab, notes that as new kinds of software and robotic automation technology are introduced to scientific labs, they might be accelerating scientific progress. The "rate-limiting step is no longer how long it will take you to run the experiment," Bonsen says, "but what better experiments can you think of to run?"

Since 2012 — the last time that BIO came to Boston — the local biotech ecosystem has been on fire. According to the Massachusetts Biotechnology Council, in 2012, venture capital firms invested about $900 million into startup companies here. Last year, that figure was $3 billion.

In 2012, one of these firms, Boston-based Third Rock Ventures, had put money into about 26 companies, which occupied about 400,000 square feet of office and laboratory space locally, according to Cynthia Clayton, the firm's head of communications. By the time this year's convention begins, Clayton says Third Rock will have helped launch about 50 companies that occupy 1.3 million square feet of space around town.

Proximity matters, which is why companies pay a premium to be in Cambridge. Professors need to find it easy to visit the startups they start, venture capitalists to visit companies they fund, and everyone else has to be close by — making it easy to meet over lunch or coffee to keep one another apprised of their progress.

Phillip Sharp, a Nobel laureate, MIT professor, and a cofounder of Biogen and Alnylam, says that big pharmaceutical companies were once content to have their labs "hidden away in the countryside," in states like Connecticut, New Jersey, and Pennsylvania. "Now, the science is moving so fast, and the opportunities are emerging so fast, that being close to the heat is essential. That is how this whole industry is now structured." And it's why pharma giants like Pfizer, Novartis, and Bristol-Myers Squibb run research centers here. (At right, Biogen and Akamai buildings line Cambridge's Binney Street in a 2015 photo.)

The result is a city where newly formed startups have to hunt for affordable office space, and where all those university grad students and researchers working on the next generation of scientific breakthroughs have to hunt to find an affordable place to live, Bonsen notes. In the shadow of Boston's biotech boom are other problems — like income inequality, aging subways and packed highways, a dearth of skilled job candidates, and the inconvenient fact that many of these innovative companies create incredible drugs that prolong lives but often cost $100,000 or more. Those are complex challenges for policy makers and their constituents.

At first glance, mayors and biotech industry innovators might not have that much in common. But both are playing a long game — shaping cities, shepherding new treatments to market — that needs to be played with a sense of urgency. The next election, the next crisis, the next cash crunch is never far off. Voters and investors are perennially on the verge of being dissatisfied — or mutinous. And there are no quick fixes or simple answers.

You know you've won if you stay focused on the future, and in a few decades (or centuries), you look back and see something good in the rearview mirror.

A Cambridge Courtyard at the Center of the Action

Published in the Boston Globe, October 9, 2015

Most cities would kill for a meeting place as magical as the open brick courtyard behind the Charles Hotel. It's a simple enough spot: benches and planters, a portal leading to Harvard Square, and two restaurants with patios, Legal Seafoods and Henrietta's Table.

But it's the place where fast-growing startups like Recorded Future, which helps businesses anticipate cyberattacks, and Formlabs, which makes a 3D printer, first connected with investors. The travel site Kayak was born over a lunch at Legal's, the two founders agreeing to put in a million bucks each and toasting with gin and tonics. In the spring of 2004, two Harvard undergrads, Eduardo Saverin and Mark Zuckerberg, ate breakfast at an outdoor table at Henrietta's and talked to a junior venture capitalist about their month-old startup, Thefacebook. His Waltham firm, Battery Ventures, passed.

Oops.

Los Angeles has Hollywood & Highland, Manhattan has the Crossroads of the World, and Boston has the courtyard at the Charles Square complex. It's a place that holds a mirror to what we're good at, and how we could get even better.

Sitting on a bench in the courtyard on a recent Friday morning, checking my e-mail, I was greeted by venture capitalist Jo Tango. He told me about a lunch at Henrietta's that led to the formation of Vertica, a database software company acquired by Hewlett-Packard for $350 million in 2011. As we were talking, we noticed Paul Sagan, the former chief executive of Akamai Technologies and a member of the board of directors of EMC and VMware, crossing the plaza.

"Being open to possibility" is important as an investor, says Tango, who was coming from a meeting at General Catalyst

Partners, a venture capital firm located in the complex. "Some of my best deals have come from serendipity."

Paul English had a meeting at General Catalyst in December 2003, and afterward, one of the partners there introduced him to Steve Hafner, a co-founder of the travel site Orbitz who was working on a new idea. English and Hafner had lunch at Legal's. "Within 45 minutes, we agreed to become 50/50 partners" in the business that would become Kayak, English recalls. The company went public in 2012, and was acquired later that year by Priceline for $1.8 billion.

My favorite story about the courtyard involves another meal at Legal's. Mitch Kapor, the venture capitalist and founder of Lotus Development Corp., the company that popularized spreadsheets and collaboration software, was having dinner in 2011. At a table nearby, a pair of newly minted MIT grads were pitching a new 3-D printer to an executive from BestBuy's venture capital arm. Kapor tweeted, "Overhearing 2 entrepreneurs pitching low-end 3D printer to a VC."

After noticing the tweet, entrepreneurs David Cranor and Max Lobovsky arranged to meet Kapor. He eventually put money into their startup, Formlabs. (BestBuy didn't.) The company now employs 105 people. (At right, Formlabs founder Max Lobovsky in Charles Square with Dan Bricklin, inventor of the first spreadsheet software, VisiCalc.)

More recently, in 2013, former Zipcar CEO Scott Griffith had breakfast at Henrietta's – egg whites and wheat toast – with Jon McNeill, chief executive of the Needham software startup Enservio. The two decided to form Censio, a startup developing software that will run on mobile phones to monitor driving, and reward safer drivers with lower insurance rates. This week, Boston-based Censio announced its first $10 million in funding.

On a sunny fall morning, everything can seem perfect. But that's if you block out the elephant in the courtyard – missing Facebook.

"No one knew how to invest in college kids," says Larry Cheng, the venture capitalist who invited the founders to breakfast. His analysis of the fledgling company was that if everything went right, a social network for young people might be worth a few hundred million bucks to a company like Yahoo or

AOL. His firm, Battery Ventures, already invested in a social network called Friendster, opted not to put money into Facebook.

The resident venture capital firm in the complex, General Catalyst, has shifted its focus to New York and California in recent years. Of the dozen companies it showcases on its website, just two are headquartered in Boston. And why wouldn't you brag about putting money into Snapchat, Airbnb, and Warby Parker, the online specs merchant?

Where does that leave Boston? "We have great businesses here," says Cheng, now managing partner at Boston-based Volition Capital. "You could make an argument that pound-for-pound, our companies have more substance than many companies in other cities. But that doesn't create headlines. This is a great town for innovation and investment — other towns would love to have what we have."

I concur. But we still have a lot of work to do to create truly world-class clusters, make sure people outside of Boston know that they're world-class, and ensure that founders have the support they need to build great companies.

In life sciences, "we just are the center of that universe now, and you don't need to evangelize it," says Andy Palmer, an entrepreneur and investor who lives in a condo at Charles Square, and eats breakfast every morning at Henrietta's.

But in areas like robotics and digital health care, "a little effort and evangelism would go a long way," he says. In those areas, plus 3-D printing and design, big data and analytics, and cyber-security, we can do more to trumpet what's happening here.

I'd love to see a group of our most promising companies go on the offensive, organizing a recruiting trip to Silicon Valley or New York, highlighting the more reasonable cost of living and better public schools here. Palmer says our greatest deficiency is "big, independent pillar companies, built by entrepreneurs" - think Amazon, Google, or EMC, the Hopkinton data storage company. Those companies serve as role models to the next generation, Palmer says, sending the message that you, too, can build something big if you take a leap.

We're very good at starting things, taking ideas out of the lab, and sculpting them into companies. The scaling up, the drive to really dominate an industry sector over the long haul, is something we can get better at.

. . .

[Author's note: Austin-based Dell acquired EMC a few days after this column ran, paying $67 billion. To see where the Charles Courtyard is, along with other key locations mentioned in this book, visit http://bit.ly/innoeco-map.]

The Story of an Acquisition, in a Fishbowl

Published in the Boston Globe, June 9, 2013

This is the story of Puffer, a sprightly little pufferfish who lived in an office building in Cambridge. Puffer was the mascot of a company called Endeca. Every day, when the software developers would show up for work on the 15th floor, the first thing they would see when they got off the elevator was Puffer, swimming happily in her tank.

All the employees loved Puffer. They put her picture on posters that promoted companywide parties. And when she puffed up — which was not very often — people took pictures and e-mailed them to their co-workers. The employees who helped take care of Puffer, feeding her krill and algae, loved her even more. She would follow them whenever they walked past her tank, sometimes bonking into the glass.

But one day in 2011, one of the richest men in the world decided to buy Endeca. He paid more than $1 billion for the company, which created software to help businesses analyze their operations or organize the products sold on their websites. And that's when things changed for Puffer and her friends.

This is the story of Puffer, but it's also the story of those thousand tiny changes that big companies often make when they acquire smaller ones. And about how those changes often lead to the loss of the very same talent the big company hoped to bring on as part of the deal.

Puffer wound up at Endeca through happenstance. The fast-growing company was subletting a new office in East Cambridge in 2001, and the prior tenant "had a few things they were trying to sell us," recalls Ken Papa, Endeca's former head of facilities. "We got their pool table, their security system, a reception desk, their saltwater fish tank, and six fish for about $5,000."

No one remembers the other fish. But Puffer "became this cult legend at the company," says Papa, whose brother, Steve, founded Endeca. "When we had a party, she'd be on the posters wearing a sombrero and drinking a Corona," says Ken Papa.

When the company moved, first to Alewife, and then to Kendall Square, Puffer came, too, in a 5-gallon pail.

In October 2011, the California tech giant Oracle, run by billionaire Larry Ellison, announced it would acquire Endeca. Most of the company's administrative employees, including Ken Papa, were told they would no longer be needed after Endeca was integrated into Oracle.

"I knew I was losing my job," Papa says. "But I helped them out as best I could." One day, in a meeting with Oracle executives overseeing the integration of the two companies, they mentioned that Oracle has a no-animals policy at its offices.

Papa tried to persuade Oracle to leave the fish tank alone. It cost about $5,000 a year to have a vendor come in to clean the tank and deliver Puffer's food. "My advice was, if they took the pufferfish, it was going to make them look like bad guys," Papa said. "But they didn't heed my warnings."

The vendor helped Papa find another home for Puffer. In January 2012, Papa sent out an e-mail letting everyone know it was Puffer's last day at the company. Some came to say goodbye, but others said they couldn't bear to watch.

The tank just gathered dust. Then someone drew a picture of Puffer on the glass with a permanent marker. The tank "sat there empty as a reminder of the Endeca that was," says Rob McDonald, a former Endeca engineering director.

Plenty of other things changed at Endeca, many much more significant. Steve Papa no longer ran the company, and there were "more layers of management," says Steve Fredette, who oversaw Endeca's mobile products.

The old formula for calculating end-of-year bonuses, which everyone understood, was altered, and "it became fuzzier and unknown," says McDonald. There were new policies about which specific snacks and sodas could be stocked in Endeca's kitchen.

But among all the changes, Puffer's disappearance was the most visible. When employees announced that they were leaving, the fish often came up in their exit interviews. "I know it seems like a silly thing," says Rob Gonzalez, a former product manager at Endeca. "But the pufferfish was part of the family."

Endeca's 150 or so engineers were the company's crown jewel: They wrote the software and knew how to maintain it and make it better. Many of them stuck around for a while after the acquisition, trying to give it a shot even though they didn't consider themselves "big company" people, says Fredette.

But when McDonald and other ex-Endecans looked at an old employee list recently, they calculated that about two-thirds of the engineers had split since the Oracle purchase. Some, like Fredette, have started their own companies. McDonald is working for a Cambridge data analytics start-up, Hadapt. (Oracle declined to comment on anything related to Endeca or its policies pertaining to fish.)

Puffer moved to a retirement center, the Fall River Jewish Home, where she lived out her final days. She passed away peacefully around Christmas of last year, says Ed Warman, owner of Aqua Vision, the vendor that took care of Puffer's tank. Ken Papa knew that, but when a bunch of Endeca alumni got together last month for a Cinco de Mayo party, he didn't have the heart to tell them. Even for that party, Puffer's face was on the poster.

Oracle eventually decided to make an exception to its policy about animals, according to former Endeca employees. Perhaps a belated attempt to revive the team's *esprit de corps*? Oracle wouldn't say. There's a new saltwater tank in the middle of the office where the engineers work. But no Puffer.

. . .

[Author's Note: For a video of Puffer, visit https://vimeo.com/68068427]

Kendall Square's Transition from Building Railroad Cars to Discovering New Drugs

Published in the Boston Globe, October 3, 2014

The three-story brick building at the corner of Main and Osborn streets in Cambridge, on the edge of Kendall Square and the MIT campus, captures three distinct eras in the city's innovation history. In the early 1800s, it was the site of Kimball & Davenport, the first builder of passenger railroad cars in America. (In the photo at right, there are pieces of railroad track subtly embedded above the building's windows.)

After World War II, it was the epicenter of the Massachusetts tech boom, home to the office and private lab of Edwin Land, Polaroid's founder. In between, Thomas A. Watson strung a wire from Boston to Cambridge, and set up the equipment to receive the first "long distance" phone call, in 1876.

Today, the building at 700 Main Street is home to LabCentral, a nonprofit that rents space to 26 fledgling biotech companies. It is surrounded by new buildings and buildings under construction for the pharmaceutical giants Pfizer and Novartis. And one-year old LabCentral itself hopes to expand soon, more than doubling in size to about 70,000 square feet.

If Kendall Square in the 19th and 20th centuries was about manufacturing and then technology, in the 21st century it is definitively about life sciences — the business of discovering and developing new medicines. The neighborhood has reached a new inflection point in the past two years, with many more biotech companies and investors finding they can't afford not to have a presence there.

Meanwhile, growing tech companies are hopping — or getting pushed — across the river to Boston. As a result, Kendall Square has transitioned from tech to biotech center.

"It's dramatically different now," says Peter Hecht, chief executive of Ironwood Pharmaceuticals. "It's way past a tipping point."

If Nashville is the nexus of country music, and Hollywood the entertainment biz, Kendall Square is the global hub for transforming scientific insights into new drugs. How strong is the gravitational pull? For Pfizer, having scientists based at Alewife was just not close enough, so it built a new $300 million building and moved them to Kendall.

Last week, Illinois-based drug company Baxter International said it would rent space in Kendall for a research division that will employ about 400 people. In June, the chief executive of Paris-based Sanofi, which in 2011 paid $20 billion for the biotech firm Genzyme, said he was relocating to Cambridge. Almost every new construction project underway in the neighborhood involves office or lab space for the biopharma business, which assumes that more big players will follow — and today's young start-ups will grow.

What actually happens inside the R&D hive of today's Kendall Square? Everything from early academic work into the origins of disease and the best ways to attack it, through venture capital funding, company formation, and the partnerships between small companies and large ones that provide the money to keep developing a drug, test it in humans, and eventually sell it.

What doesn't happen in Kendall? Running those human trials, since there isn't a hospital, and manufacturing, packaging, and distributing the drugs.

The building that houses Wendy Winckler's lab is part of the Technology Square complex; it once housed companies like Polaroid, the supercomputer maker Thinking Machines, and the Massachusetts Institute of Technology's computer science and artificial intelligence labs. (Before that, there was a soap factory on the site.)

Now, Winckler's Next Generation Diagnostics lab at Novartis uses computers and DNA sequencers to better understand tumors. Tumor tissue is shipped to the lab encased in paraffin wax, sliced thin, and put onto slides so technicians can separate tumor cells from normal cells. Technicians then use special equipment like a nucleic acid extractor — a bit smaller than a microwave, but costing $700,000 — to remove and sequence tumor cells' DNA.

The objective is to better understand different types of tumors so more precise treatments for individual patients can be prescribed. "The hope is that we'll be able to see more lasting effects with these approaches — and hopefully cures," Winckler says.

About 37 people work in Winckler's lab, about half managing the data spit out of the sequencers. By late next year, the group will move into a vast new Novartis campus that will stretch from Massachusetts Avenue to Main Street, effectively connecting Kendall Square and the University Park biotech complex to the north of MIT. Novartis, a Swiss firm, was one of the first "big pharma" companies to put down stakes in Cambridge, in 2002.

As more players come to Kendall, rents for office space are creeping toward $70 per square foot, says Roy Hirshland of the commercial real estate firm T3 Advisors. Many growing tech companies are considering less expensive office space near North and South Stations and in Downtown Crossing, Hirshland says, leaving Kendall to life sciences and a few bigger tech companies, like Google and Microsoft.

So why are biotechs willing to pay? "The networking is an intangible," says Nick Leschly, chief executive of Bluebird Bio, which moved into a new building near the CambridgeSide Galleria last year. "I go with my laptop and sit at Fuji in the afternoon, and I meet four people that I'd been meaning to see."

When I interviewed Michael Gilman, a serial biotech entrepreneur who works a few blocks away, he had just returned from a board meeting in the building that houses Fuji, a Japanese restaurant. The building was originally built for the tech company Palm Computing in the early 2000s, but Palm never moved in. Today it houses three biotechs.

Gilman's latest company, Padlock Therapeutics, hopes to develop drugs for autoimmune diseases. It has raised several million dollars in seed funding, and, if it can prove its approach, Gilman is hopeful he'll attract more.

An R&D executive who runs the Kendall Square office of Pfizer, Jose-Carlos Gutierrez-Ramos, chooses a great word to describe what is happening in Kendall: interdigitation — a tight weave, like when you clasp your hands together.

Gutierrez-Ramos first began working in the neighborhood in 1996. In those days, scrappy biotech start-ups often talked like guerrilla fighters who were going to seize the riches of big pharma; now, they're often collaborators. Why is that?

Today, academic researchers worry about the future of government funding, big pharma companies worry whether they have enough new drugs in their pipelines, and biotechs worry about the amount of money, typically hundreds of millions, required to bring a new medicine to market.

"All these constituents have moved out of their comfort zones, and they're much more open to interactions," Gutierrez-

Ramos says. "It feels like we've joined teams, and we have common goals."

Gutierrez-Ramos works across a courtyard from the old brick building at 700 Main Street. In the same way that Davenport & Bridges once made railroad cars, or Polaroid cranked out cameras, Kendall today makes new medicines. And instead of helping us get around or preserve memories, the goal is to help us stay healthier and live longer.

Singing the Praises of a No-Frills Building on Kingston Street

Published in the Boston Globe, September 15, 2016

Walk up Kingston Street from the newly rehabbed Chinatown Park toward Downtown Crossing, and you'll see Sparkling New Boston on your right and Gritty Old Boston on your left.

The tower on the right offers $3,000-a-month studio apartments and an excellent restaurant, Townsman, that dishes up a $33 duck breast from the Hudson Valley. The six-story building on the left has no restaurant, no Starbucks, no central air conditioning, no marble-lined lobby, and no commanding views. Built in the late 1880s by a cousin of Ralph Waldo Emerson's, the Kingston Building has elevators so old they still have metal accordion doors and require operators to level them off at the right floor.

Boston these days is Crane City, with new Class A office buildings popping up like Pokemon all over the Seaport District and Kendall Square, and condo and apartment towers for overseas investors and the six-figure set being erected everywhere else. It's easy to overlook the value of something that is increasingly scarce: cheap, unpretentious office space. Also, buildings that look and feel like Boston, as opposed to a mirrored box that would fit in fine in Phoenix.

But I'm not just making a case for distinctive architecture or historic preservation. The block between Essex Street and the new park is mostly filled by growing architecture, design, and urban planning firms, and startup companies and a venture capital firm. Many were driven out of Kendall Square by rents that only the likes of Google, Johnson & Johnson, and Amazon can afford.

In Kendall, you can rent a swell office for $60 and up per square foot; on Kingston Street, when startups began migrating across the Charles, some found space for less than $15 per square foot, though today's prices are closer to $30.

Buildings like the Kingston Building "really sustain the startup scene," says Matt Bellows, chief executive of Yesware, a Boston company that creates software for salespeople. "It's got a great location, nice open space, windows on three sides, and it's cheap." After spending two years in the building, Bellows says, "we only moved out when we got over 50 people, and the lines for the two tiny bathrooms became too long."

When one tenant moves out, or gets acquired, it often sells (or bequeaths) office furniture to the next company that moves in. And Susan Hunt Stevens, chief executive of WeSpire, a maker of human resources software, says she has been a customer of several other businesses in the building, like Moo, which makes business cards and paper products, and Price Intelligently, which helps companies analyze and perfect their pricing structure. (At right, Kingston Street's 19th century block faces a 21st century building.)

The building's earliest tenants were dry goods merchants, hatmakers, textile companies, and bonnet frame makers. When owner Ron Druker's family acquired it in 1947, some of the tenants produced neckties and handbags. And while many of today's companies craft websites or digital models of college campuses, some still make stuff. One street-level space is home to Fortified Bicycle, which makes rugged bikes for city riders, as well as theft-resistant accessories. Upstairs, a company called Airmada is designing an automated landing pad and pit stop for aerial drones, so that they can be maintained without much attention from human operators. Moo prints its cards not far away, at a facility in Lincoln, R.I.

Katie Rae and Reed Sturtevant are both former Microsoft Cambridge employees who started an early-stage investment fund, Project 11 Ventures, on the campus of MIT, where they were teaching a course. At the Kingston Building, they invite companies they back, like Airmada, to work out of their space until they grow to 20 employees — one company just moved out this month. Often, traveling friends and colleagues drop by to borrow a desk and mooch off the Wi-Fi. Instead of dining across the street at Townsman, Rae says, the startup set is more likely to head to the Chicken and Rice Guys, a popular Middle Eastern storefront nearby, or Gracenote Coffee for an espresso fix. A former tenant in the Project 11's third-floor digs, Phil Beauregard, says he put in such long hours working on a venture that made software for restaurant managers that he occasionally slept in the office — "probably more than I'd like to admit."

The types of businesses in the Kingston Building are those that you might expect to find in the waterfront area that the late Boston Mayor Thomas M. Menino dubbed the Innovation District (better known as the Seaport). But that neighborhood is now dominated by larger companies like Vertex, John Hancock, State Street, and the accounting firm PwC, all occupying brand-new buildings. That has created "the odd situation," writes Gregory Janks by e-mail, "where we could get a great space (grungy!) in a location with mature transportation options and great restaurants for a cheaper price" than the Innovation District. Janks is cofounder of DumontJanks, a planning and design firm in the Kingston Building.

The Kingston Street block has about 100,000 square feet of space, says Druker, president of the Druker Co. All but 2,500 square feet are occupied, and he says the last bit might get leased soon. (One issue the prospective tenant raised: extending the hours the elevator operators are on duty.)

Back in 2012, several of the building's tenants watched — and felt the tremors — as a brick building across the street was demolished. The quaintly named Dainty Dot Hosiery Building was also built in the 1880s. But it was acquired by developers in 2006 and knocked down after the Boston Landmarks Commission chose not to grant it historic status. In its place came the $130 million, 26-story high rise that contains Townsman and the Radian apartments.

As a result, there are persistent rumors that the Kingston Building could be endangered, too. (Like the Dainty Dot, it also lacks landmark status.)

Druker says he was "upset" that the building across the street had to come down and said he "feels no pressure whatsoever" to sell or make any major changes to the string of buildings he owns on Kingston. "I like the way they are, and the buildings are very financially successful for us." He says he has avoided making changes to some of the vintage signs on the building's exterior — one of which, Farley Harvey Co., advertises a dry goods company founded before the Civil War. Druker adds, "We have no plans to do anything there, but who knows what the future will bring?"

That's true of many hot neighborhoods these days, in Boston, Cambridge, and Somerville. Which makes it important to remember that while shiny, new buildings are nice for impressing out-of-town visitors or luring Fortune 500 companies, gritty old cheap space is essential if we want to be a city that has room for fledgling companies focused on the future.

. . .

[Author's Note: Townsman has closed. Project 11 Ventures didn't last, but Rae and Sturtevant are now running a venture capital fund for MIT, The Engine. The Kingston Building endures.]

A Microcosm of the Biotech Industry in One Building

Published in the Boston Globe, March 13, 2011

If you live in the Boston area, you've no doubt driven past the Riverside Technology Center hundreds of times. An unassuming, brown brick building, it sits on the banks of the Charles River in Cambridge, across from Genzyme's castle-like manufacturing plant.

Every tenant of the five-story building, it turns out, is a biotech company, and riding the elevators to visit the occupants, as I did last week, offers a good feel for the high-risk, capital-intensive, painstakingly slow, and scientifically dazzling life sciences industry. For these companies, it isn't unusual to talk about needing $100 million or more to get a new drug within spitting distance of Food and Drug Administration approval, at which point it can be prescribed by doctors.

And while the teams of 20 or 30 employees at each company may devote a decade or more to developing new treatments for conditions like cancer, autism, or sickle cell anemia, they do it knowing that a tiny ripple of bad data received after testing in humans could undercut investors' confidence, and lead to the company's swift demise.

Still, behind every glass door at the Riverside Center, the hope is that they might not only be creating a drug that will change lives, but also laying the foundation for the next Genzyme Corp. (recently acquired for $20 billion) or Vertex Pharmaceuticals Inc. (a Cambridge company with a market value of $10 billion).

"The timelines and the gestation period are just different from anything else," says Nick Leschly, a former venture capitalist who is now chief executive of Bluebird Bio Inc., developing gene therapy treatments for rare diseases. "This probably isn't the quickest way to riches or stardom. There is no Facebook in life sciences."

Leschly mentions that he fielded a phone call earlier in the day from a father eager to get his son into one of Bluebird's clinical trials.

"Part of what motivates us is that what you're doing is important," he says.

Bluebird is a 30-person company trying to succeed in a field littered with failure: Despite two decades of research at Genzyme, and intense efforts by dozens of start-ups, the FDA has yet to approve a single gene therapy treatment. In Bluebird's case, gene therapy involves extracting stem cells from a patient's bone marrow, inserting a normal version of the gene that is causing the disease into the stem cells, letting them replicate in a dish, and then re-injecting the healthy cells into the patient.

Like Genzyme before it, Bluebird is starting small: It published research last year showing how one patient with a blood disorder called beta-thalassemia had been able to forgo his normal monthly blood transfusions and go back to his job as a chef after being treated with Bluebird's gene therapy.

The company got its start in 1991, and has raised about $75 million, some of it from the investment arm of Genzyme. Still, Leschly says the company will spend the next few years testing its therapy in more patients and collecting data to present to the FDA.

One floor up is Cerulean Pharma Inc. The company is developing what chief executive Oliver Fetzer calls "the ultimate Trojan horse," a nano-particle designed to hold potent drugs, find its way to tumors, and release the drug over time. Fetzer estimates Cerulean's drug could be as much as 20 times better than current cancer drugs in reaching tumors without being absorbed by healthy tissue along the way (a major cause of drug side effects). But, he acknowledges, science can hold surprises, and Ccrulean has already abandoned a more complicated, difficult-to-produce version of its nano-particle.

Epizyme Inc., also focused on cancer drugs, is employing new insights into the way disease-causing genes are turned on and off by mechanisms other than DNA. Its chief executive, Robert Gould, spent more than 20 years at the pharmaceutical giant Merck & Co.

Unlike most of its neighbors, Seaside Therapeutics Inc. hasn't raised millions in venture capital. Instead, it has relied on grants from the National Institutes of Health, funding from patient advocacy groups, and donations from philanthropists. In developing drugs that could help patients with autism and the related Fragile X syndrome, Seaside hopes to outmaneuver much bigger players like Novartis and Roche.

The building doesn't feel anything like a biotech frat house. But there's a good deal of interaction among the tenants. One of the Seaside founders, Kazumi Shiosaki, was also a founder and temporary chief executive of Epizyme. When one of the building's tenants planned layoffs, the company passed resumes along to another firm, Aileron Therapeutics, which hired one of the scientists. (Aileron moved out of the Riverside Center in October.) Aileron chief executive Joseph Yanchik also recalls some high-quality networking with an executive from a major pharmaceutical company during a fire drill at the building.

The building's owner, Abbey Group of Boston, purchased it in the late 1980s. During the recession, occupancy dropped to about 50 percent, says Abbey Group managing partner Bob Epstein. But in 2011, he says, "we're probably 70 or 75 percent rented."

One hazard of renting to biotechs is they sometimes get acquired by large pharmaceutical companies that move their operations elsewhere. (The bigger companies are hungry for new products as patents expire on their older drugs.)

That's exactly what is happening with Alnara Pharmaceuticals, a company developing enzyme replacement therapy to help people suffering from chronic pancreatitis and cystic fibrosis. Last summer, Alnara was acquired by Indianapolis-based Eli Lilly & Co for $180 million, with the possibility of another $200 million should the drug win approval and do well in the marketplace.

In January, however, an FDA advisory panel rejected the drug, contending the company hadn't proved it works well enough. That may force Lilly to conduct more trials and collect more data.

Only a few of Alnara's 25 full-time employees will stay with Lilly and move to Indianapolis when Alnara vacates the center at the end of the month, said Robert Gallotto, Alnara's chief business officer. "Many of the folks here are local, Cambridge-based folks," he says, "and they're used to more of a small company environment."

Could some of them end up finding jobs elsewhere in the building? "Sure," Gallotto says. "I could definitely see that happening."

...

[Author's note: Bluebird Bio went public in 2013, and by 2019 was on its way to winning approval for a gene therapy treatment for a rare blood disorder. Epizyme also went public in 2013, and as of 2019 was still working to get a treatment for non-Hodgkin's lymphoma and other cancers to market. Cerulean went public in 2014, but its primary drug candidate washed out of clinical trials, and the company laid off its employees and merged with another firm in 2017. Aileron Therapeutics went public in 2017 and is still testing several cancer drugs. Seaside Therapeutics wound down at the end of 2013. The Riverside Technology Center is included on the map of key places in this book, at http://bit.ly/innoeco-map.]

Turning the Lights Back on in a Chelsea Factory

Published in the Boston Globe, January 1, 2012

On a January morning in 2011, after a blizzard had covered the city with a foot of snow, Glenn Batchelder showed up for his first day of work at an old factory complex in Chelsea.

The one-time box factory, built in 1908, had been converted into a pharmaceutical manufacturing plant, but it had been vacant since 2008 when all the employees were abruptly laid off. Martin Freed, who accompanied Batchelder into the dark, cold building on that January day, kept making references to "The Shining," the horror movie set in an empty Colorado hotel.

Batchelder and Freed were there to turn the lights back on, and attempt to make a new product for people suffering from Parkinson's disease. About 1 million people in the United States have been diagnosed with Parkinson's, a neurological disorder that causes tremors, muscle rigidity, and difficulty moving. The story of the Chelsea company, Civitas Therapeutics, traces back to 1997, and it illustrates the incredible twists and turns that life sciences companies often take.

Like most life sciences companies around Boston, Civitas's story begins in university labs. Professors at MIT and Penn State had worked on a new kind of particle that could carry a drug deep into the lungs, allowing it to be delivered through an inhaler. "The really appealing idea was that you could get away from the needles that patients need, sometimes several times a day," Batchelder says.

A company was formed, Advanced Inhalation Research, and it raised $2.1 million from Polaris Venture Partners, a Waltham venture capital firm.

Less than two years after AIR was founded, the 30-person start-up was acquired for an astonishing $125 million by another local company, Alkermes, which viewed it as a way to diversify its products beyond drugs delivered by injection. "Delivering drugs through the pulmonary system was the rage," Batchelder recalls.

As part of Alkermes, the AIR team evaluated more than 50 drugs that could be delivered via the lungs. And, as is often the case with smaller pharmaceutical companies, Alkermes sought a bigger partner to help finance the research-and-development costs, get the product approved by the Food and Drug Administration, and eventually distribute and market it. They found Eli Lilly and Co., the Indianapolis maker of Cialis and other drugs.

The two companies explored ways to deliver insulin, human growth hormone, and osteoporosis drugs with an inhaler. The insulin project moved ahead quickly, in part because of the potential. Many diabetics inject themselves with insulin several times a day, and Lilly was already in the business of selling injectable insulin, giving it a vast sales force.

The partners renovated a derelict building in Chelsea, with tax breaks from the city and state, and began preparing to make the inhalable insulin powder there.

Lilly and Alkermes used a plastic inhaler that was a bit fatter and shorter than a cigar. It didn't need to be cleaned, and was cheap enough to be tossed after 30 days. They were close to the finish line, running Phase 3 clinical trials, when Lily suddenly decided to call it quits.

The 75 people who worked at the Chelsea plant were laid off, along with another 75 Alkermes employees working on the Lilly partnership. In the press release, Lilly's president offered only the vaguest explanation.

"One day, they were talking about adding another hundred jobs here, and it seemed like the next day, the building was being moth-balled," says Jay Ash, Chelsea's city manager.

But executives at Alkermes were hoping to find someone to adopt the technology for the inhaler and the special drug formulations that it could deliver. "Our life would've been a hundred times easier if the technology just didn't work, and we could've just cut off our arm and moved on," says Alkermes vice president Blair Jackson.

Instead, Alkermes talked to other pharmaceutical companies, but none would commit. But Batchelder and two AIR alumni were interested, and they spent almost two years assembling a plan, with Alkermes, to spin out the technology.

As Batchelder tried to recruit others who had been involved with AIR to join the new company, Civitas Therapeutics, he thought of the Blues Brothers driving around Chicago, trying to get their old band back together. (Today, almost half of Civitas's 20 employees are veterans of AIR or the Alkermes/Lilly project. Batchelder wasn't one, but he knew many of the key players.)

Early last year, Civitas announced $25 million in funding from three venture capital firms, along with a grant from Michael J. Fox's Parkinson's research foundation. Alkermes also received a significant stake in the company and a seat on the board.

Instead of insulin, Civitas is focusing on a drug called L-dopa, which has been used by those afflicted by Parkinson's disease for decades. It helps supply the brain with dopamine, a key neurotransmitter that controls motor functions, and is lacking in Parkinson's patients.

The company believes the inhaler could deliver the drug more quickly than pills, helping patients who are slipping into an "off state," when they become stiff or can't move.

"When you inhale L-dopa into the lungs, the effect is immediate," Batchelder says. "It's a more direct route to the brain."

The company believes the inhaler has the potential to generate $1 billion in worldwide sales. It plans to win FDA approval and launch the product without a partner to bankroll clinical trials or handle marketing and distribution, a rarity in the life sciences business.

"We're doing it in a way that allows us to control our own destiny," Batchelder says.

Last month, Civitas began the first stage of clinical trials of the Parkinson's inhaler. At the factory in Chelsea, scientists were once again buzzing around the labs. Shiny metal silos for making the L-dopa powder, and two-story-tall machines that can pack it into 100,000 capsules an hour stood ready, waiting to produce something that will finally find its way into a pharmacy.

. . .

[Author's note: Civitas was acquired by another biotech company, California-based Acorda Therapeutics, in 2014 for $525 million. In 2019, Acorda finally got the inhaled L-dopa, dubbed Inbrija, approved by the Food & Drug Administration. Acorda still uses the Chelsea factory for production.]

Gifts of Invention & Ingenuity

Published in Yankee Magazine's 80th anniversary issue, September 2015

The mosaic-making robot doesn't have fingers, just a single suction cup that has a sure touch with glass and ceramic tiles. It plucks them from a tray and places them into a 12-inch by 12-inch grid, creating abstract patterns or recognizable images. Standing next to the steel cage that houses the robot is Ted Acworth. He points to a next-generation robot across the room.

"It's ten to twenty times faster than the original one," he says, "but we haven't filed the patents on it — so no pictures."

If Acworth had started a company two centuries earlier, no doubt it would have been a water-powered textile mill, turning the craft of weaving into a high-volume business. In 2015, his company, Artaic, is having much the same effect, reducing the cost and speeding up the time required to create a custom-designed mosaic for an office lobby or the master bath of a vacation home.

Artaic and the other start-up businesses that are its neighbors in a former Army supply depot on the edge of Boston Harbor are only the youngest shoots from a tree that has been growing in New England for a few centuries now. Just across the water from Artaic was the shipyard where Donald McKay built the fastest vehicles on earth, Clipper ships, in the mid-1800s. Go up the Charles River a half-mile and you're at the Massachusetts Institute of Technology, whose labs designed the radar systems that helped the Allies win World War II, and also the guidance computer that helped Apollo spacecraft reach the moon. Further up the river in Waltham is Route 128, the highway that in the 1980s was home to many of the companies that first introduced computers and productivity software to the workplace.

New England doesn't have a monopoly on ingenuity and entrepreneurial drive, of course, but we've been at it longer than many parts of the world. And almost every week, you can bump into a delegation visiting from Madrid or Dubai, poking into the labs of Harvard and the start-up workspaces nearby, trying to figure out the formula that produces both important scientific breakthroughs — like cancer-hunting nanoparticles — and also high-paying jobs.

The formula is not complicated, just very hard to copy: start a few universities, and give them a century or three to get very good at attracting the best professors and the smartest students, and also research money from government agencies and large corporations. When students or professors start businesses, make sure there are investors nearby willing to take risks on unproven ideas. Lawyers who can file patents are essential, as is cheap office space in old mill complexes or Army warehouses.

It gave us the telephone; Alexander Graham-Bell was a Boston University professor renting cheap space above a telegraph supply shop. It gave us "The Wizard of Oz"; two of the three founders of Technicolor were MIT alumni whose first office was in a railroad car, so they could hook it to a train and go wherever someone might be crazy enough to want to make a motion picture in color. Harvard was less supportive of entrepreneurial faculty in the 1980s than it is today, so one of the founders of Biogen left his faculty position for a few years to help pioneer the modern biotech industry. The company today sells several drugs that treat multiple sclerosis, and may be getting close to one that slows the progress of Alzheimer's disease.

Most of New England's entrepreneurial activity orbits university campuses like electrons. In Burlington, Vermont a team of recent Middlebury College graduates is building software that can convert architectural plans into three-dimensional digital environments; put on a virtual reality headset and you can amble through structures that haven't yet been built, turning your head to see out windows or down hallways. In Manchester, Southern New Hampshire University is filling brick mill buildings with software developers, designers, and counselors who run two different online colleges, with faculty and students spread across North America. Two Brown University seniors built a website that would collect orders for t-shirts, and only produce them once enough orders came in. They have now raised more than $55 million in venture capital funding for their company, Teespring, headquartered in Providence.

A few blocks from the heart of the MIT campus in Cambridge, there's a two-story brick building called LabCentral that is filled with 29 young biotech businesses that share expensive lab equipment. One tenant is Vaxess Technologies, which is using a protein found in silk to stabilize vaccines, so that they can be transported and stored without refrigeration. The founders are from Harvard, though the original scientific breakthrough was made by professors at Tufts University.

Leading a tour of LabCentral, co-founder Johannes Fruehauf mentions that one of the building's prior tenants was Edwin Land, the inventor of instant photography, who maintained his private research lab here.

But as is often the case in New England, there are layers beneath layers. Before Land's lab, the building was on one end of the first "long distance" telephone call, between Alexander Graham-Bell in Boston and his assistant Thomas Watson in Cambridge. And the rails that serve as lintels for many of the building's windows refer back to the original tenant: Kimball & Davenport, the first builder of passenger railroad cars in America.

The building, and the region, has always been home to "people who aspire to do great things," in Fruehauf's words. And something about the history, Fruehauf says, needles his tenants a bit when they show up to work every morning: "Guys, there have been smart people here before you. You've got to live up to the challenge."

2. Links Between Today and the Past

How Cambridge Became the Life Sciences Capital

Published in the Boston Globe, March 17, 2016

If you happened to wander through Kendall Square on a summer Saturday four decades ago, you might have encountered an open-air marketplace. You could have bought vintage clothing or a rock painted with President Gerald Ford's face.

You might also have seen MIT and Harvard professors and students demonstrating some laboratory tools and talking about the potential of gene splicing. Nearby was an anti-gene splicing booth manned by a Harvard grad student, Scott Thacher.

The dueling information booths were part of a debate that sprang up in Cambridge in 1976 about the new field of recombinant DNA — the ability to blend genetic material from several sources and grow it inside a living organism. "There was a sci-fi element" to the discourse, Thacher recalls, with politicians like then-Cambridge mayor Alfred Vellucci fretting about scientists creating new kinds of Frankenstein monsters.

Thacher says he felt at the time that there were "reasons to be cautious about recombinant DNA research," and he was joined in that opinion by Nobel laureates like George Wald, who suggested that wide-open deserts — rather than dense urban centers — would be more appropriate for such research.

The debates of 1976 marked the start of a five-year period that shaped the local biotech landscape. If you've ever assumed, as I had, that biotech companies cluster in Cambridge only because they want to be close to Harvard and MIT — well, that's only part of the story.

In June 1976, a newspaper article sounded the alarm about Harvard's plans to build a new lab with a higher level of safety and containment; the objective was to allow researchers to conduct experiments with recombinant DNA. Vellucci, a frequent jousting opponent of Harvard's, was outraged to learn about the university's plans from the paper. He chaired a hearing at Cambridge City Hall featuring researchers from Harvard and MIT, and an official from the National Institutes of Health.

"Is it true that in the history of science, mistakes have been known to happen?" Vellucci asked. "Do scientists ever exercise poor judgment? Do they ever have accidents?" A smattering of applause broke out in the packed hearing room.

Vellucci hoped to pass a two-year moratorium on gene splicing in Cambridge. Instead, the council passed a three-month moratorium, and created a board of nine Cambridge citizens — including a nun and a nurse — to explore whether the work should be allowed, and if so, what safeguards would be necessary. A few days after the board was created, the pro and con tables showed up at the Kendall Square marketplace.

At the time, says Phillip Sharp, an MIT professor, Cambridge felt like a manufacturing town that had seen better days. He recalls being surrounded by candy, textile, and leather factories. Sharp hosted the citizens review committee at MIT, explaining what the research scientists there planned to do. "I think we built a relationship," he says.

By early 1977, the citizens committee had proposed a framework to ensure that any DNA-related experiments were done under fairly stringent safety controls, and Cambridge became the first city in the world to regulate research using genetic material.

That early creation of a clear regulatory structure led to the Swiss biotech company Biogen opening up a lab in the city in 1982; Sharp was a co-founder of the company. Mayor Vellucci even showed up for the ribbon-cutting, declaring that he now had "no fear of recombinant DNA as long as it paid taxes," according to a history of the era, "Consensus from Controversy."

But in cities like Somerville and Boston, the atmosphere surrounding DNA research remained emotionally charged and politicized into the early 1980s. When a Harvard spin-out, Genetics Institute, tried to set up an office in Somerville in 1981, a public hearing aired concerns about rats and roaches carrying newly invented organisms out of the labs and into a nearby supermarket.

"The two founding scientists just said, 'Forget about this,'" says Gabe Schmergel, the company's long-time chief executive. When Genetics Institute instead moved into a mostly-abandoned hospital building in Mission Hill, Ray Flynn, then a Boston city councillor, led a protest outside the building.

"He was running for mayor, and one of his platforms was to be against biotechnology," says Schmergel, who snuck out the back door to avoid an unpleasant confrontation.

By contrast, "Cambridge was willing to put out the welcome mat," Schmergel says. His company bought an old warehouse at Alewife, and set up labs to develop drugs for cancer and hemophilia. When Genetics Institute was acquired by drugmaker American Home Products in 1996, it had grown to about 1,200 employees in Cambridge and Andover. (American Home Products eventually became part of Pfizer Inc. of New York.)

Today, the largest private employer in Cambridge is Novartis, the Swiss biopharma company that opened a $600 million expansion of its research campus in December. And Biogen, depending on the day, has either the biggest or second-biggest market capitalization of any Massachusetts company. (At right, three of Biogen's CEOs pose with co-founder and Nobel Laureate Wally Gilbert, second from left, who also served as CEO. Photo courtesy of Phillip Sharp.)

Meanwhile, Somerville has no biotech cluster to speak of — though Mayor Joseph Curtatone has hustled for nearly a decade to create one. "Our strategy is really a long-term play," Curtatone says.

In 2011, one of Cambridge's big drugmakers, Vertex Pharmaceuticals, was lured to Boston with an incentive package worth $60 million. Not many others have followed Vertex across the Charles River.

Yes, Cambridge had the benefit of MIT and Harvard nudging it to create a permitting system for DNA experimentation, but it also had "a major public immersion" in the topic — and it started early, says Sharp, who was awarded the Nobel Prize in 1993. That's an important lesson for elected officials regulating new fields like airborne drones, car-sharing services, Airbnb rentals, or the newest scientific frontier, gene editing.

Move too slowly, or react out of fear, and the economic repercussions can endure for decades.

Forty years after the pro- and anti-DNA research tables showed up in Kendall, I rang up Scott Thacher. Today, he runs a pharmaceutical startup in San Diego. I asked if he'd been back to Cambridge recently to see the growth of the biotech cluster, and he said that he had. This time, instead of manning a table, he was making a pitch for funding to one of the city's many biotech venture capital firms.

The Wizards of '78

Published in the Boston Globe, February 2, 2018

Long-time Bostonians remember 1978 as the year of the big February blizzard. But it was also when the modern biotechnology and software industries began to take shape in Cambridge. You'll no doubt read lots of recollections of the snowstorm as we mark its 40th anniversary, but let me explain why '78 marked an important turning point in shaping the state's innovation economy.

All we need to do is walk about a mile — from the campus of Harvard Business School on the Boston side of the Charles River to Divinity Avenue on the Cambridge side, near the Harvard Museum of Natural History.

In 1978, high-tech in Massachusetts meant mainframes and minicomputers — not PCs. One of the biggest tech companies in the world was Digital Equipment Corp., headquartered in Maynard.

An MIT alum named Dan Bricklin took a job at Digital because, he says, he failed to land a spot in a top computer science graduate program. At Digital, and at MIT before that, Bricklin had been exposed to software for both word processing and newspaper typesetting, so he knew how easy it could be to add or remove text on a computer, and see the rest of the document adjust automatically. Bricklin eventually did get accepted by a grad school, and while at Harvard Business School in 1978 he had what, to him, was a pretty obvious idea. When students made a tiny mistake calculating the expenses and revenues of a company— using pocket calculators at the time — they had to go back and start over. Why, Bricklin wondered, wasn't doing math more like doing word processing?

"I sort of imagined a magic blackboard, where when you erased one number, everything recalculated, like word processing," Bricklin says. "I had this image of an idea ... word processing the numbers." He created a prototype version in the spring of 1978, using one of Harvard's Digital minicomputers that sat "down in the basement," he recalls.

Bricklin's idea evolved into a $100 software program called VisiCalc. It was the first electronic spreadsheet software, and VisiCalc initially only worked on computers made by a Cupertino, Calif., startup, Apple Computer. VisiCalc was the first software package that gave small businesses and sole proprietors a reason to buy a personal computer, so they could do basic bookkeeping.

(At right, VisiCalc co-creators Bob Frankston and Dan Bricklin. Photo courtesy Dan Bricklin and Jim Raycroft.)

VisiCalc is now regarded as the original "killer app" — a piece of software that helped spur adoption of a new technology product. It transformed the personal computer from a plaything of nerds to a useful business tool. "If VisiCalc had been written for some other computer," Apple co-founder Steve Jobs told a television interviewer in 1990, "you'd be interviewing somebody else right now."

VisiCalc was eventually superseded by products from Microsoft and Lotus Development Corp. Both had ties to Cambridge: Microsoft was conceived by Bill Gates and Paul Allen in 1974, after Allen bought a copy of Popular Electronics magazine in Harvard Square and saw that the era of personal computers was dawning; Lotus was founded by Mitch Kapor, a former programmer at the company that distributed VisiCalc. Lotus was headquartered in Cambridge. It introduced an early business e-mail system, Lotus Notes, and grew to about 5,500 employees before it was acquired by IBM in 1995. By that time, Cambridge had a strong reputation as a place to start and grow software companies that aimed to address business headaches; today, big employers in the city include HubSpot and Pegasystems.

As Bricklin was prototyping the first version of VisiCalc in 1978, Harvard was preparing to open a new science lab on Divinity Avenue. It would allow researchers to work with recombinant DNA, combining genetic material from multiple kinds of organisms, and it had been controversial from the moment it was proposed. Cambridge's mayor, Alfred Vellucci, spoke out against it repeatedly. He worried that scientists would create some kind of Frankenstein monster in the lab that would threaten citizens.

"I have made references to Frankenstein over the past week, and some people think this is all a big joke," Vellucci said at a 1976 hearing at Cambridge City Hall. "This is not a laughing matter ... we could have a major disaster on our hands."

Luckily, rather than banning the work with recombinant DNA, as some had advocated, Cambridge instead formed a committee to study the risks — and potential benefits. In 1977, it became the first city in the world to issue a set of regulations for working with genetic material. Perhaps appropriately, the Harvard lab that touched off the whole debate opened around Halloween 1978.

Because of the regulations, "an incoming biotech company could say, 'If we come to Cambridge, we need to do X, Y, and Z,'" says Gavin Kleespies, director of programs at the Massachusetts Historical Society. "The fact that the city laid out a consistent road map made it really attractive to companies. And that was the product of Al Vellucci saying, 'We're all going to die from super bugs.' It was political theater, but in the end, it had this huge impact on the city."

One of the Harvard professors working with recombinant DNA at the time was Walter Gilbert. His research was focused on producing synthetic insulin for diabetics, and in 1978, he published a paper showing how a genetically-modified strain of bacteria — exactly the stuff Vellucci feared — could make insulin for rats. (Ultimately, a different approach to producing synthetic insulin for people won out.)

Gilbert was also one of the scientific founders of an early biotech company that was incorporated in Geneva, Switzerland, in 1978. "We had $750,000 in initial funding from the venture capitalists, but only $375,000 of it was in cash," Gilbert recalls. (At right, Gilbert in a 2018 photo.)

The company was called Biogen, and it eventually opened a lab in Cambridge in 1982. By that point, Gilbert had both won the Nobel Prize in Chemistry for his work in DNA sequencing in 1980, and also taken over as Biogen's chief executive the following year. Mayor Vellucci was present for the lab's ribbon-cutting.

"Cambridge was the obvious place to put it," Gilbert says, "because we'd been through this discussion before," referring to the debate over safety regulations.

Today, Biogen makes drugs for multiple sclerosis, and it is developing potential treatments for Alzheimer's disease. The company has about 2,100 workers in Cambridge, now its global headquarters.

In fact, most of the 25 largest employers in Cambridge — aside from the universities and hospitals — are in the business of developing biotech drugs or software for businesses. In biotech, Cambridge is regarded as the leading hub anywhere in the world. In software, it is home to branch offices of Microsoft, Oracle, and IBM, among others.

And it all traces back four decades, to 1978.

From a Factory in Peabody to the Surface of the Moon

Published in the Boston Globe, January 13, 2019

One of the most improbable and impressive companies that Boston has ever known is run out of a single-story brick building in Peabody.

Its product was invented in 1957, but still sells for hundreds or thousands of dollars. The product has been manufactured in Massachusetts consistently since around 1960. And it currently sits on the surface of Mars, on the moon, in the International Space Station, and in operating rooms and factories here on earth.

My bet is you've never heard of the company, Harmonic Drive, or its product, the strain wave gear. I hadn't, either — and I've been covering tech in Boston for more than two decades. But Harmonic Drive is a company that has remained relevant through several generations of innovation, and is still relevant today — not to mention growing.

What's nice about Harmonic Drive is that most of the gear units it makes will fit in the palm of your hand. They're made of stainless steel, so they have a heft to them. There are a couple dozen ball bearings inside that spin pleasingly as the gear rotates. Aside  from the bevy of ball bearings, the circular gear unit has just three parts, each of which sits inside the next. It's designed to be light and compact, but the piece produces a huge amount of torque and extremely accurate movements. That's pretty important, for instance, if the gear is inside a surgical robot that is performing hip replacement surgery on your mom. (Photo at right courtesy of Harmonic Drive.)

"Typically, gears are big, bulky, heavy, solid devices," says Douglas Olson, Harmonic Drive's CEO. They also have something called "backlash," which refers to the extra space and movement between the teeth of two interlocking gears. Harmonic Drive says its gear units operate with no backlash, which makes them precise. The design was created by Clarence Walton Musser, an inventor who received more than 200 US patents before his death in 1998. And it was created for one of the most dominant

Massachusetts companies of the 20th century, United Shoe Machinery of Beverly, which not only made equipment for shoe production, but also developed tank and aircraft turrets during World War II.

Like a lot of other inventions, no one was sure initially what to do with the strain wave gear. There were explorations of whether it was feasible to use the new gear to drive helicopter rotors or to remotely move fuel rods in nuclear power plants. But Harmonic Drive "really started to grow," Olson explains, in the mid-1970s, as robots found their way onto assembly lines and evolved from being powered by hydraulic fluid to electricity.

The company, which began life as a division of United Shoe Machinery before spinning out, also saw some early success in selling to NASA: One of its gear units was used to drive the wheels on the lunar rover that traveled to the moon as part of the Apollo 15 mission in 1971. That year, astronaut Buzz Aldrin dropped by the Harmonic Drive office to thank the employees for their work on the rover. (Aldrin is seen signing a poster in the photo at right. Courtesy Harmonic Drive.)

Olson nonchalantly mentions that you can also find Harmonic Drive's gear units onboard just about every GPS satellite that orbits the planet, "typically to move solar panels or communication antennae," as well as on the Mars InSight lander, which touched down on the planet in November 2018. NASA also built the company's gears into Mars 2020, another rover that is scheduled to launch next summer.

Own anything with a microchip inside? Harmonic Drive's gear units can often be found inside the automated equipment at chip fabs, the production facilities that make microchips. Inside Harmonic Drive's own factory in Peabody, there's a small gray-and-blue robotic arm helping to assemble gear units; yes, there's a Harmonic Drive gear unit inside the robot that makes Harmonic Drive gear units.

Harmonic Drive is owned by a Tokyo-based parent company, Harmonic Drive Systems, which was originally the Asian licensee of the strain wave gear that United Shoe Machinery developed.

The company as a whole has been on a tear: its revenues nearly doubled from 2017 to 2018, hitting about $500 million, though its stock has been dropping over the past year after an extended rise.

It's pretty hard to think of technology products invented in 1957 — the era of black-and-white TVs and Elvis Presley on "The Ed Sullivan Show" — that are still sold today. Much less made in the United States.

Olson tries to explain the long stretch of success. "There's that cliché that our people are our most important asset," he says. "But it's a fact. It's not easy to produce a product like this, and we're continually innovating. The talent pool in this area is excellent."

(It also helps that some of Harmonic Drive's gear units are sold to secretive agencies of the federal government, which must purchase from domestic suppliers.)

When I dropped by last week, there was a "now hiring" banner on the front of the building, and not a single empty spot in the parking lot. (Harmonic Drive currently employs 132 people in Peabody.) Olson apologized on our tour of the plant that some of the walkways had gotten narrower, since there was now equipment sitting in what had once been aisle space.

What's driving the company's growth?

"It's definitely driven by the advancement of automation," Olson says, and especially by lower-cost, easily-programmed "collaborative robots" that can work alongside humans.

And, he posits, more robots in US factories may help keep manufacturing activities here, or even bring them back from countries where the costs of human labor are lower.

"The US has lost so many manufacturing jobs to China or Mexico," Olson says. "But the cost to operate a robot in the US and China is the same. It levels the competitive advantages of one area versus another."

Harmonic Drive was born in 1960 in Beverly, at "the Shoe," as United Shoe Machinery's vast campus was known. This summer — almost 60 years later — it plans to move back to town, into a newly built facility that will double the company's current footprint. Its parent company was merged into obscurity in 1976. But Harmonic Drive has managed to survive — and thrive.

The Incredible Endurance of the Shoe Biz

Published in the Boston Globe, April 28, 2019

If you want to understand the incredible story of the modern shoe business in Massachusetts, the best place to start might be Inman Square, Cambridge, in 1906.

That was the year a Russian immigrant, Abraham Hyde, started a business in the back of a laundry, making slippers out of scraps of carpet and selling them for a dime.

The company survives today as Saucony, based in Waltham, which next month plans to release a $120 running shoe called the Ride ISO 2 ("reliable comfort on any run.")

It's tough to find industries doggedly chugging along in 2019 that date to the days when John Fitzgerald, JFK's grandfather, was Boston's mayor.

And the shoe business is becoming even more high-profile now that companies that were once based in the suburbs, like Reebok and Converse, are building headquarters closer to the city. Puma will be the newest arrival; it's consolidating its US headquarters at Somerville's Assembly Row, along with about 550 jobs. Scheduled opening date: 2021.

Of course, the biggest change since 1906 is that few companies actually make products locally — though New Balance has production facilities in Brighton and Lawrence, along with three in Maine, and Alden Shoes cranks out shiny penny loafers in Middleborough. Some suppliers, like Quabaug Vibram Innovation and Jones & Vining, which produce soles and other shoe components, also still have factories here.

The business that Abraham Hyde started in Cambridge was a typical 20th century entrepreneurial success story: Immigrant founder without much capital discovers a business opportunity, and then others. His company, A.R. Hyde, began to make fashionable shoes for women, then boots for soldiers during World War I. It made ice skates between the wars, and boots again during World War II.

"Then," says John Fisher, the founder's grandson, "my grandfather made the decision that the fashion industry had too much cyclicality and trendiness, so he started making athletic footwear only: bowling shoes, skating boots, ski boots, basketball shoes, baseball cleats."

Hyde grew by acquisition, buying brands like Spot-Bilt. (It made athletic shoes, including a cleat worn by O.J. Simpson called the Juicemobile.) The company supplied shoes to NASA, and a pair of its boots were worn during the first space walk. In 1968, Hyde purchased the Pennsylvania-based Saucony brand of sneakers, in part so it could add additional production capacity. In the 1970s and 1980s, the US running boom put the wind at the company's back. (At right, Hyde-made ski boots from around 1950. Photo courtesy of John Fisher.)

But the company was always "a small brand in a big brand world," says Fisher, whose first job at Hyde was in the advertising department, around 1971. Making athletic shoes, he says, was "a fair industry. If you built a good shoe, and you charged a fair price, and sold it through the legitimate channels of distribution, you could carve out a place for yourself."

Fisher assumed the CEO role in 1991, around the time the company changed its name to Saucony, its most recognizable brand.

Fisher says Nike was the company that helped popularize the idea of making shoes overseas, and then marketing the heck out of them. "They really disrupted the industry," he says.

Nike, founded in 1964, grew into the shoe industry's colossus. Its revenues last year were $36 billion, and in 2003 it acquired one of the oldest sneaker-makers in Massachusetts, Converse, for $305 million.

Converse was one of the original marketing innovators, hiring basketball star Chuck Taylor in the 1920s to be a traveling salesman for its high-top sneaker. (Converse dates to 1908 in

Malden; it introduced the All-Star, one of the earliest athletic shoes, in 1917.) Under Nike, Converse's annual revenue has grown impressively: from about $200 million to nearly $2 billion.

"Nike is so large that not to call Portland the center of the industry is foolhardy," says Fisher. "But the origin of athletic footwear was here, and still is here." (Germany is home to two of the biggest brands, adidas and Puma, founded by two estranged brothers. The former company chose Oregon for its US base of operations, and the latter initially chose Brockton.)

Fisher says his company was still making product in Massachusetts and Maine up through the mid-1990s. Then, there was a dust-up with the Federal Trade Commission over using the phrase "Made in America," he says.

Because many of the industry's suppliers had moved to Asia, and buying components from them was much less expensive, Saucony was purchasing components overseas and assembling them in Bangor, Maine. After a few consumer complaints about representing those shoes as being "Made in America," the FTC charged both Saucony and New Balance with misrepresenting their products as being entirely domestically made. The company closed the Bangor factory, which had employed 300 workers, and, like the rest of the industry, started working with contract manufacturers abroad, which own the factories and employ the workers, but will make shoes to a company's specifications. That move "freed up a huge amount of capital," Fisher, says.

These days, the industry is searching for new customers in China and trying to cope with the closing of many of the brick-and-mortar stores in the United States that once sold its products.

"Hopefully, the downsizing of wholesalers and retailers has hit bottom, knock on wood," says Tom Carleo, a New Balance vice president who has also worked for Saucony and Nike. Then there are fads and customer preferences, which can change as fast as New England's weather.

Carleo says the talent base that has grown up working in the shoe industry in Massachusetts is one reason it has remained rooted here. There are also technologists and entrepreneurs, he says, thinking about how new technologies, like 3-D printing, will change the way shoes are made.

And one last reason: "Boston is one of the top running cities in the world," Carleo says.

It doesn't hurt to have that annual road race every April, bringing 30,000 runners to town from 100 countries.

These days, Fisher is out of the shoe business. He teaches marketing at Boston College's Carroll School of Management, often relying on his experience to supply real-world examples. And though he sold Saucony for $170 million in 2005 — it's now part of a publicly held Michigan company, Wolverine Worldwide — he still owns a small piece of history: When the company decamped from its original Cambridge building in 1987, eight decades after it was founded by Abraham Hyde, Fisher took a brick with him. He still has it.

The Mystery of the Last Candy Factory

Published in the Boston Globe, May 4, 2018

On the walk from Kendall Square into Central Square, you'll pass the last remaining candy factory in Cambridge. It's a boxy cream-colored building, with opaque windows. A small sign out front whispers that the facility, Cambridge Brands, is owned by Tootsie Roll Industries. You need sharp eyes to read it from the far side of Main Street.

For a few years now, I've wanted to unwrap the mystery of the Cambridge Brands factory, and find a way to get inside. I succeeded at one of those goals.

My starting point: Everyone in Cambridge assumed that the factory probably made Tootsie Rolls or Tootsie Pops — or maybe both — given its corporate parentage. And the small sign incorporates Tootsie's familiar white, red, and brown color scheme.

For the first half of the 20th century, Cambridge was the rich, creamy center of the nation's candy industry. Factories cranked out Charleston Chews, Necco wafers, Squirrel Nut Zippers, Sugar Daddies, and an array of chocolates and cookies, including the Fig Newton. According to the Cambridge Historical Society, 1946 was the apex of the city's candymaking era, with 66 different companies dotted around Cambridge. At the time, the area in which Cambridge Brands is located was known as "Confectioner's Row." The Cambridge Brands facility was built in 1927 by the James O. Welch Company, which invented Sugar Babies, Sugar Daddies, and Sugar Mamas — all caramel-intensive treats. Welch was eventually acquired by Tootsie Roll Industries in 1993.

In the second half of the 20th century, the candy industry consolidated, manufacturing moved out of the city, and many of the dustier brands fell out of fashion. Still, even in the early 1980s, "My first memory of the neighborhood was how sweet it smelled," Gus Rancatore remembers. "The Necco factory was still making candy, and I think two other factories were still in business." Rancatore was a cofounder in 1981 of Toscanini's Ice

Cream, whose original location is diagonally across the street from Cambridge Brands. But Rancatore told me that he'd never been inside the factory. "Wish I could be more helpful," he said.

I asked the public relations representatives of Tootsie Roll Industries, headquartered in Chicago, whether anyone could tell me about the factory in Cambridge, or perhaps give me a glimpse inside. I waited, and called, and e-mailed again. I rang up the CEO's office and left a message.

I read everything I could about Tootsie Roll Industries, which the Wall Street Journal described in 2012 as a "secret empire." It's a publicly traded company — the stock is down about 20 percent over the last year — but does the bare minimum of publicity. The company has 2,000 employees, and the Cambridge factory is the smallest production facility it owns. Two years ago, there was a rare accident at the Cambridge factory — a candy-wrapping machine severed a worker's fingertip — and the Occupational Safety & Health Administration levied a $46,000 fine for workplace safety and training violations.

I eventually tracked down one person who'd been inside the factory: Jeff Lemberg, a Curry College communications professor who wrote a 2002 story about it for the Globe, just before Halloween. "I was hoping to find chocolate rivers and Oompa-Loompas," Lemberg said, "but it was just a bland factory run by a small team of Central American women in hair nets." The noise from the machinery was so loud that everyone wore ear plugs. Lemberg also happened to meet the CEO and COO of Tootsie Roll Industries, Melvin and Ellen Gordon, who gave him a personal tour. "By coincidence," Lemberg explained, they just happened to be in town from Chicago.

Actually, it turns out that the top two executives of Tootsie Roll Industries lived part-time in Wellesley and had strong ties to the area. Melvin Gordon was born in Dorchester, and earned degrees from Harvard College and Harvard Business School; Ellen Gordon studied at Wellesley College and earned a degree at Brandeis.

The Gordons had overseen acquisitions that included Dots gumdrops, Charms Blow Pops, Dubble Bubble gum, and Andes chocolate mints — as well as the purchase of the Cambridge Brands facility in 1993. While the company is headquartered in Chicago, the Gordons seemed to spend a good deal of time in Wellesley; Tootsie Roll Industries paid about $12,500 a month to rent them an apartment in the Windy City, and between $800,000 and $1.2 million on their private jet transportation, according to Securities and Exchange Commission filings.

When Melvin died three years ago, at age 95, Ellen took over as the company's CEO. She is now 86. "Mrs. Gordon is vigorously engaged in the day to day operation of the Company's business and strategic planning," according to a March SEC filing. "In addition, Mrs. Gordon has advised the Board that she has no present intention of retiring from her current positions as an officer and a director."

There are continual questions about whether Tootsie Roll Industries will be gobbled up by a larger company. But Ellen Gordon, her late husband, and her father before her have been at the helm since the 1950s. Gordon and her four daughters own about 60 percent of the company.

No Wall Street analysts cover Tootsie Roll Industries, in part because the company is so reticent — it doesn't hold investor conference calls, for instance. But in 2017, the activist investment firm Spruce Point Capital Management issued a "strong sell" recommendation on the company. "Tootsie dates back to the early 1900s and its brands are withering along with its core customers," the Spruce Point report said. "Sales haven't grown in six years, and we estimate it is losing market share in North America."

After waiting two months for a response, I finally got an e-mail from the public relations firm that represents Tootsie Roll Industries. They answered five questions, informing me that the answers came from the CEO herself.

About 200 people work at the Cambridge factory, making 26,500,000 pieces of candy a day. Of those, about 14,560,000 are individual Junior Mints. (The Cambridge Brands facility is the world's only source of Junior Mints, Sugar Babies, and Charleston Chews — but it doesn't make Tootsie Rolls or Tootsie Pops.) How is it that Cambridge Brands has continued to operate as everything else has closed down? "The company has invested millions of dollars in automating packaging, processing lines, and materials handling equipment, and we will continue to do so," Gordon wrote. (Gordon's photo at right is courtesy of Tootsie Roll Industries.)

Why doesn't Cambridge brands offer tours, or even let the occasional reporter (like me) inside? "As is typical in the manufacturing industry," Gordon explained, "for food safety, proper sanitation, and hygiene, the facility operates a closed plant."

Its neighbor on Massachusetts Avenue, the New England Confectionery Company, decamped from Cambridge in 2003, moving its plant to Revere. That company is in dire straits: It filed for Chapter 11 bankruptcy protection in April, and an auction is scheduled for May 23. The company could be acquired by someone who wants to continue running it, or it could be sold for parts. Necco's former factory is now occupied by the Novartis Institutes for Biomedical Research, a pharmaceutical research center that is now Cambridge's biggest private employer.

That leaves Cambridge Brands as the last vestige of an industrial era when Cambridge made things, from railroad cars to carriages to soap to woven hoses to bolts.

It still makes Junior Mints.

. . .

[Author's note: Unfortunately, the Necco factory in Revere shut down in July 2018, laying off 230 workers. As of Halloween 2020, Ellen Gordon was still running Tootsie Roll Industries as she approached her 90th birthday. The Cambridge Brands factory is included on the map of key places in this book, at http://bit.ly/innoeco-map.]

In Boston, the Keynote to Apple's Turnaround

Published in the Boston Globe, August 28, 2011

To appreciate the scope of what Steve Jobs accomplished during his second stint as Apple's chief executive, you have to rewind the tape — or rather, spin back the iPod's wheel — to an August morning in Boston 14 years ago.

More than 1,500 of the Apple faithful filled the Park Plaza Castle to hear Jobs deliver his first MacWorld Expo keynote since returning to the company the year before. I was in the front of the hall, covering the event for *Wired* magazine's website. It felt like a conclave of Shakers, devout but dwindling.

"I came today to give you a status report on what's going on, and to try to fill you in on some of the steps we're taking to get Apple healthy again," Jobs began.

It was a resonant, return-of-the-prodigal-son moment. But it wasn't at all clear that Jobs could save the company he cofounded. Apple had brought him back to the fold after a 12-year absence by purchasing his failed start-up, NeXT Inc. Just a month before MacWorld came to town, Apple's board had sacked the chief executive who had made that decision.

Jobs had not yet assumed the position of Apple's interim chief executive; he introduced himself that day as chairman and CEO of Pixar.

There was very little good news for Jobs to report. The company had been within three months of running out of cash and declaring bankruptcy. Sales had dropped precipitously.

Things were so bleak that when Michael Dell, founder of rival computer maker Dell Inc., was asked what he would do if he ran Apple, he said that he would "shut it down and give the money back to the shareholders." There were about 8,000 fewer people attending the MacWorld trade show that year.

When Jobs told the crowd that Microsoft was making a $150 million investment in Apple — money that would help sustain the company — the audience booed. They kept booing as Bill Gates's face appeared on a huge screen, looming above Jobs, to assure everyone that Microsoft would continue producing Office software for Macs. Jobs chastised the audience: "If others are going to help us, that's great, because we need all the help we can get."

The audience was full of Apple retailers, software developers, and clone-makers: Apple had allowed companies like

Power Computing and Motorola to crank out generic-looking computers that ran its Macintosh operating system. Jobs would eventually put an end to those clones, which cannibalized Apple's own sales without doing much to spread the gospel of Mac. But on that morning, he said nothing much about the future, outlining a bland strategy of getting Apple focused on markets where it was strongest: creative agencies and schools.

Did Jobs want to run Apple? According to the book *The Second Coming of Steve Jobs*, he "thrust himself into the power vacuum and quickly took control" after the company's prior chief executive, Gil Amelio, was ousted. But Harvard Business School professor David Yoffie, who has written extensively about Apple, tells a different story. "I heard from insiders at the time that Steve was ambivalent," Yoffie says, "but to my knowledge, the board wanted him."

At the time of the Boston keynote, Michael Oh was a 24-year-old who ran Tech Superpowers, an Apple retailer and service provider on Newbury Street. "We were ready for someone to take the helm and make change, so we could follow — anyone with a good plan," he said. "Then came Jobs, and he was, for lack of a better term, the messiah for the Macintosh platform."

Jobs was named interim CEO of Apple in September 1997. The following year, he introduced the first major product of his second term in office: the candy-colored iMac, which packed the workings of the computer into a Jetsons-style TV unit. (The "i" stood for Internet, and the company had designed a radically simple, two-step process to connect to the network.) It was the start of a Barnum-esque parade of products, including the iPod music player, iTunes online media store, iPhone, iPad tablet computer, and the ultra-thin MacBook Air.

In 2001, the first Apple Stores opened in Virginia and California; there are now 333 around the world, and consumers regularly line up outside for the privilege of being the first to own a new Apple product.

Jobs became the undisputed heavyweight champ of new product introduction, forbidding leaks in advance of announcements and getting the attention of the world's media focused on him. Apple lovers practically salivated when, at the end of a Jobs keynote, he would pause and say, "One more thing," always saving the biggest news for last. (In Boston, there had been no "one more thing.")

In 1997, Apple was begging Microsoft and others to keep writing software for the Macintosh. Today, the iPhone and iPad are the dominant mobile devices, as far as software developers are concerned. There are at least 425,000 apps available through the iTunes Store, and whenever a developer decides to charge for an app, Apple pockets one-third of the price.

The 1997 MacWorld keynote was the last time, as far as I know, that Jobs gave a public speech in Boston. The trade show moved to New York the following year — closer to creative industries like advertising and design, and better for generating media coverage.

Much has been written about the culture of innovation, sly industry disruption, and savvy marketing that Jobs fostered at Apple over the past 14 years. For a brief moment earlier this month, Apple was the most valuable company in the world, measured by market capitalization.

Back in 1997, in the Park Plaza Castle, even the truest of true believers could not have imagined such a renaissance. It was one of those moments that many of us have faced, when you are handed a horrible situation and expected to work miracles. Few of us will do as well as Jobs did.

...

[Author's note: This column was published the week that Steve Jobs resigned as Apple's CEO. Jobs died less than two months later, in October 2011.]

YankeeIngenuity.com

Published in the Boston Globe Sunday Magazine, November 7, 1999

From the highest part of his Christmas tree farm in Swiftwater, New Hampshire, Mike Garvan can look north into the White Mountains — to Bethlehem, Franconia, and Twin Mountain — where he used to work for the US Forest Service. It's the last day of August, and on his way up to this overlook, Garvan has passed row upon row of Frasier and balsam firs, each tagged with a different colored plastic ribbons to indicate its quality. Occasionally, he pulls out a pair of orange-handled clippers from a holster on his belt and snips at a tree so that it will grow more evenly.

"By the early '80s, I was moving into a desk job with the Forest Service, and my next promotion would have been to West Virginia," says Garvan, who has an eaglelike nose, wavy dark-gray hair, and, a white beard. "I wanted to stay in New England, so I started looking for farms I could lease. I struggled at first to make a go of it, like many small businessmen."

Today, Garvan's Mountain Star Farms has about 75,000 trees on 80 acres. It's larger than most New England Christmas-tree operations, but in Garvan's words, it is "still a very small business, with modest sales revenues."

But that's starting to change. Last year, Garvan began selling his Christmas trees over the Internet. He sold 200 trees, boxed in heavy, waxed cardboard and shipped via United Parcel Service, and earned roughly 50 percent more profit on each than he would have if he had sold them wholesale. This season, Garvan expects that he'll sell between 400 and 800 trees through his Web site. Those transactions will account for 15 percent of his total volume (but 30 percent of his revenue), and his spreadsheet projections indicate that those Web sales with their high profit margins could represent half of his business percent of his business — or more — within five years.

"The business was doing fine before the Internet, but the Net gives the business an added dimension, added profitability," Garvan says, walking down the hill toward Swiftwater Cottage, a former housekeeping cabin painted white with green shutters. It now serves as an office and welcome center for people who come to the farm in November and December to cut their own trees. Garvan is accompanied by Ben Hoyt, the farm manager, who started working at Mountain Star in 1983, shearing trees as a 13-year-old hired hand. "It's also made it possible for me to make a generational transfer of the business to Ben."

Throughout New England, the Internet is changing the dynamics of business, making communication more efficient and opening up global markets. But the medium's effects are most startling among smaller enterprises, the farms and home-based businesses that have allowed New Englanders to carve out a living for centuries. Not only does the Net permit entrepreneurs throughout the region to live where they want while selling their products around the world, but it's making cottage industry far more financially rewarding. Of the fifteen entrepreneurs I spoke to for this story, only one — a grouchy golf-club maker in Vermont — said his Web site wasn't generating substantial new income.

More representative is Anne Kaye, a spirited 70-year-old antiques maven in North Providence, Rhode Island, who sells mahogany bedroom sets and carnival-glass punch bowls on eBay, the popular on-line auction site based in San Jose, California. Before she bought a computer and taught herself how to surf the Web, Kaye says she would buy a bedroom set for $700 and sell it to a wholesaler for $850; on eBay, she sells the set directly to a consumer, who pays as much as $1,300 or $1,400 for it. "The last person in the chain makes the most money," explains Kaye, "and right now, we're the last person in the chain."

"Before, I had hamburger every day," she continues before executing a perfect vaudevillean pause. "Now, I have steak!"

Even the most perfunctory Internet search turns up hundreds of small New England businesses that have ventured into the wilds of e-commerce. There are shops in the Berkshires that sell antique tools, landscape painters in central Vermont hawking their art, New Hampshire firms that sell architectural elements salvaged from old houses, a blacksmith, used snowmobile dealers, flower growers, maple syrup merchants, and bed-and-breakfasts galore. One typical B&B; owner, Bob Bonkowski, who with his wife, Sue, runs the Heron House B&B; in Southwest Harbor, Maine, says that his Web site is responsible for 70 percent of all new guests.

"People who consider the rural countryside a haven have always sought to try to make a living there," says Tony Elliott, co-founder and vice president of SoverNet, an Internet service provider in Bellows Falls, Vermont. "The Net provides a link, makes it easier to sustain a cottage industry. You don't have to be in the big city anymore to do the kind of commerce that you need to support yourself. The Internet brings you in touch with all of the people and the resources you need." Elliott says that an increasing number of SoverNet's customers are inquiring about on-line storefronts.

While cottage industry in New England may never have been endangered, the Internet — by making it more remunerative — seems to be fortifying it for the next century. "Cottage industry is very representative of New England," says Laurel Ulrich, the Philips professor of early American history at Harvard University. "People love the independence of having their own land. But most of New England has such bad soil — it's just rock. So going back to the Colonial period, it was always a matter of patching together a little bit of farming, a bit of trapping, some fishing, lots of weaving and spinning."

In contrast, though, the new wave of Internet-enabled cottage industry allows its practitioners to focus on fewer things. When asked whether she's surprised at the extent to which the Internet is super-charging small businesses like Garvan's, providing them with a reliable, profitable stream of orders, Ulrich says she isn't. Why? Her two sons, both PhD engineers, run a small business in Lee, New Hampshire, that makes high-performance kick scooters called Xootrs. "They're a form of personal transportation," Ulrich explains. "They are to old-fashioned scooters as Rollerblades are to roller skates." And where can one buy a Xootr? On the Web, of course.

Walking into the converted three-car garage in Carol Coski's side yard is like entering the barrel of a kaleidoscope. Every wall is covered with brilliantly colored cotton fabrics: batiks from Bali, pastel plaids, and offbeat prints, like hogs on Harleys, duded up in leather jackets. In one corner is a jumble of red-white-and-blue priority envelopes from the US Postal Service. Coski stands behind a counter, in a short-sleeved shirt and shorts that she made herself, helping a customer who has driven here, to Westminster, Vermont, from her home in Western Massachusetts.

Before Coski's shop took over the garage, her husband, Jim, used to raise sheep and rabbits in it. The Coskis have always been an entrepreneurial pair; before starting her fabric shop, Quilt-a-way, five years ago, Carol ran a singles club in Rhode Island and made neckties. Together, they've bred dogs and sold homemade dog biscuits, an operation that at one point employed 40 people.

"My daughter, Jan, is a computer programmer at Brown University," Carol Coski says, taking a break at a picnic table just outside the shop where, in good weather, she teaches classes in fabric painting. "She always used to say, 'You're nobody if you don't have a Web page.' I was doing e-mail but not the Internet, and eventually I said OK. So Jan made me a Web page for Mother's Day.

"I wasn't expecting that it would give me anything more than Web presence, but to my surprise, people started ordering." These days, Coski says, 70 percent of her business comes from the Web site in the summer, and 85 percent in winter, when her local customers are less inclined to venture outside. Visitors to the site can browse among roughly 1,000 fabrics and order them using a secure form.

While Coski enjoys meeting her customers face-to-face in the shop and participating in the quilting community through classes and competitions — her own quilts win prizes at fairs around New England — she says that the Westminster area can't really support a retail store that doesn't also have an Internet outpost: "Initially, I thought I would be serving just the local community."

But, she continues, "If it weren't for the Internet, I'd be out of business already. Quilt-a-way doesn't just appeal to quilters in the area. I'm appealing to quilters around the world."

Every night after dinner, Coski and her husband process the orders that come in from the Web site — anywhere from five to 45 a day. "On a slow day in the store, I might sell $36 in fabric," Coski says. "But that night, I'll do $650 on the Net. Some nights, we've had orders for over $1,000."

Coski has loyal customers in Canada, the United Kingdom, Australia, and Hong Kong. She explains that often, they can find a better selection of fabrics at better prices on line than they can in their local retail stores, even when shipping costs are factored in. "We have orders that I've stumped my postmaster with," Coski says, watching a glossy blue Volvo pull into her driveway. It's after 4 p.m. — closing time — but she'll open up the store anyway. "I come in and say, 'Bernie, where is United Arab Emirates?' And he says, 'I don't know, I'll look it up.'"

Since Coski isn't interested in running a purely virtual enterprise — she would miss the interaction that comes with helping customers with their projects — Quilt a way is just about the perfect business for her. The Web provides the financial stability to do what she loves. And she can live where she wants, on four acres just off Interstate 91 in southern Vermont, with a brook on the property. She and Jim can still breed dogs; a gaggle of shar peis romp around the yard, sniffing at everything. Every January, the Coskis decamp for a month to Tampa, Florida, where Carol teaches a class at a quilting store run by a friend. When they return, even though the store has been locked up, they've got a queue of several hundred orders waiting in the e-mail in-box.

That kind of mobility is one of the most appealing characteristics of a Web-oriented business, but it also means that Web proprietors can easily uproot their business and take it elsewhere — a possibility the Coskis think about whenever their driveway ices up. "If we decide to move to North Carolina because of the winters here," says Jim, "75 or 80 percent of the business comes with us."

How does the Coskis' backyard business compare with their earlier endeavors, like the dog-biscuit company? There isn't the pressure of having employees or overhead, says Jim, who adds that he and Carol are earning more than they ever have. A new Jeep Grand Cherokee in the driveway, with "Coski" vanity plates, is evidence.

Forrester Research is a Cambridge company that tracks technology's impact on business and also makes estimates about how fast electronic commerce is growing. According to Forrester's projections, small and medium-sized local businesses sold $680 million worth of goods and services on the Web in 1998 — a number that, by 2003, Forrester expects will grow to $6 billion.

While those numbers sound impressive, Forrester analyst Charlene Li explains that small and medium-sized local businesses, over that span of time, will actually be losing a share of on-line purchases to their bigger competitors. According to Li, while the local small fry sold 9 percent of everything consumers bought on line last year, by 2003, they will represent only about 6 percent of Net purchases. In the off-line world, Li adds for comparison, fully 50 percent of all retail sales are handled by small and medium-sized businesses.

"The local players got to the Web first," says Li. "But they don't have the infrastructure, the back-end systems, the marketing money. So when the big guys come along, they have this huge infrastructure, lots of inventory, and powerful brands. It takes longer for them to set up on line, but once they do, they dominate. Most of the volume [in any product category] will go through the five biggest players."

That doesn't spell doom for the Quilt-a-ways of the world, though. Small-business people tend to be savvier than, say, the 25-year-old founder of a Silicon Valley start-up with $5 million in venture capital in his pocket. Rural entrepreneurs, Li says, "can't afford to put their money into a black hole. If the money isn't generating profits, they won't spend it."

There is room on the Web for the garage entrepreneurs and backyard tycoons, Li says. "They do have a niche, even if they're not making very much of a dent [in the overall e-commerce figures]. Those that can find a place on the Web will sell more than they've ever sold before."

To the CottageIndustry.com CEOs, that's hardly bad news.

At Jock's lunch counter in the tiny town of Fairfield, Maine, the waitress knows exactly what Frank Tozier Jr. wants: a burger, no fries, and a bottle of Poland Spring water. Tozier works just up the road, and he drives his red pickup to Jock's every day for lunch.

"What do you think, Michelle?" Tozier asks the waitress. He looks as if he could be the actor Woody Harrelson's younger brother.

"I try not to," Michelle answers.

Tozier's company, AC Antiques, is an example of how the Net is creating small businesses from scratch. Tozier grew up on a dairy farm in Fairfield, and he worked it until he was 30. After a short stint working for a friend who manufactured wholesale gift items, like wooden duck decoys, Tozier began to hear about people who were selling antiques on eBay. Earlier this year, Tozier, an antiques neophyte, tried his hand at listing a few items on the site.

Like Anne Kaye in North Providence, he was astonished at the prices antiques could command on the Web. Before long, he was buying in much larger volumes; on one day in early September, he had 103 items up for bid on the site, from Victorian marble-topped tables to Art Deco wardrobes to antique phonographs. Every month this year, Tozier says, his sales on eBay have doubled.

"I've shipped a bunch of stuff to Hong Kong and several pieces to Alaska," he says, driving toward the rented warehouse where he stores most of his unsold inventory. "Everybody's on the Net. I'll ship anywhere you can send me a check from."

When asked whether his business is doing better than the antiques shops in nearby Waterville that don't sell on line, Tozier, not an eager conversationalist, nods.

"There's no place to have a store that gives you the same reach as the Internet," he says, as if it should be obvious.

Before AC Antiques, Tozier had never been a boss; now, he has five employees, three of whom handle crating and shipping, one who cleans the merchandise, and one who handles paperwork. This month, the business's main location, where the antiques are readied for shipping, was slated to double in size, from 4,000 to 8,000 square feet.

"I always just assumed I'd be a farmer," says the accidental antiques mogul. "They wouldn't have predicted this in my yearbook."

For others, like Deborah Evans, running a Web business makes it possible to escape from high-pressure metropolitan careers. Evans, who along with her business partner, Dede Johnson, runs the site MaineNeedle point.com, had been a construction manager for high-rise buildings in Hartford, Boston, and New York.

"We wanted to do something fun, because we were too old to get up in the morning and hate going to work," says Evans, who is dressed as if she's ready for an afternoon of sailing, in a polo shirt with the collar turned up, boat shoes, and an eToys baseball cap. "And we both knew that we couldn't work for anyone else anymore."

Now, they spend their days in Johnson's converted dining room in Blue Hill, Maine, with a dog at their feet, a wall covered with various hues of needlepoint wool, two large-screen monitors, and several printers and scanners. "We're a design studio, a manufacturer, and a retailer — all in one room," Evans exclaims. But there's no sign in Johnson's front yard advertising MaineNeedlepoint.com's existence; the Web is their primary retail outlet, and all of their needlepoint patterns are designed on the computer and produced on the premises.

Customer response to MaineNeedlepoint.com has been so positive that Evans has started to write a business plan, and the partners are making plans to incorporate and find outside investors to fuel the company's growth. Even more exciting, to Evans, is the chance to teach technology skills and business sense to high school students and recent graduates in the area.

"One of the things that we hope we can offer, as we grow, is an opportunity to see a career that isn't picking blueberries or lobstering," Evans says. "If you've never touched a computer before, we'll mentor you. It would be really nice to give back to this community."

Inside a large rust-colored barn with two walls open to the elements, Mike Garvan and his farm manager, Ben Hoyt, are getting their packaging equipment ready for the 1999 holiday season. First, to calculate shipping costs, they weigh the tree using a hanging scale. Then, they place the tree on a machine that vibrates and shakes it vigorously, which causes any leaves, brush, or brown needles to fall to the floor. Then Hoyt pulls a 7-foot-long cardboard box from a pallet in the corner. He lays the box horizontally on a work table and then feeds a cable with a loop at the end through the box. Garvan attaches the loop to the base of the tree, and Hoyt uses an electric winch to pull the tree, base first, into the box. It's amazing to watch the tree fold up into itself as it disappears into the box.

Garvan slips some freebies into the box with the tree. There's a pamphlet about Mountain Star Farms, along with care instructions for the tree, a tree-disposal bag, and, for the first hundred or so customers, a tree ornament. Then, he uses his PC and laser printer, loaded with software from UPS, to create a shipping label for the box. (He makes a point not to ship trees on Thursday or Friday if he can help it, since he knows they'll spend at least part of the weekend sitting in a heated warehouse, which causes the trees to dry out.) This 7-foot Frasier fir, which would have sold for $23 to a wholesaler, or $28 to a customer who came to the farm to cut it himself, will sell for $40 to a Web shopper.

Who is it, exactly, who uses the Web to buy a Christmas tree? Garvan admits that picking out a tree, for many people, is an even more personal choice than picking out fruits and vegetables at the supermarket. But he notes that Web-based grocery delivery firms are finally gaining momentum, and he brags that once people see the quality of his trees, they will become customers for life:

"I think about the guy who works on Wall Street who doesn't want to carry a tree home in the snow, or the retired couple in Florida struggling with the tree and putting it on top of the Miata. That's as opposed to the guy in the brown suit showing up at your door and saying, 'Here's your tree.'"

Garvan's sales pitch is pretty well honed. He's also enthusiastic about expanding his on-line offerings and is considering selling wreaths, ornaments, and tree stands, in addition to the tree itself. Now that the Net has enabled a direct relationship between Garvan and his customers — he's like the Michael Dell of the north country — anything is possible.

"Finding customers was always a barrier to growing our business," Garvan says, sitting at his desk in the cottage. "The Internet has solved that."

Ulrich, the Harvard professor and the Pulitzer Prize-winning author of *A Midwife's Tale: The Life of Martha Ballard*, says that this direct channel from cottages and farms to customers is a new wrinkle for New England entrepreneurs.

"In the 19th century, cottage industry meant piecework," she says. "You'd get raw materials from somewhere else, you'd process them, you'd send them to the storekeeper, he'd send them to Newburyport, and they'd go off to some kind of market." Having a closer relationship with the customer is not only a way to hold on to more of the profits, according to Ulrich; it provides more of an opportunity for the CottageIndustry.com CEOs of the next century to "be more creative and do something that they love. They can take advantage of the attraction of being able to live here and not have to commute to a city. There's something about the freedom there that's new."

What Happened to the Real Animal House

Published in the Boston Globe, September 24, 2019

Hanover, NH — It's a quiet September morning on the Dartmouth College campus. The students are trickling back from summer break, but classes haven't yet begun.

And there's no evidence of activity at 9 East Wheelock Street, not far from the school's central quad. The stately two-story brick building with green shutters was once Alpha Delta house, the fraternity that inspired the movie "Animal House."

Today, there is no band playing on the building's broad front porch, no one hanging out in the Gentleman's Bar on the first floor, no one in the infamous party basement, and not a toga in sight.

But on the second floor, once home to the brothers of Alpha Delta, there are men and women tapping out emails, taking conference calls, and huddling for meetings.

Alpha Delta house has gone corporate. The fraternity was de-recognized by Dartmouth in 2015, after a branding incident and other disciplinary violations. The house sat empty for several years, as lawsuits and zoning squabbles played out. And then this spring, startups began to move in. There are now five of them — all with some kind of tie to Dartmouth — paying $200 a month for an office that was once a double dorm room.

John Pepper, who as an undergrad served as the fraternity's social chair, and lived on the third floor, greets me at the front door: "Welcome to the AD Innovation Center."

When I inhale deeply at the threshold — it's a beautiful fall morning, and I've left the city — Pepper quickly asks, "You don't smell anything, do you? It took us months to get rid of the smell. Most of the old furniture is gone." Pepper is known in Boston as the founder of the Boloco chain of healthy burrito shops, but he lives just across the Connecticut River from the Dartmouth campus, in Norwich, Vermont. He's chairman of the corporate entity that owns Alpha Delta house, and also chair of the selectboard in Norwich.

Alpha Delta house dates back to 1920, and the fraternity goes back even further, to the 1840s. In the years after "National Lampoon's Animal House" was released in 1978, making the phrase "double secret probation" a catch-phrase and launching John Belushi's film career, the fraternity tried to distance itself from it. But dig just a little, and you discover that the writer who spun tales of his frat days in National Lampoon magazine, Chris Miller, was an Alpha Delta brother. Miller was also one of the writers of the movie, and in 2006 published a memoir titled, "The Real Animal House: The Awesomely Depraved Saga of the Fraternity That Inspired the Movie."

The movie, says Scott Snyder, another alumnus of Alpha Delta, is "an embellishment that took all the craziest things that Chris experienced and imagined, and condensed them into one narrative." He adds that "there are many fraternities you could go to and have that kind of experience, if that's what you were interested in." Snyder is now an architect in Vermont who helped oversee the recent renovation, and serves on the board.

"If you'd seen the house four or five years ago," Snyder says, "it was totally abused, and in really bad disrepair. First, we had to make it safe and code compliant." Pepper estimates they spent about $75,000.

The renovation didn't eliminate all traces of Greek life: there's still some spray-painted AD graffiti on a brick wall in the basement, and some rooms still feature murals created by past residents, like a screaming eagle spreading its wings in front of a Stonehenge-like structure. (The letters underneath stand for the fraternity's semi-secret motto: "Sickness Is Health. Blackness Is Truth. Drinking Is Strength.")

But on the mantles of the fireplaces in various offices, beer bottles and textbooks have been replaced by business tomes like *Crossing the Chasm* and *The High Growth Handbook*.

All of the current tenants have some kind of link to Dartmouth: their founders include alumni, professors, and college employees who are developing startups in their off-hours. For Bill Hudenko, a psychology professor and researcher at Dartmouth, part of the appeal is that the AD Innovation Center is a five-minute walk from his office on campus. But he also appreciates getting informal advice and support from other entrepreneurs; one of his board members, Kevin McCurdy, runs a startup located just across the hall. Hudenko's startup, Trusst, has built a secure app that lets people communicate with mental health professionals for a monthly fee, without having to schedule or show up for in-office visits.

Vidigami is a startup that helps schools collect and share the photos they capture throughout the year. Resolve aims to help consumers negotiate when they receive exorbitant medical bills. Worthee, the company that Pepper and McCurdy run, is a mobile app designed to help low-wage workers better manage their careers. CampersApp, run by a husband-and-wife team that have day jobs at Dartmouth's business school, enables campgrounds and RV parks to communicate with their guests through a mobile app, and fill some of their campsites with last-minute discounted bookings.

"It's cool being with a bunch of other startups," says Heather Gere, CEO of CampersApp. Travis Gere, the startup's Chief Technology Officer, adds, "Brainstorming solutions and having a sounding board is something we don't have when the two of us are working together from home."

One dynamic that the denizens of the AD Innovation Center have adjusted to is fraternity alums dropping by to give their families a tour. It can get busy during the college's homecoming week or during winter carnival.

A more vexing problem that Pepper says he continues to deal with: break-ins. "We have surveillance video of twenty students breaking in on different occasions, looking for some memorabilia they can go hang in their room and say, 'This is from Alpha Delta,'" he says. "The last one is from three weeks ago." (He says the break-ins haven't affected the office tenants — and that aside from reprints of historic photographs, there isn't much memorabilia left to take.)

Pepper posits that turning the former frat house into an incubator has helped strengthen the fledgling startup scene in Hanover — even though he is not sure how long it will be used as office space. Snyder says they've considered creating a "small boutique hotel" on the as-yet-unrenovated third floor. Pepper wants to host more Dartmouth student and alumni events in the building, and says that he recently received an inquiry from a Presidential candidate's campaign looking for office space and event space.

And could the Alpha Delta fraternity ever be resuscitated? The school's administration made it clear in 2017 that once banned, fraternities can't be unbanned. "Their official word is 'never,'" says Pepper. But he adds, "There's no such thing as never." (John Belushi as Bluto: "Nothing is over until we decide it is. Was it over when the Germans bombed Pearl Harbor?")

This past April, an Alpha Delta alumnus rented the house to celebrate the renewal of his wedding vows. "They had a seven-piece band, and there was dancing," Pepper says. It was a one-night revival, a trip back in time.

And the guests wore togas.

3. Failures, Conflicts & Challenges

What Happens When Startups Go South

Published in the Boston Globe, July 20, 2018

When things start going south at a startup, no one wants to talk about it.

The stream of self-congratulatory press releases and social media messages dries up, and executives suddenly stop replying to interview requests. Laid-off employees have typically been asked to sign nondisparagement agreements, so they clam up, too.

Those reasons combine to make it tough to write about the most challenging stage of a startup's existence: when it has burned through its bankroll, and will either die, get acquired by another company, or figure out some way to survive.

It's happening right now at two Boston startups that together have raised more than $160 million in funding from local venture capital firms, and trace their roots to the MIT Media Lab: Jibo and Jana.

Jibo is the higher-profile of the two. Founded in 2012 by a MIT robotics professor, Cynthia Breazeal, it set out to design a countertop robot that would serve as a kind of household concierge. The company's launch video featured a chipper assistant able to serve as a photographer at parties, facilitate videoconferences, and even order Chinese takeout.  But the product didn't hit the market until last fall — and when it did, it couldn't do many of the things promised in the video. And then there was the price: $900. (At right, Cynthia Breazeal with early Jibo employee Jonathan Ross.)

Despite landing on a Time Magazine list of the "25 best inventions of 2017" and garnering lots of other fawning press notices, Jibo wasn't exactly a hot seller — especially when an Amazon Echo intelligent speaker was selling for about $100 and could do many more things than Jibo. (The Echo was unveiled in 2014, after Jibo was in development.)

"We talked a lot about what our killer app was," says a former Jibo employee, who requested anonymity. "I don't think we had a good enough answer, and that created a challenge for marketing. Why was it worth it? At our price point, you had to be able to justify the cost."

"A robot is one of the hardest pieces of tech to get out the door," robotics entrepreneur Gui Cavalcanti said, "because it's a combination of advanced mechanical, electrical, and computational systems that all have to work together. Jibo wasn't ready for producing robots at scale quickly, and the lag time killed their relevance in a fast-moving market." That market is now dominated by less-expensive smart speakers from companies like Amazon, Google, and Apple.

Jibo's vice president of marketing, Nancy Smith, confirmed that the company laid off employees in June, "to allow ourselves additional time to secure additional funding or pursue an exit." ("Exit" is startup lingo for an acquisition or IPO; the latter is not a realistic option for Jibo). When I dropped by Jibo's office midday Wednesday to return a loaner robot, no one was visible working inside, and nobody came to the door. Jibo has raised more than $70 million in venture capital funding, much of it from local firms that included Flybridge Capital Partners and CRV. (At right, Jibo's office on the day I arrived to turn in my robot.)

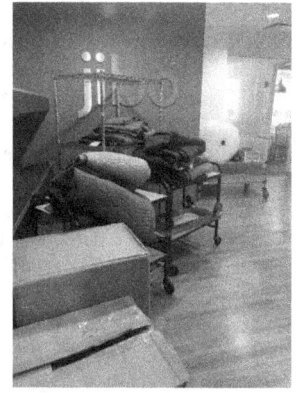

Jana has raised even more money from investors — about $90 million, according to Crunchbase, a startup funding database. It launched a mobile app for Android phones called mCent, which helps defray the cost of mobile phone usage in emerging economies like India and Brazil. How? Users interact with marketing messages or install an app that is being promoted, and they get a few rupees knocked off their monthly bill.

But several things took the wind out of Jana's sails, according to a former employee. The cost of mobile data packages started to drop in the markets that Jana was targeting, and the ad rates that Jana could command were plummeting as well. Plus, Google started rolling out free Wi-Fi access in hundreds of train stations around India. That reduced consumer interest in Jana's major market. There was also "a revolving door" in Jana's leadership ranks, says the former employee, who asked for anonymity.

The company had about 100 employees at one point, and investors valued it at $300 million, according to the former employee. But in late June, there was a severe round of job cuts, and efforts are underway to either sell the company or reboot it with a different strategy. Nathan Eagle, the CEO and cofounder, didn't respond to e-mails or phone calls seeking comment.

What is typically happening at this point in a startup's life? "There are a lot of closed-door meetings," says David Chang, an angel investor and serial entrepreneur who has been part of both successful startups (TripAdvisor) and failures (Mobicious, a photo sharing service for mobile phones.) "The energy changes. The founders aren't around. When people sense that the ship is sinking, it's really hard to get them focused." Board members and investors may be offering conflicting advice about the best course of action, Chang says. The founder is typically trying everything he can "to keep the lights on," he says.

Sometimes, Dipul Patel says, the founders of a startup aren't aware of how bad things are until it's too late. "You don't realize that you're on death's doorstep as quickly as you should," Patel says. "It's like looking in the mirror one day and realizing that you got fat. Well, it didn't happen all of a sudden." In 2016, after several rounds of layoffs, Patel sold his Boston startup Ecovent to a larger company, ConnectM Technology Solutions of Marlborough.

There may be a face-saving sale that gives the investors a bit of their money back — but no profit. A bigger company may want to "acqui-hire" the startup's team of engineers, paying a nominal amount of money to save the larger firm the trouble of recruiting engineers on the open market. Sometimes a venture capital firm forces one of its troubled startups to merge with a healthier startup working in a similar arena. And sometimes, there is manna from heaven — a miraculous new source of funding that comes in at the last possible moment.

But before any of that happens, things often go quiet. Very quiet. "It's perfectly understandable why people aren't spending a lot of time promoting the demise of the venture," says Steve Kane, a Boston entrepreneur. "People have committed so much of their lives, and everything is wrapped up in this endeavor. If it doesn't work out, it is this very heavy emotional situation. It is a humbling experience for the team, and the investors lose everything."

A Bold Attempt to Reinvent Solar Power

Published in the Boston Globe, July 8, 2012

Bic Stevens can remember his first glimpse at some dazzling solar power technology developed at the University of Massachusetts Lowell back in 2001. Scientists had produced a "little quarter-sized solar cell, entirely out of plastic, and it made a little propeller go," Stevens says. The appeal of a "dirt-cheap," pliable, and easy-to-manufacture solar material was that almost anything, from the roof of a bus to the top of an Army tent, could start generating electricity from the sun.

Stevens put the first $50,000 into creating a company that would commercialize the UMass research, and helped recruit a Nobel prize winner in chemistry to advise the new venture, Konarka Technologies. (The company was named after a temple in India built to honor the sun god Surya.)

Over the next 11 years, Konarka raised $170 million from private investors including Chevron Corp.; secured millions in grants, tax credits, and loans from Republican and Democratic administrations in Massachusetts and Washington; bought an old Polaroid plant in New Bedford to make its "Power Plastic"; hired and then laid off 100 employees; and filed for bankruptcy protection in early June. Konarka's creditors will meet Tuesday to discuss the disposition of the company's assets.

Unlike another New England company that is being sold for parts, Providence video game start-up 38 Studios, Konarka was the kind of company that fit perfectly into this region's research-and-design sweet spot.

While 38 Studios employed artists and game designers to craft a digital fantasy realm, Konarka built a team of PhD's in chemistry and materials science to develop a solar cell with a wide array of practical uses.

And while 38 Studios was led by a novice entrepreneur, retired Red Sox star Curt Schilling, Konarka's chief executive, Howard Berke, was a serial entrepreneur who'd previously been involved with videoconferencing and medical imaging companies. 38 Studios was banking on a Hollywood-style blockbuster. Konarka was applying brainpower to bring a scientific breakthrough to market.

So what happened at Konarka?

Employees and investors alike were attracted by the idea of cranking out inexpensive, flexible solar material using a "roll-to-roll" process similar to printing.

But, says Dan Roach, an early Konarka employee, "the unanswered question was always how efficient the product would be" — that is, how much of the available sunlight could it turn into electricity?

Another issue was how long Konarka's Power Plastic would last, since plastic tends to degrade in sunlight. "If there was a case study written about Konarka," says Roach, "it might say that this left the academic lab too early. A lot of the venture capital money was spent doing research, and not developing the product."

While the Army tested Konarka materials for use atop tents, and the company pitched a transparent version of Power Plastic for use on buildings' windows, only two products ever saw the light of day. One was a $180 messenger bag, made by a German retailer, that used Konarka material on the front flap to recharge digital cameras and mobile phones inside. And an Australian company called Sky Shades put Konarka's material on top of a $10,000 patio umbrella, the SolarBrella, which could supply juice to laptops and other portable electronics. Konarka's factory in New Bedford was largely idle.

The last outside money that Konarka raised came in 2010, when Konica Minolta Holdings of Japan invested $20 million. When I visited Konarka later that year, the company said the efficiency of its solar cells was still at 3 to 4 percent, while traditional silicon cells were able to hit 15 to 20 percent.

But Berke was selling the vision: "Imagine putting a plastic strip on the back of a smart card and having it power a display on the front." (He declined to comment for this story.)

"It was hard for Konarka to find that unique place where its product would win out over the alternatives," says Jonathan Melnick, an analyst who tracks the solar industry at Boston-based Lux Research. "They were very good at raising money, but they almost raised so much that it became a hindrance. It forced them to go to market before they were really ready."

Daniel Cohen, a former Konarka scientist, says that his team had managed to achieve 9 percent efficiency in the lab earlier this year. "We had good things to show investors," he says, "and we had more orders in the first month of 2012 than all of 2011." A partnership with 3M was in the works, too. It felt like the company might pull a rabbit out of a hat once again.

But on May 23, Berke called a company meeting and told employees that Konarka hadn't been able to raise more money, and would cease operations. (Coincidentally, Schilling laid off 38 Studios' employees the following day.)

Could someone — perhaps even Berke — acquire Konarka's assets at a bankruptcy sale and continue investing in the technology? I think it's possible. Melnick at Lux Research says, "There's certainly some value in their intellectual property, but whoever acquires it just needs to have a longer vision for when they'd expect to turn a profit. It's not going to be in two years."

During this year's presidential contest, Mitt Romney will no doubt be asked about the $1.5 million grant the state gave Konarka in 2003, when he was governor.

And his successor, Deval Patrick, will most likely lose $3.3 million in taxpayer money that his administration lent Konarka to set up its New Bedford plant. Both governors clearly envisioned that a solar material that could be plastered on just about anything would create plenty of jobs in the state.

But, says Stevens, "it was a very tough nut to crack. You look at the amount of money that has gone into the solar industry, and you see it's a very hard business unless you're incredibly good and incredibly lucky."

On Founders, Venture Capitalists, and Competition

Published in the Boston Globe, November 22, 2009

On July 20, 2006, Sheila Marcelo and Nick Beim flew from Boston to Chicago to visit a company called Sittercity. The business, which charged parents to access an online database of sitters and nannies, had been launched in Boston five years earlier.

"We took the meeting to talk about an investment," says Genevieve Thiers, the Boston College alumnae who founded Sittercity. She'd met Beim, a partner at Waltham-based Matrix Partners, that year at a trade show. "Nick talked about how Matrix worked with companies and founders," Thiers recalls.

Marcelo was serving as an entrepreneur-in-residence at Matrix, hoping to join or help start a business that Matrix would back. "I wanted to do family, health, or education - those areas were my passion," Marcelo says.

Three months after the trip, Marcelo started a website, Care.com, to compete directly with Sittercity. Matrix Partners and several prominent investors poured capital into her new company - totaling more than $16 million so far. It wasn't until late last year that Sittercity raised its first round of venture capital.

The two companies are now vying to become the go-to marketplace when families need someone to provide in-home care - essentially, the Monster.com of hiring a Saturday night sitter. And while both Marcelo and Thiers say they'd rather put ancient history behind them, their 2006 meetings shed light on the sometimes-thorny relationship between entrepreneurs and investors who are looking to put their money to work in a particular business sector.

While an undergrad student at Boston College, Thiers did a bit of baby-sitting to earn extra money. One day on campus, watching a pregnant woman posting fliers to hire a nanny, Thiers decided to see what websites existed to connect parents with caregivers. She didn't find much. She borrowed $120 from her dad to register the domain Sittercity.com.

After she graduated, Thiers landed a job with IBM's Lotus division in Cambridge, and she ran Sittercity as a side project. The seed funding for the business came from her salary, mainly.

"To get baby sitters onto the site, we printed out fliers at Staples and put them up at every dorm in 33 colleges around

Boston and the suburbs," she recalls. By September 2001, when the site launched, she had 600 sitters in her database. The following year, when she was laid off from IBM, she decided to focus on Sittercity. She also followed her soon-to-be-husband to Chicago.

Those years, she says, were "the evangelism period for the site. I just ran around the country and did hundreds of interviews with local papers and TV stations, explaining how the site worked." She has appeared on "The View," "The Today Show," and "Ellen" as an expert on hiring and managing caregivers.

Marcelo had been general manager of TheLadders.com in Manhattan, a website that lists jobs with salaries of more than $100,000. Matrix is one of the backers of TheLadders, and Beim, the Matrix venture capitalist, invited Marcelo to join the firm as an entrepreneur-in-residence in May 2006.

She says she started researching services such as pet-sitting and eldercare and discovered that women make most of the decisions about whom to hire. She started developing an "umbrella portal concept" to bring many of those home-based services together on a single website.

Once a company had established a relationship with a customer, she figured, it might be able to sell additional services - such as tutoring or finding a housekeeper.

"The market was extremely fragmented," Marcelo says, with no one site offering a wide range of services. (Thiers says Sittercity had begun to branch into tutoring, housekeepers, and other areas a few years before.)

Marcelo acknowledges meeting with several companies that were running care-oriented sites, including Sittercity and Sitters.com, a Virginia company founded by a former AOL executive.

"We were pretty upfront with anyone we talked to," Marcelo says, adding that Matrix was considering investing in or buying an existing company that Marcelo could help run. "We said that this was an idea I was working on and that it was an umbrella organization that would go beyond just baby-sitting."

But Thiers says that while she was aware that Matrix was talking to other sites and might put money into one of them, the idea of Marcelo starting a company "never came up" in three meetings with Marcelo and Beim.

Mike Cravens, founder of Sitters.com, says he also had multiple meetings with Beim and Marcelo — which included discussions of Marcelo becoming the chief executive of his company following an investment from Matrix. But as to mentioning the possibility of Marcelo starting her own business, Cravens says, "That's an absolute lie." In an e-mail Marcelo sent

Cravens on Oct. 7, 2006, she pleaded with him to do a deal with Matrix and wrote that "out of respect for what you have done and despite my passion for the broader 'care' business, I would not entertain starting it on my own." (Marcelo recalls sending the e-mail but says she can't confirm the date.)

Marcelo launched her own company that month, after she and Matrix decided against buying Sitters.com or investing in Sittercity. When Thiers heard about the launch of Care.com, now based in Waltham, she says, "I was totally surprised."

A Matrix spokesperson writes via e-mail, "We can appreciate that the companies in question do not like competition, but we do not believe that their claims of unfair treatment are at all merited because both Sheila and we said from the earliest discussions with these companies that we were considering competitive options and not to share any information with us that they were not comfortable sharing." (Beim would not comment, saying he did not want "to engage in that kind of mud-slinging.")

Business plans, of course, can't be protected by patents, and whatever information the founders of Sitters.com and Sittercity shared was of their own volition. Marcelo writes in an e-mail, "The idea that 'trade secrets' gleaned from anyone else's business helped Care.com or hurt anyone else's business is, frankly, false."

Thiers raised $7.5 million for Sittercity in December 2008, in part from Providence-based Point Judith Capital. Both she and Marcelo now claim to be the leading site for finding caregivers online, and Thiers says, "There's no valid industry in this world without competitors." She says one new job is posted every five minutes on her site and as many as 2,000 caregivers sign up with Sittercity each day. Care.com claims more traffic to its site and counts 40 employees at its office and another 40 moms who work full time from home.

Both companies charge $30 a month to use their sites and emphasize that they provide background checks to help parents weed out bad apples. Both try to get media coverage (Care.com has also been on "The Today Show"). Both are now angling to sign up corporate customers, who pay to give their employees access to the sites.

About that difference of opinions, Marcelo says, "I realize that all entrepreneurs believe that no one else had the idea before them, but a large part of whether you succeed is execution."

Is there a lesson here for other entrepreneurs? It may be that no question is impolite during a meeting with investors. "It's fair game to ask who they've seen, who they're talking to, what they're incubating," says Eric Hjerpe, a partner at Waltham-based Kepha Partners, who wasn't involved with any of the three companies.

"Asking lots of questions is what differentiates a novice from a pro."

. . .

[Author's note: Care.com went public in 2014, and quickly grew to more than 500 employees. Sittercity is still privately-held, with about 50 employees. In 2010, Sittercity acquired Sitters.com for an undisclosed sum.]

The Intern Who Started a $9 Billion Company

Published in the Boston Globe, August 05, 2012

Several summers ago, an MIT student named Drew Houston showed up for an internship at Bit9, a Waltham network security company. After graduation, he landed a job there as a software engineer, but left in May 2007 to do his own start-up.

Since then, Bit9 has had a pretty good run. It has grown to 150 employees and set up sales offices in Europe and Asia. Among the customers it helps protect from hacker attacks are the Air Force, 7-Eleven, and Toyota Financial Services. Last Monday, it announced a fresh round of venture capital funding: $34.5 million, bringing the total amount Bit9 has raised to more than $70 million.

But the business that Houston started in 2007, Dropbox, has proven to be a rocket ship. Dropbox helps more than 50 million people store and synchronize digital files so the latest version can be accessed from any device. Investors have pegged the San Francisco company's current value at $4 billion. Steve Jobs, the late Apple chief executive, tried to acquire it. Dropbox has raised $257 million in venture capital — some of it from Sequoia Capital, the same Silicon Valley venture capital firm that just put money into Houston's old employer, Bit9. (At right, Houston pictured in 2013.)

Has there ever been a summer intern who has done so much, so quickly? (Forbes estimates Houston's net worth at $400 million. He is 29.) And how did Houston become the latest product of the Bay State to become an entrepreneurial rock star in California?

Houston was born and raised in Acton, where, by age 5, he was playing with an IBM PC, and by 14, working for an online game company in exchange for equity. While studying at MIT, he started an online SAT prep company, Accolade. He also met Arash Ferdowsi, his Dropbox cofounder.

"Drew was a down-to-earth guy who had tremendous passion about what he was doing," says Mark Roberge, who met Houston at MIT. "At the time, he wanted to revolutionize SAT preparation."

Houston's LinkedIn profile says Accolade was profitable, but after he graduated, he went to work for Bit9. The company's software is modeled after the human immune system, in that it understands what is normal activity on a corporate network, but treats anything it doesn't know as dangerous.

Todd Brennan, one of Bit9's founders, says it was clear that Houston was "destined for greatness." By the end of Houston's first summer as an intern, Brennan used to joke, "Be nice to Drew. We'll all be working for him someday."

Houston started working on the idea for Dropbox on the side, inspired by a bus ride from Boston to New York. He'd left some crucial files on a USB drive at home, and he started thinking about a service that might solve that problem. Why not store the latest versions of important files in a special folder — a Dropbox — that could be accessed from anywhere and shared easily?

Houston had connections at Atlas Venture, then in Waltham. It was the first investor in Bit9, and after Houston left the company, he'd occasionally show up at Atlas's office, sometimes to use a conference room. "He had a strong vision for Dropbox," says Pete Shannon, then a principal at Atlas. "He wanted it to be unobtrusive, and he didn't want it to take a lot of work for the user."

Jeff Fagnan, the Atlas partner who oversaw the investment in Bit9, says, "At the time, Drew wanted several hundred thousand dollars to hire a couple of developers" in order to make faster progress.

Atlas didn't invest, and neither did General Catalyst, a Cambridge venture firm that also had Houston on its radar screen. Houston showed Dropbox at Web Innovators Group, a regular Cambridge demo night organized by venture capitalist David Beisel. "The first incarnation was certainly raw," says Beisel. He didn't invest.

Neither did a roomful of Boston and New York venture capitalists who saw Houston present Dropbox in August 2007 as part of a three-month finishing school for entrepreneurs called Y

Combinator. I saw that demo, and it wasn't clear to me, like many in the room, how a two-person start-up would compete against bigger companies that might do the same thing, from Google to Microsoft to Apple to Carbonite, a Boston data backup company.

Dropbox's founders moved to San Francisco shortly after that — Y Combinator's guru in chief, Paul Graham, recommended the move to the companies that participated in his program — and they raised their first $1.2 million from Sequoia, the Silicon Valley firm that bankrolled Apple, Google, and Oracle.

Last year, Forbes reported that Dropbox's revenue was on track to reach $240 million — even though 96 percent of its customers use a free version of the service. (Dropbox's PR firm confirmed some statistics in this story, but wouldn't make Houston available for an interview.)

Fagnan at Atlas is bullish on Bit9: "My personal feeling is that they will be a flagship IPO in Boston," he says, noting that every new cyberattack helps sales. As for passing on Dropbox, Fagnan says he wasn't convinced that Houston could build a file storage, synchronization, and sharing system better than Google or Microsoft.

"We screwed up," Fagnan says. "When you see somebody of Drew's ilk, you should fund them even if they are doing SteakKnives.com."

Since then, Atlas has moved to East Cambridge, just a few blocks from MIT. And Fagnan says the firm has made it easier for its partners to make so-called seed investments of less than $1 million. "We want to be able to bet on first-time entrepreneurs," he says.

The start-up ecosystem in Boston is definitely getting better. But when we don't put money into companies — whether Dropbox or Facebook — we don't get a vote in where they put down roots.

I did find one person in town who believed in Houston's vision enough to invest in the company's earliest funding round: Todd Brennan, the Bit9 founder who originally hired Houston as a summer intern.

. . .

[Author's note: Dropbox beat Bit9 to an initial public offering. Its stock began trading in March 2018, and by 2020, the company had attained a market cap of $9 billion. Bit9 changed its name to Carbon Black, and engineered a successful IPO two months later, in May 2018.]

Y Combinator, WebInno, and Supporting Fledgling Ventures

Published in the Boston Globe, April 5, 2015

A decade ago this month, Alexis Ohanian and Steve Huffman showed up for an interview at a former candy factory not far from Harvard Square to pitch their idea for a startup called My Mobile Menu, which would allow diners to order food with their phones and skip the line at restaurants.

The roommates from the University of Virginia hoped to be accepted into a new program called Y Combinator, which was described in an online announcement as "like a summer job, except that instead of salary, we give you seed funding to start your own company with your friends." Ohanian and Huffman got rejected.

But the next day, Y Combinator called back, telling the two friends they'd get a spot in the summer program if they came up with a better idea. They did, conceiving of a "front page for the Internet." They called it Reddit. Today, the site attracts 174 million visitors each month and hosts Q&As with the likes of President Obama, Bill Gates, and Buzz Aldrin.

Neither Reddit nor Y Combinator stayed in Boston, nor did most of the other founders who participated in the entrepreneurship program's first cohort in 2005. But another initiative for startups that hatched that year in Cambridge, Web Innovators Group, did stay, and it developed into a central fixture of the local startup scene.

How these initiatives progressed over the past 10 years says a lot about the cultures and attitudes of the innovation communities on opposite coasts. Between YC and WebInno, as the programs are known, they have helped launch companies such as Dropbox, Birchbox, Airbnb, RunKeeper, FlipKey, Twitch, and CustomMade.

Their alumni have raised hundreds of millions in capital, and one company, the privately held lodging site Airbnb, might be worth as much as $20 billion. But the most successful and fastest-growing of the bunch are, such as Facebook, Airbnb, and Y Combinator, no longer headquartered in Boston, hiring people and minting new millionaires somewhere else.

So can Boston somehow become stickier?

Y Combinator created a model since mimicked by hundreds of other "accelerators" around the world — a 12-week program that supports founders with small amounts of funding as they turn rough ideas into working prototypes, test them with customers, and present them to an audience of investors at a "demo day."

In 2005, Ohanian says, "starting a startup wasn't as cool as it is today, and there were far fewer resources for total novices like us." They got access to the tech-savvy founders of Y Combinator. The young entrepreneurs ate together and compared notes on Tuesday nights, when Y Combinator founder Paul Graham would make a crockpot of chili.

At the first demo day in 2005, Reddit raised $70,000; the following year, it was acquired by the publishing company Conde Nast. Today, Reddit, of San Francisco, operates independently, with investors such as the rapper Snoop Dogg and Peter Thiel, the original backer of Facebook.

Until 2009, Y Combinator ran a summer program in Cambridge and a winter one in Silicon Valley. I went to demo days in 2007 and 2008, and I saw companies present to an audience of about 60 "angel" investors and venture capitalists. Most of the investors seemed to be window shopping and kept their wallets in their pockets.

When I interviewed him in 2008, Graham was frustrated with the passivity of the local investors. "What happens when you're conservative in the technology business?" he asked. "You lose. That's what the implication is for the future. They're gonna lose."

The following January, Graham announced that he and his wife, Y Combinator cofounder Jessica Livingston, were expecting their first child, and the program would move to the Valley year-round.

"Boston just doesn't have the startup culture that the Valley does," Graham wrote in a blog post.

Last month, 115 startups attended YC's demo day in Mountain View — so many that the "demo day" stretched over two days, with about 500 investors in the crowd. YC has become the Harvard of technology entrepreneurship — albeit tougher to get into, with an acceptance rate under 3 percent.

"Given their past track record, the most promising companies will apply to Y Combinator first," says Nick Tommarello, chief executive of WeFunder, an online fund-raising site that was born in Cambridge, participated in YC in 2013, and is now in San Francisco. After graduating YC, Tommarello adds, entrepreneurs can tap into a network of alumni — much like Harvard.

Web Innovators Group, also founded 10 years ago, stayed in Boston. It has become one of the central networking events for the tech set. Those events, held quarterly at the Royal Sonesta Hotel in Cambridge, fill the largest ballroom. It offers young companies an audience for what is often their first public product demo, but unlike YC, it doesn't provide seed funding. There don't tend to be many investors in the crowd, either.

But it fills a big void, giving the startup set a place to gather, and a way to build buzz, recruit employees, and connect with prospective customers. Presenting at WebInno "directly led to a few key early customers signing up," says Raj Aggarwal, chief executive of Localytics, a company that helps creators of mobile apps better understand their users. Late last month, the Boston company raised $35 million.

Another entrepreneur, TJ Mahony, says audience feedback and online mentions of his startup, FlipKey, helped "put the wind in our sails." The year after Mahony presented FlipKey, which focused on reviews of vacation rental homes, Newton-based TripAdvisor acquired the company for an undisclosed amount.

In Boston, "people are more supportive today of these first-time entrepreneurs than they were in 2005," Jo Tango of the Waltham investment firm Kepha Partners says. "But change comes slowly."

For entrepreneurs focusing on mobile apps, social sites, and whatever comes next, the pull of New York or Silicon Valley is intense — especially when they want partnerships with big tech or media players. They also want access to investors willing to pour gasoline on the fire when things get going.

Can we get these consumer tech companies to stick here? Some say Boston should build on its strengths — and nurture biotech, robotics, business software, and infrastructure companies. "Instead of focusing on what we're not good at," says Bill Warner, a Cambridge entrepreneur and angel investor, "I'd understand what we are good at."

I'm not ready to wave the white flag on all the rest. We've seen initiatives founded in the last five years such as Bolt, Blade, Launch, and Harvard's Innovation Lab that all try to provide office space, guidance, and initial funding to nascent businesses, many of which are developing products for consumers. We can do more — especially when it comes to helping startups build awareness and hire more quickly. It only takes one big success to start the flywheel spinning, creating wealth that can fund the next generation of companies.

In the decade since YC and WebInno got started, Boston has become a more hospitable place for starting Web, social, and mobile businesses. But as they grow, startups want to see the equivalent of a well-paved superhighway — a route that lots of others have traveled before. Boston's is still under construction.

...

[Author's note: WebInno changed its name to Boston Innovators Group, shifted from quarterly to "every so often"... and then eventually petered out in 2017. Y Combinator endures. Recent cohorts of Y Combinator have included more than 200 startups. When Airbnb went public in late 2020, it had a market cap of $82 billion.]

Two Duffel Bags, a Shovel, and the Hunt for a Breakthrough Cancer Drug

Published in the Boston Globe, June 19, 2011

John Walker remembers a colleague stopping him in the hall, sometime in the summer of 2004, to ask about his plans for week. There wasn't much on the schedule, said Walker, who was a 27-year old "informatics analyst" (a/k/a IT guy) at Infinity Pharmaceuticals Inc. in Cambridge. The next day, he was aboard a plane to Boise, Idaho, on an unusual mission.

"I got into Boise, rented a car, and drove about four-and-a-half hours to this little town called Frenchglen, Oregon," Walker says. "I stopped at an Army-Navy store to buy two duffel bags and a shovel, and then I met up with a retired botany professor who we'd found on an online discussion board."

The professor had promised to lead Walker on a hike into the mountains of Oregon to find a poisonous plant called *Veratrum californicum*, sometimes called the corn lily. Ranchers knew it as a plant that, when ingested, caused sheep to give birth to one-eyed lambs. Infinity wanted to see whether a substance contained in the plant might become part of a new cancer drug.

You don't need to read too much about the pharmaceutical industry to know drugs are insanely expensive to develop. A decade can pass between the time a new drug enters trials and when it is approved by the Food and Drug Administration. Yet when you get a bleak diagnosis, or when someone you love gets sick, you want there to be some incredible new treatment, fresh from the lab.

Sometimes the story of how a new drug makes its way to hospitals or doctors has so many twists and turns, it reads like an installment of the "National Treasure" films, if only Nicholas Cage played a chemist instead of a historian.

The story of one of Infinity's drugs, known as IPI-926, started not with Walker's trip to Oregon, but a few months before, in the Back Bay. Julian Adams, chief scientific officer at Infinity, wakes up at 4 a.m. most mornings. "I have insomnia, I guess, but that's the time when I can do my best reading of scientific journals," says Adams. "There's utter silence, which is great."

One morning, Adams was intrigued by an article in the journal *Nature* that discussed a substance called cyclopamine —

extracted from the corn lily plant — that affected a bit of genetic circuitry that can cause cancer in animals. Adams decided he wanted to get some, to run tests in Infinity's lab.

Small problem: "We found out that there was about 10 grams of it in the world, available from one supplier," Adams says. "And it cost $22,000 a gram." The company bought a gram, to have a sample to work with, and dispatched employees like Walker to Oregon and Idaho to fill duffel bags and U-Haul trucks with corn lilies, so Infinity could produce its own cyclopamine for research.

At times, it felt like a smuggling operation. Driving a truck full of the unusual plants across the Nevada border to a processing plant in California, former Infinity executive Andy Palmer thought it would be wisest to cross late at night. So he and a colleague stopped in Vegas, and passed a few hours playing blackjack.

But the cyclopamine that Infinity extracted from corn lilies wasn't potent enough, breaking down too quickly in the body. So scientists started sketching the molecular structure of cyclopamine on whiteboards, and making guesses about how to alter it to make it better.

They developed 30 or 40 upgraded versions of cyclopamine, testing them on samples of cancer cells. Of that group, only three candidates, including IPI-926, seemed worthy of further testing in animals. To produce these drugs in the lab, a chemical reaction was required; unfortunately, it was so explosive that no outside contractor would do it. So Infinity collaborated with a chemist at the University of Montreal to develop a less-volatile method.

Like many biotechs, Infinity doesn't yet have a product on the market. In 2009, its most advanced drug, intended to treat stomach tumors, collapsed during a clinical trial; patients taking it were dying at a higher rate than those who weren't. Between 2006 and 2010, Infinity spent $80 million nudging forward IPI-926, which the company hopes will one day win FDA approval to treat pancreatic cancer. (Much of that money was supplied by larger pharmaceutical companies such as Connecticut-based Purdue Pharma LP., in exchange for the right to sell the drug outside of the United States.) Infinity lost $50 million last year.

Infinity's chief executive Adelene Perkins, observes that trying to develop drugs for pancreatic cancer has been "a graveyard" for pharmaceutical and biotech companies. Charles Fuchs, a physician who runs the Center for Gastrointestinal Oncology at the Dana-Farber Cancer Institute, says he has been involved with 14 experiments involving pancreatic cancer. "I wouldn't say that they were all failures," he says, "but none of those has resulted in a new drug approval."

Fuchs is one of the doctors leading clinical trials of IPI-926, when patients voluntarily test a new drug. The theory is that 926 serves as a sledgehammer, breaking down the wall that surrounds tumors, and letting standard chemotherapy drugs in to kill tumor cells.

At a medical conference in Chicago earlier this month, doctors overseeing early tests of IPI-926 presented encouraging data from 16 patients who used it in combination with a standard chemotherapy drug. Five experienced "meaningful" reductions in the size of tumors.

Barbara Shuffman of Boston is one of 120 patients taking part in the next stage of clinical trials. She is 60, and was diagnosed with pancreatic cancer in early May. (Nationally, about 40,000 people get that diagnosis each year; of those, about 20 percent survive more than a year.) Thirty years ago, her father contracted the same disease. He died about seven months after his diagnosis.

"The hope is that this will give me a better option of getting farther along," Shuffman says. "I don't want to leave any stone unturned." Shuffman plans to participate in a walkathon this September, to raise money for pancreatic cancer research

At Infinity, there's cautious optimism about 926. "We're intrigued, but it's still very early," Adams says.

We don't yet know how this movie will end.

. . .

[Author's note: IPI-926 was abandoned in 2012, after a clinical trial found that patients receiving a placebo were outliving those taking the experimental drug. Infinity continues to work on other cancer drugs.]

Getting a License Plate for a Flying Car

Published in the Boston Globe, October 19, 2008

Like many motorists, Dick Gersh found it a bit of a hassle to get a license plate from the Registry of Motor Vehicles.

Gersh's company, Terrafugia, Inc., is apparently the only company making automobiles in the state of Massachusetts, and so there wasn't an established "auto manufacturer" category when he went to request a plate.

Oh, and the vehicle Terrafugia is building will also be capable of flying, at 115 mph.

"It takes regulators quite a while to get comfortable with who we are and what we're doing," says Gersh, vice president of business development at the start-up. "At the Registry, or the Department of Transportation, or the Federal Aviation Administration, none of the regulations really contemplated a flying car." (The plate finally showed up in June, after nearly six months of discussions.)

Want a big entrepreneurial challenge? Try to design an aircraft and bring it to market. (As of 2007, there were just under 600,000 licensed pilots in the U.S. who might buy your product.) Want an enormous entrepreneurial challenge? Design an aircraft that can also fold up its wings, drive off the runway, and travel safely at highway speeds. Success is so absurdly improbable it is like asking the clerk at the local pet store to sell you a parakeet that can also bench-press 400 pounds and play the trombone. (At right, a view of the back of Terrafugia's prototype vehicle.)

The last serious attempt to bring a car-airplane hybrid to market was the Aerocar, in 1949. According to Carl Dietrich, CEO of Terrafugia, the company built six prototypes. It needed 500 orders in order to gear up for mass production, but never got there.

But Dietrich, who, along with his wife and co-founder Anna is a graduate of MIT's aeronautical engineering program, is not deterred. In a small workshop in Woburn, they're building a single-engine aircraft with a carbon fiber body that will be able to carry two passengers through rush-hour traffic — or the wild blue. It's sleek, white, angular, and very futuristic looking, with a black propeller in the rear. If you plucked off the wings, the body would look like a cross between a Mini Cooper and a Volkswagen Beetle – complete with moon roof. Nearly everything does double-duty; the front canard (a small wing) also serves as a bumper, and a horizontal stabilizer in the rear also contains the tail lights – and that hard-to-obtain license plate.

They hope to fly the thing before 2008 is out, and last week they were at the Lawrence Municipal Airport, doing some high-speed driving tests on the ground.

Dietrich doesn't like the term flying car. "People hear that term and immediately it's associated with the Jetsons, Back to the Future, and Blade Runner," he says. "They think it will be in everybody's garage." Instead, Terrafugia uses the term "roadable aircraft." Dietrich explains, "This is an aircraft you can also drive – a more useful airplane." It still requires a pilot license, but the company is hoping the plane will fit into a relatively new category the FAA calls "light-sport aircraft." It takes only about half the time and money to obtain a pilot's license to fly light-sport aircraft, compared to a traditional pilot's license, but the speed of the planes in this category are limited to about 120 miles per hour, they can only carry two people, and pilots can only fly them in clear weather. (At right, Carl Dietrich shows off an early prototype at a Massachusetts Technology Leadership Council event.)

Still, the population of so-called "sport pilots" are growing. In 2005, there were just 135 in the U.S., and by the end of this year there will be about 4200, according to Chris Dancy, a spokesman for the Aircraft Owners and Pilots Association.

Dietrich says that aside from the coolness factor, the design of Terrafugia's vehicle, known as the Transition, will address some of the problems that pilots encounter when they try to use their aircraft for actual travel, as opposed to weekend sightseeing. When they encounter bad weather in the Transition, they can simply land at the nearest airport and continue their journey on the road. (The company's goal is a top speed of 70 to 80 miles per hour, in car mode.) The engine uses premium unleaded, instead of pricier aviation fuel. Pilots don't have to rent hangar space, which can cost $1000 or more a month, since they will be able to drive the Transition home and keep it in a standard-sized garage. And when pilots land at most of the country's 5000 small airports in a traditional aircraft, they need to call a taxi to get into town, since car rental counters are a rarity.

"It can be hard to explain the value of this to non-pilots," Dietrich says, "but when you're a pilot, the problems of high costs, limited mobility on the ground, and weather sensitivity are in your face, all the time." Their target price is $198,000.

Dietrich says the company has raised a bit more than $2 million so far. To get to low levels of production – say 20 vehicles a year – he'll need another $7 million.

But even some investors and well-off entrepreneurs who also have pilot's licenses are a bit hesitant about putting money in the company. Paul Maeder, managing general partner at Highland Capital Partners in Lexington, passed on the deal, Dietrich says, because he wanted to see the Transition fly first. When I asked Maeder about that, he alluded to problems that aircraft manufacturers can encounter even after they've taken to the skies and been approved by the FAA. "I admire their persistence and optimism," he wrote via e-mail, adding, "A lot of people passed on the Wright Brothers, too." Philip Greenspun, a software entrepreneur, blogger, and flight instructor, wrote in an e-mail that "the idea of financing a new airplane company is ridiculous, from an investment point of view...the best case is maybe to get one's money back."

And raising money from individual investors won't be a breeze in the current environment, when many once-wealthy individuals are feeling substantially less wealthy.

Another challenge, observes Ed Crawley, is keeping the weight of the aircraft down; to be considered a light-sport aircraft, it needs to have a weight at take-off of no more than 1320 pounds. "They're trying to do a lot more than other manufacturers in that category," says Crawley, a professor of aeronautical engineering at MIT. "They need bumpers, and an automotive suspension." (Above, Terrafugia employees. Carl Dietrich is on the left; co-founder Anna Dietrich is in the white scarf. Dick Gersh is third from the right.)

Like many pilots, Crawley says he's enchanted by the concept. "How cool would it be to be the first guy to fly into an airport, fold up the wings, and drive out of the gate?" But he adds that while "the coolness factor" will attract some buyers, "the ultimate commercial success will hinge on the thing's utility."

The Terrafugia team understands the headwinds they're facing, but they're energized by trying to accomplish the nearly-impossible.

"For me, this was an opportunity to assist a talented group of engineers in getting something literally into the air," says Gersh. He previously worked in the insurance industry, so he has a good understanding of risk. "If this were easy, somebody would've done it before."

...

[Author's note: Terrafugia was acquired by a Chinese company, Geely Holding Group, in 2017. As of 2020, Terrafugia has still not earned FAA certification or delivered a flying car to a customer, though it has test-flown the Transition. Both Carl and Anna Dietrich have left the company, as has Dick Gersh.]

Waking Up from a Biofuel Dream

Published in the Boston Globe, September 1, 2017

In the decade since it was founded in 2007, Joule Unlimited made a lot of amazing claims about the future of fuel, and raised a lot of money to try to back up those claims.

Joule was designing a system that would produce diesel fuel or gasoline using nothing more than the sun, carbon dioxide, water, and a genetically-modified bacteria. It would be available for about $1.20 a gallon — without government subsidies. The Bedford company would begin construction of a 1000-acre production plant in New Mexico in 2017. Joule's tag line said that it was "solving the energy crisis with affordable, renewable clean fuel," and the company managed to attract $200 million in financing from investors, including Cambridge-based Flagship Pioneering and the German carmaker Audi, which was eager to test Joule's sustainable fuel.

Last month, though, the company was auctioning off its New Mexico facility. Nearly all of the company's 120 employees were laid off — the most recent round happened in the spring — after Joule was unable to raise more money. The company's investors are now looking for a buyer interested in the company's patents.

When it comes to producing "biofuels" from natural substances that can compete on price with fuel extracted from the ground, "there's probably no approach that's new under the sun that somebody hasn't attempted," says Robert Rapier, an analyst who runs the website R-Squared Energy. "Billions and billions of dollars have been put in" by big oil companies and startups, without producing anything that you can actually put in your gas tank.

Joule got its start in the offices of Flagship Pioneering, as a concept: what if you could take a kind of bacteria that is sometimes called blue-green algae, tweak a few genes, and get it to excrete fuel? "It was a major, major scientific endeavor," says Flagship founder Noubar Afeyan, and one that involved academic collaborators like George Church of Harvard and Jim Collins of Boston University, both co-founders of Joule. Since the bacteria that Joule was working with relies on photosynthesis to survive, a research paper published by the company's founders in 2011 was headlined, "A New Dawn for Industrial Photosynthesis."

Joule's prize patent, #9,034,629, was issued in 2015 — just as the company was starting to fall apart. It covered the genetically-modified bacterium Joule had developed, and a process for using it to convert carbon dioxide and water (including brackish or sea water) and make fuel. The CO_2 used by Joule's process, incidentally, could be piped in from a factory that would otherwise release it into the atmosphere — a big environmental benefit.

But many observers, including Rapier, questioned Joule's claims. "They were saying that they would produce 20,000 gallons of fuel using an acre of land," he says. But he questioned those numbers, simply based on the amount of solar energy — one of the required ingredients for the Joule process — that falls on the surface of the earth. "Many people were very skeptical that they could pull off what they were trying to pull off," Rapier says.

The company was trying to prove that what worked in the lab would also work at a larger scale, at first using a 1/10th acre system in New Mexico. And it was making ethanol first, rather than diesel or gasoline, because that was an easier first step. (Ethanol is blended into other fuels, rather than used on its own.)

The challenge of the work, says Afeyan, is that "you're competing with a commodity. On one hand, you have a hundred billion gallons of something" like crude oil, and the production efficiencies that have accrued to that industry over a century, and "on the other hand, you've got a couple gallons" of a biofuel made in a custom-built, one-of-kind facility. "You have to show not just feasibility," Afeyan adds, "but economic viability. It proved quite challenging."

Making it even more challenging were oil prices that plummeted, in 2014, from $112 a barrel to about $60 a barrel by the end of the year. Prices continued to drop in 2015. That was also the year that it was revealed that Audi's parent company, Volkswagen, had created software to enable its cars to cheat on emissions tests. That scandal, coupled with less pressure to look for alternatives to oil, may have scared off the bigger oil companies and utilities that Joule hoped would supply its next round of funding.

Joule attained a bit of momentary fame during the 2016 election cycle. John Podesta, Hillary Clinton's campaign chairman, had served on the board of Joule from 2010 to 2014. During that time, the company accepted funding from Rusnano, a venture capital firm owned by the Russian government. Media reports questioned whether Podesta's links to Russia had led to that investment from Rusnano, and whether Podesta had properly disclosed the stock he held in Joule when he joined the Obama administration in 2014, as an adviser to the President.

Afeyan says that the Podesta controversy "was a completely irrelevant factor" in Joule's ultimate fate, and that Podesta "was not a factor in Rusnano's investment in Joule whatsoever."

On August 15th, you could bid online to buy the equipment that Joule once hoped would coax bacteria into producing fuel in Hobbs, New Mexico, just a few miles from the Texas border. Back in April, laid off Joule employees sipped margaritas and shared nachos at the Border Café in Cambridge. One of them called it "literally the best company I've worked for. Everyone was pulling in the same direction."

John Beneman, an expert on algae-based biofuels, notes that Joule isn't an anomaly. "There are other companies out there that have raised hundreds of millions of dollars and come up with the same results – either they are walking dead, or ghosts, or resting in peace," says Beneman, who is also CEO of the consulting firm MicroBio Engineering in California.

Does Beneman believe it's just impossible to use a genetically-engineered organism to make an affordable, more sustainable kind of fuel, rather than extracting it from the earth? "I'm not saying it's impossible, just that it requires long-term work," he says. "There are a lot of technologies take years or decades to develop, and get to the payoff."

Ten years and $200 million later, we're still not there.

The Columnist and His Critic Hash Things Out

Published in the Boston Globe, June 30, 2019

"Hello, Complaints Department."

"This is Eric Paley, Managing Partner at Founder Collective. You know, the Cambridge venture capital firm that put money into companies like Uber, PillPack, Hotel Tonight, and Formlabs? I've got a few bones to pick with your coverage."

Plenty of readers think I can be too much of a cheerleader for startups or the investors who put money into them, hoping to earn a massive return. But Paley has the opposite complaint: he thinks that I focus too much on what I perceive as the shortcomings of the Boston tech scene. And that I ought to swap my cynical green glasses for a pair that are at least slightly more rose-colored.

Here's a lightly-edited transcript of a conversation we had at a conference earlier this month.

...

Scott Kirsner: You think I'm a glass-half-empty person.

Eric Paley: I think you're hurting our ecosystem.

SK: Really?

EP: Yeah.

SK: I feel like I'm a realist. I feel like we need to fight a little bit harder to retain really smart people who have ideas for companies —

EP: Boston has this incredible import of incredible talent because of the universities and the hospitals.

SK: Shouldn't we fight to keep more of it?

EP: [But] all they read about in the Boston *Globe*, despite Boston having the most exit value of any place outside of Silicon Valley, is how terrible things are going, or where are all the Boston IPOs? ["Exit Value" is the dollar value of companies that get acquired or go public.] Even though Boston has had more IPOs than anybody else, except for Silicon Valley —

SK: I think what you're whiffing on is that the venture community here has shrunk. It is still very comfortable funding the second- or third-time entrepreneur, more than the first-time entrepreneur. It is very uncomfortable with writing $50 million checks — these big king-making rounds you see in Silicon Valley, where [investors have] decided you are going to dominate 3D printing or dating or whatever. It's dribs and drabs of funding.

Let's talk about [the digital payments company] Stripe — kids who went to Harvard and MIT. Shouldn't we have figured out how to retain Stripe in Boston?

EP: If they keep reading about all the problems in Boston, they won't recognize all the good stuff that's going on.

The right comparison for Boston in tech is New York, not San Francisco. San Francisco is enormous as an ecosystem. It takes generations to build that big an ecosystem.

There was sort of a lost decade in Boston tech, largely related to VCs having enormous bias that was age-based, towards older entrepreneurs. They really missed out on some really great entrepreneurs because they were incredibly biased on age.

I don't see this issue so much that Boston has trouble with new entrepreneurs these days... Pillpack was first-time entrepreneurs, Formlabs was first-time entrepreneurs. [The former company was acquired by Amazon for about $1 billion last year; the latter is a privately-held 3D printing startup that is valued at about the same amount.]

SK: Do you feel like there are any problems that we have, other than me being too cynical, or other than there's not enough media?

EP: I would say your glasses are a concern. I'm kidding.

SK: Let's agree that robotics is a space where we have the [intellectual property], we have the smart people, we have the startups, and there's no venture fund that specializes in robotics?

Why is that? Why isn't there somebody saying, "Let's create the next iRobot"?

EP: It's General Catalyst, and Spark, and Founder Collective, and CRV, and Highland [who are funding robotics startups.] Here's my concern: you tend to take these top-down views, of, "Why didn't something organically happen that hasn't happened?" Instead of looking at the organic stuff that has happened, [which] is pretty amazing.

I think robotics is really, really challenging. It's hard to find the match between the tech and the use cases. There will be other great robotics companies. Probably the best robotics company that has ever been venture-backed, in history, is Kiva [a warehouse robotics company acquired by Amazon in 2012.] It was in Boston. Bain Capital [Ventures] was the largest investor, out of Boston.

Have you written the article about what Kiva has meant for Amazon?

SK: I've written both the article about how it's driving Amazon's efficiencies internally, and also how they took it away from all the other customers, because Amazon didn't want to be selling guns to its rivals.

EP: So you found the most cynical angle.

SK: I found the most interesting way to write about it. Isn't it interesting that a company that sold robots to Staples and Walgreens and Diapers.com, suddenly says, "No, we can't sell you robots anymore, because Amazon bought us?"

EP: I think you can start there, but I think the more interesting story is that the leading warehouse operator in the world ended up having to buy an external technology and scale it to over a million robots.

The thing I'm getting at is, New York is building a great ecosystem. Boston rivals New York as a tech ecosystem quite well. We've had bigger exits, [and] we have big stories that don't get attention. [Boston is] a very deep ecosystem in all kinds of ways. But New York is proudly rising together. And the story of New York is this super-excited, super-positive story. The story in Boston is still caught, in my opinion, in 15 years ago — the cynicism of not backing young entrepreneurs, only being enterprise [technology]... I just think that's dated.

SK: I don't think we're in opposition, I just feel like I want to aim a little bit higher in terms of, like, retaining more of those people who are obsessed with building stand-alone companies...

I write about 50 columns a year for the *Globe*. You're making it seem like 40 of them are me criticizing the Boston ecosystem. But I actually think 40 are either about new clusters that are developing, and interesting companies that are the first in a space, or companies like Toast that are now giant successes...

EP: Even in these company articles, you tend to always find this slight angle of, "Here are the big questions."

SK: Yeah, or what their challenges are going to be. A lot of startup journalism is, "These guys are rock stars. They raised $30 million."

EP: I'm not saying [write more] fluff. What I am saying is, these are really inspiring entrepreneurial stories that really matter in the community. When you finish them, which is usually what you do, by taking a slice, you do undermine the story.

You're approaching it like a political reporter. You start from a place where you say, "I'm looking not just to tell the untold story that might be exciting and positive," but to be "balanced," which is, in my mind, a loaded term...

SK: I feel like at times, I certainly have been the biggest booster of the startup economy in Boston.

EP: I definitely missed those articles.

SK: But we do have this incredible natural resource of these universities and the students that come, and a lot of businesses get started on campuses. And I just feel like, let's just retain [a slightly higher percentage of them], whether they're finding jobs in an established company, or whether we're helping them find visas, because they were born in a foreign country, or whether we're funding them.

EP: I'm obsessed with this question of how do we retain people. But I think for that to happen, we need to be telling our stories better.

The day that CarGurus went public, there was an article in TechCrunch about a marketplace for autos that raised $1.6 million. There was no coverage about CarGurus. If you're not telling that story, who's telling that story? There's no one telling that story.

4. The Valley

Over 36 Hours, a Glimpse of What Fuels the Silicon Valley Simulation Machine

Published in the Boston Globe, October 28, 2012

SAN FRANCISCO — Having beaten my checked bag to the luggage carousel, I fired up my iPhone and did something illegal. Using an app called SideCar, I summoned a complete stranger to come pick me up from the airport.

Earlier in October, a California regulatory agency ordered SideCar to cease connecting passengers with ordinary drivers looking to make a few extra bucks by playing chauffeur. The company ignored the order, and the day before my arrival raised $10 million from Google's venture capital arm and another investment firm. It took 18 minutes for my driver, Eddie, to show up at the airport. I hopped into his black Acura sedan, and we sped north toward the city.

I was in town for about 36 hours, and I wanted to get a sense for where the action was in the Bay Area, at a moment when Apple is the world's most valuable company and employees are leaving once-hot Facebook to find the next big thing. Of course, the Bay Area is also the ecosystem to which Boston regularly compares itself, and which exerts a magnetic attraction for many young entrepreneurs educated here. Here's what transpired.

WEDNESDAY, *9:30 p.m.*

My SideCar drops me in Glen Park, the hilly neighborhood where I once lived. The app suggests a "donation" of $30 for the ride, which I can adjust up or down as I see fit. I give Eddie $30, figuring I still saved a few bucks over a taxi.

I'm meeting another complete stranger, Dylan, who has agreed to rent me a room in his house for $110 a night. I used the website Airbnb.com to find Dylan's listing. The San Francisco start-up was founded to help turn ordinary people into innkeepers, and last week it raised $117 million, in addition to $120 million raised earlier. Dylan told me he teaches physical education at a public school, and the suite in which I was staying, with its own private bathroom and outdoor patio, had once been his master bedroom. Airbnb tacked a $31 service fee onto my two-night reservation.

Like SideCar, Airbnb is one of the companies trying to establish a new "sharing economy" using resources that people own but hadn't previously used to generate income. But there are questions about its legality, too: anyone renting rooms by the night in San Francisco is supposed to have a bed-and-breakfast permit. I don't care: The bed is comfy and the water pressure strong.

THURSDAY, *10 a.m.*

After 4½ years at Facebook, Don Faul left in June to join Pinterest, a San Francisco company that operates one of the hotter new social networking sites. Pinterest allows users to create an online pinboard, posting pictures of places where they might want to vacation, for instance, or desserts they might want to  serve at their next party. As with Facebook, you can connect with friends, celebrities, or people whose taste you admire to see what they're "pinning." (At right, Faul demos the site.)

The site has attracted users faster than Facebook or YouTube did: Earlier this year, it crossed the 20 million user mark. In many ways, says Faul, the company's head of operations, Pinterest is growing so fast it can barely keep up. For now, the company has 75 employees stationed at rows of simple tables in a high-ceilinged space with exposed ductwork and paper lanterns hanging down. But next door, it is renovating a much larger office that will be able to accommodate hundreds of additional employees. (At right, Pinterest's office in the SoMa neighborhood.)

Like many Web-based companies, Pinterest is trying to figure out how to best translate its product to mobile phones and tablets, while increasing the amount of time users spend on its website, Faul says. What the company isn't doing is talking about how it will make money. "We're

thinking about it, but it's not our primary focus right now," Faul says.

THURSDAY, *11:15 a.m.*

Running late for a meeting at AngelList, I hustle through the lobby of a luxe residential building across from AT&T Park, the home of the San Francisco Giants. When I arrive, founder Naval Ravikant tells me that as commercial rents in San Francisco have risen, many landlords are finding it more profitable to put start-ups, rather than individuals, into apartments.

Ravikant started AngelList to help connect entrepreneurs with prospective investors. Now, about 5,000 wealthy investors and 90,000 start-ups maintain profiles on the site, and AngelList wants to simplify the rest of the investing process.

A new feature, AngelList Docs, puts investment paperwork online, complete with electronic signatures, "reducing a company's financing to a checklist process," Ravikant says.

As for the current craze of "seed-stage investing," handing small start-ups a few hundred thousand dollars to see if they might be able to design the next Pinterest, Ravikant acknowledges that "it has gotten really frothy," with valuations of fledgling companies rising into the stratosphere.

But "angels" investing their own money can presumably afford to lose it, he says: "In the worst case, what's happening is a voluntary transfer of money from rich to poor, from old to young."

THURSDAY, *12:45 p.m.*

Celeb sighting: While I'm eating lunch at the Samovar Tea Room with entrepreneur Daniel Raffel, Evan Williams walks in and sits down at the next table over. Williams, cocreator of Twitter, is at work on a new publishing site called Medium, where creators will collaborate on articles or collections of photos. It's expected to launch early next year.

THURSDAY, *3 p.m.*

I meet Paul Graham for coffee at Coupa Café, a popular hangout among entrepreneurs located just off the main drag of Palo Alto. Before we go in, Graham spots someone across the street who is carrying a prototype of a motorized skateboard called a Boosted Board.

The creators of the Boosted Board participated in Graham's three-month accelerator program for entrepreneurs, Y Combinator. Graham mentions they've recently raised more than $400,000 from customers eager to be the first on their block to own a Boosted Board, with its six-mile range and 20 mile-per-hour top speed.

More than 80 start-up teams participated in the most recent Y Combinator program over the summer; only 2 percent of the companies that apply get in. (By contrast, the acceptance rate at Harvard, where Graham earned a doctorate in computer science, is 5.9 percent.) Y Combinator makes a small investment in each company in exchange for between 2 and 10 percent of its stock.

Already, the program has spawned companies like Airbnb and Dropbox, a popular file-sharing service.

Graham says his goal for Y Combinator is simple: "To fund a lot of the good start-ups."

THURSDAY, *4:30 p.m.*

My last stop of the day is at the Googleplex — Google's headquarters, in Mountain View. I sit across the table from Steve Lee, a director of Google X, the company's secretive research-and-development division. The company has disclosed only two projects that the division is working on: a car capable of driving itself and Google Glass, a postage stamp-size digital display attached to an eyeglass frame.

Lee gives me a chance to put on Google Glass for a few minutes and use it to snap pictures, read text messages, and get directions to a destination. Lee patiently explains that I can interact with the display by speaking commands, touching the arm of the eyeglass frame, or moving my head. It's confusing at first, but I know I'd get comfortable with it given more time.

And I am sure I would like to have the world around me annotated, with background briefings on people I encounter and historical tidbits about buildings I pass.

Will it become normal for all of us to flit back and forth between the people we're talking to and the screens of our head-mounted displays? Will it be legal to drive while wearing Google Glass? Is that why Google is working on a self-driving vehicle?

I'm mulling over those questions as I head north on Route 101, the main highway that links Silicon Valley to San Francisco. I feel like I'm living in the past, gripping the wheel of a non-autonomous Mazda, surveying the road ahead while wearing old-fashioned, non-digital eyeglasses.

What Silicon Valley does better than any other place — fueled by entrepreneurs, engineers, and investors' money — is simulate possible futures. Most of them never come to pass. But enough do to keep the simulation machine humming.

. . .

[Author's note: While Sidecar shut down at the end of 2015, Uber and Lyft both succeeded with a similar transportation offering. As of 2020, Pinterest is publicly-traded, as is Airbnb. While the first release of Google Glass didn't fly with consumers, the company still sells the device to corporate users as Google Glass Enterprise Edition, and continues to develop the technology.]

Why Facebook Went West

Published in the Boston Globe, September 9, 2007

In April of 2004, two Harvard undergrads walked into the Charles Hotel for a meeting with a venture capitalist. What happened next either highlights Boston's deficiencies as a greenhouse for a new generation of Web start-ups, or illustrates the incredible magnetism of Silicon Valley — or a bit of both.

The Harvard students were Mark Zuckerberg and Eduardo Saverin, and they were at the Charles to talk with a senior associate at Battery Ventures of Waltham. It was the senior associate's job to spot interesting companies for the partners at his firm to consider as investments. (The firm where this person now works allowed him to be interviewed only under the condition that he not be named.)

He'd heard about the website that Zuckerberg and Saverin and a few other students had built because he himself was a Harvard alum, and a few days earlier, he'd run into some current students who had told him about it. It was called Facebook, and at the time it only had 1,000 or 2,000 users.

Zuckerberg told the senior associate that he was planning to go to California for the summer, and he wasn't sure whether he would return to Harvard for his junior year. Summer was less than two months away. The senior associate was pretty sure that if Battery Ventures didn't invest before then, a Silicon Valley venture firm would discover the deal. For venture capital firms, getting in first can often mean getting a bigger chunk of a start-up for less money — especially if the start-up isn't talking to other firms. And Facebook wasn't.

After a second meeting at the Charles, and a visit to Battery's offices above the reservoir in Waltham, Zuckerberg said he thought Facebook was worth about $15 million, and was willing to accept an investment ranging from $1 million to $3 million, which would have given Battery a substantial chunk of the start-up.

But Battery had already made an investment in an earlier social networking site, Friendster, which was foundering. Zuckerberg struck some partners at the firm as a little too brash. And no one was sure whether Facebook would appeal to anyone other than college students, its target.

There were also turf issues with Battery's Silicon Valley office, which had invested in Friendster. "There was a question about whether we on the East Coast side were going to lead an investment with a sophomore in college who was considering a move to the West," says the senior associate.

The firm passed — even though Scott Tobin, the Battery partner who evaluated the opportunity, could have invested a few hundred thousand in Facebook without putting the deal to a vote of all the partners. (Tobin had earlier invested in Akamai Technologies Inc., now a member of the S&P 500 index.)

Zuckerberg, who grew up in Westchester County in New York and attended Phillips Exeter, went to California in June 2004 with two of his Facebook cofounders.

Through a chance connection, Zuckerberg was introduced to Peter Thiel, a cofounder of the online payment system PayPal, who was running a hedge fund called Clarium Capital. He met with Thiel in August, at Thiel's office in downtown San Francisco.

Thiel had also been an investor in Friendster, and he knew that the conventional wisdom was that all the social networking sites "were just fads that would come and go," he says. Thiel listened to Zuckerberg's pitch in the morning, asked him to go out and grab lunch, and by the time Zuckerberg returned in the afternoon, "we said we'd invest, and we agreed to the basic valuation parameters," Thiel says.

"It seemed like a good company," he said, adding, "Most of the time, we're not that fast."

Thiel put in $500,000 of his own money in return for 10 percent of the company.

Zuckerberg set up shop in Palo Alto, and by the end of the year, Facebook was approaching a million users. In 2005, the company took in $12.7 million from the Silicon Valley firm Accel Partners, and by the end of that year, the site had more than 5 million users, having decided to allow high school students to join.

"Facebook was perhaps the most controversial deal we've done in several years," says Jim Breyer of Accel Partners. "Some of my best friends in the business were wondering why we'd write a check to a company that had very little defensibility to their business." Indeed, anyone could potentially build a better site and lure Facebook's users away.

Last year, the company passed 12 million users, and raised another $27.5 million; this time, Greylock Partners, a Waltham firm that has a branch office in San Mateo, Calif., invested. Greylock partner David Sze, who works on the West Coast, admits that he had the opportunity to invest in Facebook in 2005, but says, "I was too busy — I just didn't have the cycles to look at it. In retrospect, that was a mistake."

Facebook now has 39 million users and is the sixth most popular website in the United States, according to the measurement firm comScore Inc. An average of 150,000 new users create a free Facebook account every day, according to the company.

A Bear Stearns analyst recently estimated that the company, which has already spurned several acquisition offers, is worth as much as $6 billion, and will bring in about $140 million in revenue this year. That's with just over 300 employees.

(Looming over Facebook's success — and any eventual public offering — is a lawsuit filed by several fellow Harvard students who allege that Zuckerberg built Facebook using software code he had originally written for their site, ConnectU.com, and that he also borrowed parts of their business plan. A Facebook representative said that none of its founders were available to comment.)

What makes Facebook so appealing is that once users join and create connections with their friends and colleagues, it becomes an incredible hub of information: friends can share photos, tell you where they are, show what music they're listening to, what parties or conferences they're planning to attend, or how much money they've raised for next weekend's charity walkathon.

Facebook also decided, in May, to allow other companies to develop applications that users can easily incorporate in their profile pages. Each of these apps — there are now more than 3,000 of them, according to the tracking firm Adonomics — adds new features without the company investing a penny. And unlike MySpace, Facebook is allowing the companies that develop these apps to use them for marketing purposes or to make money, which provides a great incentive.

So even if Boston didn't end up as Facebook's home base, there are plenty of companies here now developing applications for it. Needham-based TripAdvisor, Inc. offers a world map that you can stick virtual pushpins in, to show your friends where you've been.

Fafarazzi.com in Somerville has an app that allows Facebook users to send each other photos of celebrities, to reflect their mood. StyleFeeder Inc., a Cambridge shopping recommendation service, launched an app in June that has since been installed by 45,000 people.

"We don't want to make Facebook the cornerstone of our growth strategy, but we're happy to ride the wave," says Dina Pradel, StyleFeeder's vice president of marketing.

Could Facebook have succeeded if it had gotten an investment locally before Zuckerberg & Co. went West, and kept its headquarters here?

When I put that question to Accel Partners' Breyer, who is a native of Natick, he had a one-word answer: no.

"So many of the Facebook employees have come from top Internet companies like Yahoo, eBay, and Google that the culture that has been built at Facebook is fundamentally more consumer Internet savvy than if it would've been built anywhere else on the planet," Breyer says, after praising the engineering talent in Boston.

"Folks in the Valley are incredibly geo-centric to a point of snobbery," writes Battery Ventures' Scott Tobin via e-mail. He acknowledges that Silicon Valley is producing more companies than Boston but "to make an argument that great companies can't be built in any one place is bunk in my mind."

He mentions Microsoft Corp. in Redmond, Wash., and Qualcomm Inc. in San Diego as examples. "It just takes a good driving attitude to make it happen."

As for passing on Facebook, "that may turn out to have been a mistake," Tobin admits.

5. Profiles & Interviews

Tim Berners-Lee, the Web's Creator

Published in Webmaster Magazine, October 1996

The first big thunderstorm of the summer is rattling the windowpanes of MIT's 545 Technology Square, and the man who invented the World Wide Web is chastising me in a clipped British accent for not having read his FAQ.

"Have you looked at my Frequently Asked Questions?" the Oxford-educated Tim Berners-Lee asks, implying that one of those questions bears a distinct resemblance to my own first query. "You'd get a lot of points with me as a journalist if you'd actually looked at them first."

I stammer out an excuse: I've grown inured to FAQs; they rarely offer any real answers to my questions. But in Berners-Lee's promising view of the Web's potential, there's an answer to every journalist's question out there, coded and cross-linked in HTML. So in addition to making the Internet a place for sharing all kinds of information, the Web should render this kind of interview superfluous. And that would be fine with Berners-Lee. The director of the World Wide Web Consortium (W3C) and a principal research scientist at MIT's Laboratory for Computer Science has more important things do.

After developing the initial proposal for the Web in March 1989, writing code for the first Web server and combination browser/HTML editor in 1990, introducing the Web to CERN (the European Particle Physics Laboratory in Geneva, Switzerland) in December of that year, making it available on the Internet in the summer of 1991, and refining the specs for URLs, HTTP and HTML over the next two years, Berners-Lee landed at MIT in 1994.

His post there hasn't diminished the demands on his time and energy. He helps coordinate the activities of the 150 companies that constitute the W3C — fast-moving companies like Netscape Communications, Microsoft, Hewlett-Packard, Open Market, Silicon Graphics and Sun Microsystems — to ensure that the software standards that serve as the Web's foundation remain open and nonproprietary. The way Berners-Lee describes it, the job sounds a lot like trying to choreograph a swarm of hornets.

Somehow, though, Berners-Lee remains easygoing. A few moments after the FAQ incident, he apologizes, saying he's just getting tired of explaining the origins of the Web time and time again. Berners-Lee, dressed in a short-sleeve madras shirt open at the collar, still has the excited eyes and unruly blond hair of a college student, and he speaks very quickly when talking about the potential of the medium he created. With a whiteboard full of scribble as a backdrop, we sit down at the small round meeting table in his office, and Berners-Lee gets down to explaining the challenges of managing the Web's growth, as well as some of his expectations.

Scott Kirsner: When the telephone was invented, people thought it was going to be used for bringing music into people's homes. I'm curious as to how you envisioned the Web being used when you first began developing it.

Tim Berners-Lee: Initially, I envisioned it as a universal space in which all information could be put to get over the tremendous problems of incompatibility between servers, different data formats and different interactive databases such as VAX Notes and Usenet news. I was interested in it being very much of a space in which it was easy to add information. If you found something wrong, for example, and you had write access in that area, you would be able to go and fix it. The idea was that putting stuff on the Web should be trivial — just like reading it — and with the original World Wide Web program it was. You could make a link just by hitting a key. As you browsed, you could have many documents open at once. The target time for getting from one document to another was a tenth of a second. There would be a sort of sense of equilibrium between people and information, whether that information was Olympian information that descended from the clouds — "the CEO has just decreed company policy will be this," which nobody has write access to — or whether it was something you just scribbled down on the back of an envelope — "Hey, you should go and read this." All that information, which is part of how an organization works, is more than the sum of the knowledge of the people.

SK: Are you surprised by the speed of the Web's growth?

TBL: It's been a fairly steady exponential. The number of Web pages, somebody says, is doubling every two months. But it's been doubling every two months for years! And it'll only flatten out when something like 50 percent of American families have Web browsers. And it'll still be taking off elsewhere.

SK: At what point did it occur to you that you would be able to say that, potentially, 50 percent of American households would have Web browsers?

TBL: For the first two years, it was a hard sell, a hard push trying to persuade people to adopt it. And for a long time, within the Internet community, there was a feeling that gopher was where it was at. It was much easier to use, and hypertext was much too complicated. And then in 1992 it became clear that the Web was more exciting to people than gopher. A few people who had been writing consistently for gopher started actually producing Web sites instead. Then it was clear there was no other system competing with it. But there's no one point when I sat back and thought, "Wow! This is gonna actually do it." The analogy I use is of getting on a bobsled. For a while you're pushing like crazy, you're pushing with all your might, and then there's a certain point at which the thing is starting to run by itself. Then you have a small period of time in which you can jump in, and then you have to be thinking about the curves, and you have to actually get involved. And now we're into the curves.

But there was a period of transition as it started to pick up speed — through '93, with Marc Andreesen's efforts — and a few really good Web sites, like the Vatican's beautiful exhibit of Renaissance art.

SK: It seems like a huge number of companies have started to realize that the Web and its protocols are a great way to share information internally. Do you see that happening?

TBL: I get that question a lot: "What about the intranet? Don't you think this is really exciting?" Which is sort of a waking up to the fact, which has always been the case, that most of the World Wide Web has always been used within groups, within companies. So the companies that win are the ones that learn how to use the Web at every level: for public relations, for internal discussions and for keeping track of the silly decisions we make day-to-day, which sometimes, if you're going to reverse a decision, are very interesting.

SK: Tell me about your decision to start the Web Consortium, which is a nonprofit organization, rather than going out and launching "World Wide Web Incorporated."

TBL: Well, I obviously looked at that possibility. In 1992, I was looking at a lot of different possibilities. I was under a lot of pressure from people who were rewriting their entire business plans around the World Wide Web. They said, "We understand that the Web hinges on some specifications sitting on a disk in Switzerland. How do we know that this is going to be stable? We need something better." The call was for a vendor-neutral forum. The thing that the Web has given the world is interoperability.

Interoperability is something that has just never happened on such a scale. And if that broke, that would be a big shame. The thing spread largely because I didn't make World Wide Web Incorporated in 1991. If I had done it in 1991, it would have been just another hypertext product, another proprietary product. All the big manufacturers would have come out with lookalikes.

But the fact that the specs were open and there was an open process discussing them was why people adopted it so fast. They could reorganize their entire activity around the World Wide Web because they knew that it wasn't based on some model where World Wide Web Incorporated could suddenly turn on the licensing and say, "All right, next year everything is the same as last year but 3,000 bucks a pop."

So I went around America and Europe looking for somewhere that would be appropriate [for W3C], and a number of places, including a number of large companies, made a good play for being the World Wide Web Consortium center, but MIT had this great reputation for being open. With X Windows, the Lab for Computer Science said the X Consortium code would be available for free to anyone. And it always was. So that was an indication that the Lab for Computer Science was going to play by the rules.

SK: The Web consortium's stated mission is "to realize the full potential of the Web." How do you define that, the potential of this medium?

TBL: I don't think I like to define it in any inclusive way, because that would limit it. When I've been speaking, I've been using the word "intercreativity" recently. Because I've said interactivity, and people will say, "Oh, yeah. The Web's great because it's interactive." And they mean clicking on links, or submitting a form. I don't count that as interactivity. Interactivity is when we can sit down and we can actually build Lego blocks together in cyberspace. When we can sit around a table and draw up a plan for something together. We all have a sense of each other's presence, and we can all join in. We can all build knowledge and have our group knowledge represented on the Web. I think that's something that has got to come.

Then there is a web of trust — computers being able to understand who you trust for what. It will get to the point where a lot of the things you're going to be doing on the Web give you some exposure, whether you're buying things or sending confidential information. You don't want to have to check at every point who it is you're really talking to. You want the software to take care of the security for you. But to do that, it has to understand who you trust. There has to be a language in which people can talk to machines about trust, protocols in which machines can talk to machines about trust. That will be the basis of a lot of things. A lot of things will take off when we have that right.

SK: In terms of the more advanced stuff on the Web — especially agent technology, like the music recommendation site that came out of the [MIT] Media Lab and the BargainFinder site that Andersen Consulting developed — what do you see as the potential with those sorts of things? [BargainFinder was an early price-comparison service, which scoured the web to compare the prices of compact discs across various e-commerce sites.]

TBL: I think those are very interesting. I think agents are going to eventually make life more manageable, and be very powerful. I think the things people are doing with collaborative filtering, for example, are interesting. Using the combination of people and machines well is going to be an art. And our long-term push is to get information and machinery to a point where someone can make assertions and say, "I disagree with that document" or "I certify that this document is true" or "I certify that this person owns this house" — things that will allow you to actually verify things. For example, when you buy a house, typically in a lot of countries it involves a title search through all the deeds. The deeds are stored in land registries, and it takes lawyers a long time to go through them. And it's not only the deeds, but you have to do a search for any acts of transfer of land. If all this stuff were on the Web, and if it were in machine-readable form, you'd just be able to ask, "Is this person in this state going to be able to sell this house?"

SK: How do you see that sort of technology being applied to intranets or corporate networks in terms of decision making and communication inside a company?

TBL: One of the earliest proposals back in the pre-Web days was that one of the exciting things about getting everybody to live in a virtual world — to put their information into an information space — is that you can then use computers to analyze it. So within a corporation, there are a lot of exciting tools you can use, all sorts of forms of meeting and communication that you may never have thought of before. And also there'll be the fact that you'll be able to use computers to go and have a look at it. Can you imagine saying, "Here's our organization. Here's its home page. Now off you go, my little agent. Go and tell me what you think." And it may come back and say, "Well, pretty good organization. I can see you have a set of products here, and you have some documentation for them. And there are a few funny things. We've got a module over here that's been written by somebody that's not used by anybody at all. We've got one product over here that so far as I can tell is identical to this product over here, which is made by your Australian division. You know, that one is selling and this one isn't. Also, I've looked at the topology of your R&D; department, and, just looking at it from a long distance, it has a certain property to it. The ratio between the valency of the individual people and the diameter of the division itself and the overall connectivity I've compared with a Fortune 500 company over the last 10 years is very worrying. This looks like a division that isn't working very well. Because I've looked at your knowledge space, and the people are just not connected together properly..."

You could imagine that you would be able to make this Mr. Spock-like or, no, Bones-like little thing that looks at the body of knowledge inside an organization and trouble-shoots and tells you what's going on and in a way helps us get toward the self-managing team. And that's just talking about it at the organization level. If we can do that, it's very interesting to be able to do that at the democracy level, too. Because what we're really trying to make out of the country is a self-managing team. It's not as though we're really putting one person in charge, we're trying to make the whole thing so that we can all work together. And when you look at it on a global scale, then, even further up, you're trying to find a way that people ca n work together. So maybe we can improve things at every level.

SK: Do you see these kinds of developments as a five-year thing, a 10-year thing or something so incremental that you couldn't really keep track of them?

TBL: Well, go back to when electricity was invented. Where would you think new uses for electricity would stop being developed? It's just going to be layer upon layer. Hopefully, in a few years, people will stop talking about the Web as an application, and they'll be talking about the Web like they talk about air and water. It'll just be something you take for granted. It's information space. And exciting things will be happening within that space.

Dean Kamen, Inventor and Cultural Commando

Published in Wired Magazine, September 2000

Dean Kamen's sense of what's possible is governed by the immutable laws of nature. Everything else is up for grabs.

Kamen, 49, is a self-taught physicist and multimillionaire entrepreneur who lives in a hexagonally shaped house of his own design atop a hill just outside Manchester, New Hampshire. Invisible from the road, the estate is outfitted with a softball field, a wood-paneled library that's full of awards and honorary degrees (Kamen never graduated from college), a wind turbine to help supply power, and a pulley system that can deliver a bottle of wine from the kitchen to the bedroom.

He calls the place Westwind, and he stuffed it with a collection of toys and antiques that includes a jukebox, a slot machine, and a 25-ton steam engine once owned by Henry Ford. In Westwind's basement, there's a foundry, a machine shop, and a computer room, where Kamen often toils late into the night. He keeps a Porsche 928 and a black Humvee in one garage, two Enstrom helicopters in the other. The smaller, piston-driven chopper takes him to and from work at his offices in  downtown Manchester; the larger, turbine-driven version is reserved for longer hops, like to his private island off the coast of Connecticut. For trips more than a few hundred miles, he flies his twin-turbofan CitationJet.

Kamen has high-powered friends to match his taste in toys, and throws lavish parties that entice many powerful people to New Hampshire. Visitors have included George W. Bush, NASA administrator Dan Goldin, and, more recently, John Doerr of the VC firm Kleiner Perkins Caufield & Byers. But it's not the Rolodex, the air force, or the tricked-out Batcave that separates Kamen from the usual posse of tech multimillionaires. It's the way he's gone about acquiring it all, and the offbeat, often idealistic ways he chooses to spend it.

While Kamen won't divulge the size of his fortune, much of it stems from having invented things he decided ought to exist —

no market research necessary — like first-of-their-kind medical devices.

...

While Kamen was attending college in the 1970s, his brother — then a medical student and now a renowned pediatric oncologist — complained that there was no reliable way to give steady doses of drugs to patients. So Kamen invented the first portable infusion pump capable of delivering drugs (such as insulin) to patients who had previously required round-the-clock monitoring, freeing them from a life inside the hospital.

In the mid-1990s, he devised a phone book-sized dialysis machine — at a time when similar devices were as big as dishwashers and required patients to make regular trips to dialysis centers. Vernon Loucks, former chair of Baxter International, contracted Kamen's privately held company, Deka Research & Development, to develop the machine. "We didn't believe it could be done," he recalls. "Now it's all over the world. Dean is the brightest guy I've ever met in this business, bar none."

When he watched a man in a wheelchair try to negotiate a curb in the late '80s, Kamen wondered whether he could build a chair that would hop curbs without losing its balance. After $50 million and eight years in development, the Ibot Transporter — a six-wheeled robotic "mobility system" that can climb stairs, traverse sandy and rocky terrain, and raise its user to eye-level with a standing person — is undergoing FDA trials, and should be available by 2001, at a cost of $20,000. That may sound high, but keep in mind that the Ibot erases the need to retrofit a home for a wheelchair. Plus, mobility system is if anything an understatement: In June, Kamen saddled up his Ibot and climbed the stairs from a Paris Métro station to the restaurant level of the Eiffel Tower — then promptly called John Doerr on his cell phone.

"At first blush, you'd stay away from developing something like the Ibot, just because of the legal implications," says Woodie Flowers, a mechanical engineering professor at MIT and a friend of Kamen's. "You're going to put a human in it and it'll go up stairs? That's nuts. But he did it. He's not one to get caught up in conventional wisdom."

Lately, Kamen has broadened his work beyond health care. He believes technology and ingenuity can solve all kinds of social ills — like pollution, limited access to electricity, and contaminated water in many third-world countries, where bacteria from human feces in drinking water is a leading cause of cholera. To help ameliorate the water problem, Deka's team of 170 engineers is working on a nonpolluting engine — funded by several million dollars of Kamen's own money — based on a concept first floated in the early 1800s but never realized.

The device is called the Stirling engine; Kamen hopes it can be developed into an affordable, portable machine that will run a water purifier/power generator that could zap contaminated H_2O with a UV laser to make it safe for drinking. "It can burn any fuel, and you can do all kinds of things with it," he says. "It might be very valuable in emerging economies, giving them access to electricity, even the Net."

. . .

Another project, to be unveiled in the next year, will necessitate building "the largest company in New Hampshire," Kamen says with characteristic bravura. He's shy about details, except to say it involves a consumer device unrelated to health care and will require $100 million in financing. Among the investors: Kleiner Perkins.

But Kamen's first love and greatest passion these days is an idea that may be the farthest-fetched of all: turning engineers and inventors into pop-culture superstars. Operating through a nonprofit outfit called U.S. First (For Inspiration and Recognition of Science and Technology), Kamen works to encourage kids to pursue careers as scientists, engineers, and big thinkers. Lots of people talk about doing that, but to Kamen it's a holy crusade, and he sincerely believes he can reprioritize society to value inventors the way it values athletes.

"Our culture celebrates one thing: sports heroes," he says. "You have teenagers thinking they're going to make millions as NBA stars when that's not realistic for even 1 percent of them. Becoming a scientist or an engineer is."

Kamen launched First several years ago when he realized that many American teenagers were unable to name a single living scientist. The organization sponsors a national competition that matches high school students with engineers from local companies. The kids are given a standard kit of parts and challenged to build a working robot in six weeks. The robots are pitted against one another on a playing field, and the best-designed, wiliest bots rise to the top.

Dean Kamen, with his unconstrained sense of what's possible, has proven the skeptics wrong many times before. But honestly — replacing quarterbacks with engineers as mainstream heroes? Maybe he's been spending too much time in his Batcave.

Kamen wears the same uniform every day, whether he's in Deka's machine shop, meeting with bankers, or visiting the Oval Office: beige Timberlands, Levi's, and a cotton work shirt. With his pompadour of wavy black hair, he looks like a 1950s auto mechanic. In cold weather, he adds an olive-drab army jacket, its pockets crammed with small tools.

Kamen talks fast, and his voice retains the brassy streak of his native Long Island. He's funny and charismatic, but he has the air of someone used to shouldering big, improbable projects — driven, haunted, quixotic. He doesn't take vacations, and he hasn't paused to marry. "If I'm awake, I'm working," he says. "Deka and First are my work, my family, my hobby. They're everything."

His day usually begins by 9:30 at Deka headquarters, a renovated mill building on the banks of the Merrimack River. That gives employees "an hour of sanity without me in the morning," he says. Kamen works until 9 or 10 pm, when he breaks for dinner, bringing along a staffer or two to talk shop.

Deka projects come in two flavors: Kamen's ideas, and everything else. Everything else — mainly contract research for health care concerns — is what pays the bills. Deka designed the HomeChoice portable dialysis machine in partnership with Baxter, as well as a medical irrigation pump for Davol. Deka has also worked on a series of innovative vascular stents (shunts that keep blood vessels clear) for Johnson & Johnson. "If you've got a tough problem, there's only one place to go," says Baxter's former chair Loucks.

By comparison, Kamen's projects are far-out inventions, like the Ibot or the Stirling: grand in scope, slower in development, and often too risky to attract corporate funding. "Sometimes we crash and burn. It's better to do it in private," he says. "I'd rather lose my own money than someone else's."

When things work out, Kamen basks in his success. On a frosty day last winter, I followed him around downtown Manchester as he took an Ibot out for a spin. The Ibot moved so fast that I had to break into a trot just to keep up. It not only operates in four-wheel drive — a standard motorized wheelchair has two-wheel drive — but it has a "balance mode," in which the front wheels rise up, balancing the Ibot upward, like a dog begging for a treat.

The chair's dual processors direct the grounded wheels to move back and forth slightly, compensating for weight shifts. The Ibot is so stable in balance mode that its occupant can even win a shoving match with just about any human.

In front of First headquarters, I watched as a crowd of gawkers stopped Kamen to admire the Ibot. One man asked how the chair works: "Does it just balance with weights?" Kamen — at eye-level with the guy, balancing on two wheels — paused a moment and smiled. "Technically," he said, "it's magic."

Magic moments aside, Deka also has its failures. A project to develop an automated bedside pharmacy — tied into a hospital's computer network and able to deliver more than 30 drugs without manual intervention — is on hold after soaking up several million dollars in funding. "We ran into a lot of political problems," is all Kamen will say. "The drug companies don't want it to happen."

He might run into problems with the Stirling engine, too. The development of a marketable Stirling device has eluded the brightest engineering minds since Robert Stirling, a Scottish minister, patented the first version in 1816. The basic principle of Stirling's external combustion engine is simple: A chamber is filled with a gas that expands as it is heated by a small heat source, such as a propane flame, and contracts when cooled. The process operates a piston and drives the engine. The advantage? Cheap, local fuels can be used to run the engines, and Kamen has adapted his model to produce electricity instead of mechanical power.

But producing the thing is a more complex matter. While many have tried to use Stirlings to power drive shafts for vehicles, they have proved too expensive to manufacture on a mass scale, and they're not always efficient enough. One low tech problem is designing seals that guard against waste as the heat is transferred into a form that does useful work.

Deka's version heats a chamber containing helium, under pressure, and Kamen says it can run on gasoline, propane, fuel oil, diesel, alcohol, or even solar power — with one-fifth the emissions of a gas stove. Deka's engineers think they'll succeed where others have failed because they've ironed out all the kinks. "We looked at the history of the Stirling — all the money and time and expertise poured into it — and identified a half-dozen key goofs that previous teams had made," says project leader Chris Langenfeld. "Seventy percent of it was a materials challenge. We had to track down the right composites to use as seals."

Kamen hopes that his family of Stirlings, five years in development, will soon bring portable electricity to nations without a reliable power grid — or any grid at all. He envisions briefcase-sized Stirlings powering cell phones and cell towers, as well as purifying water. He aims to have them on the market in the next two years, and is currently working on the marketing issues — like how developing nations will be able to afford bulk purchases of the engines, which are projected to cost $1,500 apiece.

Staffing for the Stirling project alone involves about 20 people, including chemical, electrical, and mechanical engineers; thermodynamicists; particle and combustion physicists; and software designers and testing technicians.

"Deka is one of the highest-morale operations I've ever seen," says Ray Price, president of the Economic Club of New York and a close friend of Kamen's. "There's no bureaucracy, and very little structure. Dean expects performance, but how they get to solutions is up to them."

Kamen supervises the 10 or so projects under way at Deka at any given time, and is rarely at his desk. He refers to himself as "a human entropy producer," roaming the halls and labs, tossing out ideas, asking about timing, and prodding project managers.

Deka also has its mercilessly intense side. "There's a sorting process that happens at Deka," says MIT's Flowers, also an adviser for First. "You have the people who stick with Deka because they realize it's a great place to learn, to try things that haven't been done. Successful people listen to, understand, and respect Dean." But Flowers adds that he has known some MIT grads who have found the experience less than satisfying. "One of them would never cross the threshold again. Dean occasionally runs over people."

Those who stick around remain aware of the impatience that simmers beneath Kamen's surface. The same is true of those people who contract with Deka. Bob Gussin, Johnson & Johnson's recently retired chief scientific officer, convinced his former company to fund the Ibot, despite great internal resistance. He calls Kamen "brilliant," but says, "Dean is so intense and so aggressive that you always have to worry whether he'll get frustrated at not moving fast enough. Sometimes his intensity is almost frightening."

Kamen exhibited a pronounced entrepreneurial bent from an early age, as well as a dislike for rote learning. In junior high, rather than do his homework, he would read demanding primary texts like Isaac Newton's Principia on his own, and then heckle his science teacher. As a teenager, he built control systems for sound-and-light shows in his basement, and before long, he was getting contracts for installations at Manhattan's Hayden Planetarium, the Four Seasons, and the Museum of the City of New York. While still in high school, he was asked to automate the Times Square ball drop on New Year's Eve. Before graduation, he was earning $60,000 a year, rivaling the combined income of his father, a comic book artist, and his mother, a high school teacher.

...

Kamen's tendency to put his own projects before his schoolwork continued at Worcester Polytechnic Institute in Worcester, Massachusetts. On frequent trips home, he worked on his portable infusion pump, eventually dubbed Auto-Syringe. But the basement was getting crowded. Kamen needed more room. He engaged an architect to expand the basement under a newer wing of the house, and hired a crew to prop the house on stilts to make room for a Bridgeport milling machine, an arc welder, lathes, saws, and other equipment purchased from a neighborhood machine shop.

What did his parents think? Kamen sent them on a cruise during the period of heaviest construction.

After five years at WPI, Kamen still hadn't collected enough credits to graduate, so he was asked to leave. He moved back to Long Island and poured his energy into Auto-Syringe. The New England Journal of Medicine published an article about the benefits of the pump, and the National Institutes of Health ordered 100 units. In 1979, to escape taxes and overcrowding, he moved to New Hampshire. "I saw the license plates that read LIVE FREE OR DIE, and that sounded pretty good to me," says Kamen.

After two years, he sold Auto-Syringe to Baxter for an undisclosed sum. Up until that point, he'd hardly taken a salary, plowing the majority of his profits back into the business. For the first time, he felt rich. Within days of the sale, he bought a helicopter, fulfilling a childhood dream.

The helicopter led him to North Dumpling Island, a speck of land with a lighthouse, located in Long Island Sound. His flight instructor's wife, a real estate agent, told him the island was for sale. One winter day, he set out to find it. He brought the chopper down near the lighthouse tender's home. A frightened old man, part of the family that owned the island, came out to see what was going on. The young inventor befriended the man and his wife. When Kamen later bought the island (at a bargain price), he let the couple continue living there.

Though Kamen doesn't visit the island much anymore, it's a microcosm of his worldview, a whimsical combination of leave-me-alone and dreams of techno-utopia. An aerial photograph that hangs in Kamen's office at Deka bears a caption that reads "The Only 100 Percent Science-Literate Society."

When Kamen wanted to erect a wind turbine on North Dumpling and the state of New York objected, he seceded from the US. Though the secession has never been officially recognized, he signed a nonaggression pact with his friend, then-President George Bush, and enlisted Ben Cohen and Jerry Greenfield of Ben & Jerry's as "joint chiefs of ice cream." North Dumpling has its own flag, its own anthem, a one-ship navy, and its own currency. One bill, which Kamen carries in his wallet, is the value of pi. "You can't make change for it," he says with a grin. "It's a transcendental function."

After the sale of Auto-Syringe in 1982, Kamen began buying 19th-century mill buildings in Manchester and renovating them as office space (he now owns 570,000 square feet of office space in the city). He set up Deka R&D in one, and soon got to know city and state politicians, like John Sununu, the governor of New Hampshire who would go on to become a notorious chief of staff for President Bush. Today, Kamen has a direct line to New Hampshire governor Jeanne Shaheen.

"In a small state like New Hampshire, Dean is a very visible guy," says Jay Wood, president of Kana Communications, one of Kamen's tenants. "His helicopter comes buzzing down the river and lands on a building — you can't ignore that."

. . .

When it comes to First, Kamen's a complete noodge. He makes sure that the state's pols are all visible supporters, which means First events are usually peppered with political types. Every four years, when the presidential candidates roll through New Hampshire looking for votes, Kamen makes First headquarters — aka First Place — and Westwind available for rallies, parties, and speeches, and looks for a *quid pro quo* from the candidates — soliciting promises to invite First winners to the White House.

One day during my visit, Kamen and I get a chance to meet up with George W. Bush. Kamen's already been all over the Eastern time zone, but nothing is more important to him than scoring promises on behalf of First. He woke up in Cleveland before dawn, then flew to visit Bose Corporation, near Boston, to show off the Ibot and talk with Amar Bose about marketing Deka's top-secret consumer device. He picked up a banker from Credit Suisse First Boston at Manchester airport to discuss financing, then wolfed down a dinner of pizza and beer at First Place, where

George W. was giving a speech. After the speech, Kamen drags me through the crowd toward the candidate.

Apparently George W. indicated at a recent Westwind dinner that he might be able to attend the First nationals in Orlando. "I want to get him to promise to come in front of a reporter," Kamen tells me. "You're going to be my witness."

. . .

I'm standing in a parking lot near Manchester airport with Kamen's parents, Woodie Flowers, and Rich Cox, a Deka technician, waiting for Kamen to arrive. I'm looking for the Hummer. His mother knows better. She points to the sky and says, "There's Dean."

Kamen sets the little Enstrom down on the tarmac, and before long we're piling into the CitationJet. To Kamen, the Citation is a "beautiful machine," with its twin Williams-Rolls turbofans, top altitude of 41,000 feet, and maximum speed of Mach 0.7. The thing looks fast even standing still.

I'd heard a few stories about Kamen's piloting before I boarded. One was that he had a less-than-perfect attendance record at the CitationJet training program. But as a friend tells it, he missed only two questions on the final — the highest score in a class full of professional pilots. Afterward, he proved to the instructor that those "wrong" answers were actually correct.

On an unusually warm March afternoon, we're off to Ypsilanti, Michigan, the site of the initial round of First regionals. Kamen is upbeat, as evidenced by his safety speech before takeoff: "In the event of an emergency, those bimbos in the high heels who served you coffee will be of absolutely no use," he says. Of course, there are no flight attendants on the plane.

Kamen sees the lack of appreciation for science in America as a problem — but that's not to say he's calling for a revamping of the educational system. In his view, more teachers, textbooks, PCs, and Internet access won't get students jazzed about learning. "They need to have access to challenging, hands-on projects that result in a tangible product" — like building robots. And they need role models — engineers — to assist them.

Kamen refers to First as "the NCAA of smarts." The competition has no formal instructional agenda. You just have to build a bot that can play a game better than the others do. In January, groups of high school students receive kits and a description of the game. Each group has to build the robot in six weeks, working with engineers from local companies — like Du Pont, Ford, and Honeywell. There are only two restrictions: expense (no more than $425 can be spent on additional parts, supplied by a company called Small Parts) and weight (the robot can be no more than 130 pounds). At the competition, two student teams will be paired to form an alliance.

This year, the robots have to pick up basketball-sized rubber balls and drop them in bins, earning one point for yellow balls and five for scarcer black ones. Robots also earn five points for ascending a ramp in the center of the field, 10 for hanging from a chin-up bar, and 10 more for helping a partner robot hang from the bar.

Once we're on the ground, we hustle off to the campus of Eastern Michigan University, where the students are trying out their robots. Kamen has no official duties tonight, but he can't wait to see the action. Inside the field house, teams are making last-minute adjustments and sawing off vestigial robot pieces to make the weight limit. Kamen talks to a team tinkering with Chief Delphi, one of several robots sponsored by Delphi Automotive Systems. Two teenagers approach: "Can we have your autograph?"

It's just as Kamen would have it: High school kids treating an engineer like a celebrity. And it happens several times over the weekend. MIT professor Flowers, who is serving as an emcee, is equally adored.

The following morning, at the kickoff, there are pep bands and flag bearers, honor guards and spirit corps. Students stomp their feet and cheer wildly. When two opposing robots face off to get to the ramp, the screams are deafening.

Kamen watches most of the two-minute matches from the sidelines, fixated. He marvels at a robot named V Force that can grab the chin-up bar, slide laterally along it, and, with a long arm, pluck balls out of its opponent's goal and place them in its own. "Just another science fair, huh?" he mutters to me after a particularly exciting match.

In the ensuing two days, the competition will have elements of WWF aggressiveness and flashes of Nascar-style maneuvering — except that this event is rooted in mental dexterity. But that's not enough for Kamen. He wants First to attract the same attention lavished upon professional sports. That's why he spends his energy at First events needling bigwigs at sponsoring organizations. This year, GM, Johnson & Johnson, Motorola, Xerox, and NASA together are supporting 171 teams. But Kamen wants more. He wants to include every student in the country, and have the events televised. (He also wants you to enlist, as a kid or backer: firstinspires.org.)

Xerox chair Paul Allaire, who is smitten enough with the event to sit on the First board, is skeptical. "Is it totally practical? I'm dubious. But it's a good, if lofty, goal."

Another First board member, Bill Murphy, chair of Small Parts, waves off naysayers. "You watch," he says. "Dean's a schemer. He won't quit until it happens."

Walking the halls backstage at EMU, Kamen bemoans how difficult his mission to change the culture has been. "The inertia is enormous," he says. "If I'd have known nine years ago that it would've taken this much energy, I ..." He falls silent. But there's only one way Kamen can finish the thought: "Hell, I still would've done it."

When the finals begin, the excitement increases palpably. In the first game of the best-of-three finals, Chief Delphi pokes its snout into its opponent's goal, sucks out three balls, and skitters over to deposit them in its own goal. As the seconds tick away, it snatches another two points. Delphi's red alliance wins the first match, 34 to 16.

The next match goes to blue. "It happens like this every time," Kamen says gleefully.

In the rubber match, the action centers on the chin-up bar. Both blue alliance robots manage to hang, seizing the lead. But Visteon, Chief Delphi's red alliance partner, charges blue's Techno Beast, knocks it down, and, in the waning seconds, pulls itself up to the bar for the win. The audience roars.

Sly and the Family Stone's "You Can Make It if You Try" blasts over the PA, and the First judges form a receiving line. Hundreds of teens line the aisles, exchanging high-fives.

...

Heading back to Willow Run airport, Kamen is thinking ahead to the nationals at Epcot Center in Orlando. He's campaigning to get Governor Jeb Bush, who will attend the finals, to pledge that every Florida public school will participate next year.

Meanwhile, the Ibot is sailing through FDA trials and could be available by early 2001. ER star Noah Wyle is planning to make a feature film about Kamen and First. And work on the Stirling engine is going well, though, of course, not fast enough for Kamen.

On the flight back to Manchester, he cracks a joke over the intercom about pilots reporting basketball scores in midflight. "Who cares about bounce-bounce-throw?" he asks.

I ask if he knows the outcome of the First regionals at the Kennedy Space Center. "Let me call ground control," he says, mimicking a pilot-controller exchange. "Ground, this is Citation six-Delta-Kilo. Do you have the results of the First regionals in Florida?"

Everyone laughs, and then K. C. Connors, First's regional manager and Kamen's girlfriend, chimes in. "A few more years, Dean," she says. "A few more years."

. . .

[Author's Note: Of course, the secret project Kamen referred to in this piece turned out to be the Segway, the self-balancing electric vehicle unveiled in 2001. First marked its 30th anniversary in 2018. Each year, more than 600,000 students in more than 100 countries participate in the competition. Woodie Flowers died in 2019 after having heart surgery, and First organized a memorial service that was streamed worldwide. The photos accompanying this piece are courtesy of Dan Bricklin.]

Ray Kurzweil, Immortal

Published in the Boston Globe Sunday Magazine, October 31, 2004

Ray Kurzweil hasn't given much thought to his epitaph or spent an afternoon shopping for a burial plot. It's not that the idea of death hasn't occurred to him; he's 56, his father died of a heart attack at 58, and heart disease claimed his paternal grandfather. Kurzweil just doesn't plan on dying. Ever. "I think death is a tragedy," he says. "We've rationalized that it's a good thing, because we've had no alternative."

Kurzweil, one of the most influential living inventors, expects that rapidly accelerating progress in the fields of biotechnology, nanotechnology, and medical devices will eradicate the scourge that is human expiration sometime within the next 50 years. His latest book, *Fantastic Voyage: Live Long Enough to Live Forever*, coauthored with Dr. Terry Grossman and published this month, is almost certainly the first diet book that promises not just to help readers drop excess pounds but to render them immortal.

An MIT alumnus, Kurzweil knows a bit about rapidly accelerating progress. As an inventor, he has been responsible for breakthroughs in the fields of speech recognition and document scanning. He invented the first reading machine for the blind that was flexible enough to read any sort of printed matter. And prodded by Stevie Wonder, he produced the first electronic keyboard able to simulate the sounds of real orchestral instruments. Lately, he has been developing software to predict changes in the stock market — software that he plans to use to start his own hedge fund.

Sipping green tea at his office in Wellesley Hills, Kurzweil is dressed in a blue pinstripe suit; with his gray-flecked hair ending in a duck's tail, he looks like a 1960s rock musician turned CPA. He speaks in carefully crafted paragraphs, and every movement is deliberate. He is an unswerving optimist who believes that new technologies will be able to solve the most pressing problems society faces, from terrorism to energy shortages to diseases. His guiding principle is what he calls the "law of accelerating returns." Because of exponential advances in science, Kurzweil and Grossman write in *Fantastic Voyage*, "the 21st century will equal 20,000 years of progress at today's rate of progress."

Kurzweil says he knew he wanted to be an inventor at age 5. As a student at MIT in the mid-1960s, he enrolled in every computer course and operated a business using mainframe computers to match high school students with appropriate colleges. The company later sold for $100,000 and helped pay his way through school. He went on to rack up 14 patents and got rich by taking his companies public and later selling them to acquirers like Xerox. In 1999, President Clinton awarded him the National Medal of Technology. Kurzweil, who's been married for 32 years — he and his wife, Sonya, have two children — has been working with the same business partner, Aaron Kleiner, for more than three decades. His company, Kurzweil Technologies, serves as an umbrella for eight different start-ups, including KurzweilAI.net, a website that tracks technology news, and it's rare when he's not juggling multiple projects.

Kurzweil became interested in the field of wellness at 35, when he was diagnosed with diabetes and found that conventional insulin treatment produced undesirable side effects. In their book, Kurzweil and Grossman advocate an array of common-sense wellness strategies for good health, like reducing one's intake of sugar, caffeine, and alcohol; adopting a low-impact exercise regime; and taking handfuls of dietary supplements. Kurzweil pops 250 pills a day and says he manages his diabetes without relying on insulin. "I really approach this as an engineer or a scientist," Kurzweil says. "I don't just take all these supplements based on general research. I see what effect they have on my biochemistry. I really view it that I'm aggressively reprogramming my biochemistry." He spends one day a week at an alternative-health clinic in Arlington, submitting to tests and receiving intravenous injections. Getting dosed with lecithin, he says, helps keep his cell membranes pliable, allowing nutrients in and toxins out.

Taking proper care of the body today, Kurzweil believes, is a necessary step on the path to immortality for himself and his fellow baby boomers. In 20 years, he predicts, biotechnology will be able to block the circuits that cause disease and will radically slow aging. After that, what he calls the "full blossoming of nanotechnology" will allow us to replace the fragile and diseaseprone cells we were born with, swapping our fading neurons with nano-engineered neurons that keep our memory forever sharp. He plans to be around for both those revolutions, whenever they occur.

Even some of his close friends, however, trust his business instincts more than his health advice. "I'm not as healthy in my behavior as Ray," says Michael Brown, the retired CFO of Microsoft. "But if he calls up and says, 'I'm going to start a company,' I say, 'How much do you want?'"

Leonard Guarente, an MIT biology professor who has studied mechanisms in yeast and mice that extend their lives, says, "I don't throw around the word 'immortality' much myself."

Others argue that humans weren't intended to have unlimited life spans.

In Kurzweil's view, what makes us human is our quest for knowledge and self-improvement, and to his mind, there are no problems that can't be solved through the application of ingenuity. "I don't define humanity in terms of our limitations," he says, "but rather by this quality of seeking to overcome our limitations. We didn't stay on the ground or on the planet, and we're not staying within the limitations of our biology."

Joe Caruso, Angel Investor

Published in the Boston Globe, September 18, 2015

Getting an audience with Joe Caruso doesn't require sweet-talking an assistant or networking your way through friends of friends of friends. You simply go to a scheduling website and sign up for a half-hour block of time, and a few days later, you enter a small glass-walled conference room at the Cambridge Innovation Center and sit down across a wood-topped table. Caruso is tie-less in a blue Oxford, laptop open in front of him. His vibe is Peter Falk-like. "Tell me about yourself — not your business," is a typical opener.

When I signed up for a slot earlier this month, though, Caruso spent the first few minutes trying hard to convince me not to write a column about him. His reasoning: there are lots of people who offer advice and mentorship to entrepreneurs in Boston, and a sizable subset of that group are also willing to write early checks to fund businesses they feel have a shot at success. (At right, Caruso with Pamela Aldsworth of JP Morgan.)

But no one else is as accessible, humble, and willing to help as Caruso, who calls his Westwood company Bantam Group. And it's hard to find an angel investor in Boston with as diverse of a set of investments. Caruso put money into HubSpot, Constant Contact, and Carbonite, all now publicly-traded software companies. But he also invested in Coffee Connection, the early chain of cafes that invented the Frappuccino — and which was acquired by Starbucks in 1994; Sutro, which is designing a monitoring and chemical-dispensing system for pools; and Terrafugia, a Woburn company developing a flying car.

"Joe is an investor in people," says Matt Douglas, CEO of Punchbowl, a party invitation site based in Framingham. "I still don't think he really understands Punchbowl, but the product and the specifics of the technology are not that important to him."

Caruso says, "I pride myself in having a good filter for people. It hurts when I'm wrong. It's like you're the expert at selecting wines, and it turns out you paid $1000 for a bottle of vinegar." He says that he treats office hours as a separate thing from pitch meetings. At the former, he wants to be a sounding board. "I'm not here filtering for deals," he says. "If people come raising money, I want to have a separate meeting."

Caruso meets with all sorts of entrepreneurs at office hours: "Fifteen year-olds, 65-year olds, some people with brilliant ideas, and some complete whack jobs," he says. But even when someone is describing to him the small snafu that is keeping their perpetual motion machine from working as designed, Caruso says, "I throw a switch and treat them like an absolute equal."

Caruso has never actually started his own company. He was an early employee of Teradyne in the late 1960s, which was just starting to make test equipment for the microchip industry. He later ran a company that made monitoring systems for stroke and spinal cord patients, Cyborg Corp. It was a bruising experience, with the company's investors at one point suing each other.

Back then, he says, "I didn't have the benefit of a good mentor, and I'd like others to have it. It's sort of my mission."

He's omnipresent at startup showcases and business plan competitions. He seems to know about almost every company raising an initial fundraising round; sometimes he writes the first check that doesn't come from the founder's friends or family. Seth Priebatsch, founder of the Boston-based mobile payment company LevelUp, says he pitched Caruso one morning before running a marathon. "He wrote me a $5,000 check then and there, and I put it in my sock and ran back to Boston with it," says Priebatsch, who was at the time a Princeton undergrad. The money may not be a "life-changing" amount, says entrepreneur Ben Sprecher — typically it isn't more than $25,000 — but Caruso's name can be helpful in helping persuade other investors to hop on the train.

Recently, some of his companies have been acquired by Google, VMWare, and Autodesk. One startup, Crashlytics, which helped mobile app developers collect data about crashes, was acquired by Twitter within a year. That turned his $5,000 into more than $200,000, according to Crashlytics founder Wayne Chang. But Caruso's Bantam Group website also doesn't conceal the companies that croaked, designating them with a skull-and-crossbones icon.

"Anybody who says they can predict a company is going to be successful is lying," says Caruso. "I think of what good investors bring to the table as being sort of a little speck of dust on the die that biases the way it lands. It can be advice, it can be introductions. I make my little contribution, and some other people make theirs, and we bias things in the direction of success."

In 2000, "I was a first-time entrepreneur, and Constant Contact was my first time raising venture money," says Gail

Goodman, chief executive of the Waltham digital marketing company. "Joe was everything I needed — he helped me tune the [slide] deck and tune the pitch. He was that perfect coach." Constant Contact today employs more than 1400 people.

"He has a 'how can I help?' attitude, as opposed to a 'how can I make money?' attitude," says Sprecher, whose couponing startup, Incentive Targeting, was acquired by Google in 2012.

Caruso says that his typical Thursday at the Cambridge Innovation Center starts at 10 AM and runs through 6 PM. (He holds similar office hours at his alma mater, Northeastern University, as well as MassChallenge, Techstars, Harvard, and the WeWork shared office space. "Wherever people want me, I go," he says.) According to his calendar, he has met with more than 250 entrepreneurs in 2015 so far.

When my half hour with Caruso was up, I noticed a group of people lingering outside the conference room — three entrepreneurs from Spain. It was their turn for thirty minutes with Joe. Maybe it'd be just another meeting. But maybe it'd be one they'd later realize had altered the roll of the die.

6. True Crime

Catch Me If You Can

Published in Fast Company, August 2003

Jay Nelson parked his wife's white Jeep Cherokee in a garage near Hartford's Bradley International Airport and dashed toward the terminal. It was Valentine's Day 2001, and he was worried he'd miss his flight.

This was Nelson's first day as a fugitive.

The following day, Nelson was expected to appear in federal court in Concord, New Hampshire to face arraignment for fraud related to his ingenious home-based business: running auctions for computer equipment on Yahoo and eBay and rarely delivering the merchandise. It was a business, Nelson now says, built on a "100% profit margin."

Before leaving home early that morning, Nelson had written a note to his wife, Krista, who was pregnant with their first child. In the note, he explained that he was leaving because he didn't want to cause problems for the family.

When Nelson stopped to check his luggage with a redcap outside the terminal, the redcap told Nelson that he'd have to go inside — his name had been flagged because he'd bought his ticket the day before. "I was worried that they would catch me before I got onto the plane," Nelson says. He was traveling with $10,000 in cash and about $4,000 in gold and platinum coins.

But if he was on any computerized watch lists, the agent at the US Airways counter didn't notice. Nor did the agent balk when Nelson handed over his New Hampshire driver's license, even though it didn't match the name he had used to buy the ticket on the Web, Jay Elson. Nelson boarded the plane just before the cabin door closed, and a few minutes later, he watched with relief as the airport began blurring past the window.

Eventually, however, Nelson's real name would feature prominently on another list: the most-wanted roster of the U.S. Postal Inspection Service, which is responsible for investigating most online-auction scams. He'd be charged with conducting more than $200,000 in illicit auctions, using 15 different screen names and ripping off 1,700 victims. "He found a method that worked," says Tom Higgins, the postal inspector who was the sole investigator who built the case against Nelson — and who tracked him down after he fled. Nelson could produce new online identities almost at will, and "he could commit Internet fraud faster than we could investigate," Higgins says.

Though Nelson never wielded a gun, Higgins started thinking of him as the John Dillinger of the Web — someone who excelled at a particular kind of crime and was brilliant when it came to eluding capture. In contemporary terms, Nelson's case was the Internet version of *Catch Me If You Can*.

Nelson is just one of the individuals who have decided to make a living by swindling bidders on eBay and Yahoo — albeit one of the most successful. Auction fraud has been the biggest source of consumer complaint to the Internet Fraud Complaint Center, run by the FBI and the National White Collar Crime Center, every year since the center was created in 2000. Fraud is also a sticky problem for eBay, the Web's biggest auction site. (Although Nelson operated on both Yahoo and eBay, eBay's business is far more dependent on auctions than Yahoo's is.) EBay's virtual auction house hosted nearly $15 billion in sales of merchandise last year, generating $1.2 billion in revenue for the company. EBay says that only an infinitesimal fraction of its auctions are fraudulent, but ensuring that its marketplace is a safe arena for buying and selling merchandise is crucial to the company's continued growth. And catching serial scammers like Nelson is a good place to start.

COMPLAINTS TRIGGER AN INVESTIGATION

There wasn't anything exceptional about the Jay Nelson file when it first showed up in Tom Higgins's interoffice mailbox, courtesy of his supervisor, in May of 2000.

Higgins, 45, has worked for the U.S. Postal Service since he was in college, when he took a job as a letter carrier in the town of Andover, Massachusetts, north of Boston. He had always wanted to be a federal agent — maybe in the Secret Service or the FBI — but the path to becoming a postal inspector seemed a little clearer. Despite the dweeby title, postal inspectors are indeed feds: Higgins packs a 9-millimeter Beretta Centurion whenever he leaves the office. "We're not as well-known as the FBI," shrugs Higgins. "That doesn't bother me." He has a low-key personality, a spiky gray brush cut with a shock of white in front, and a reputation around the office as a tenacious investigator.

Postal inspectors ferret out crime that takes place within the ranks of the postal service, but they also work on cases that involve drugs and bombs sent through the mail, as well as mail and wire fraud — the category that online auctions fall into. Part of Higgins's job is to sort through complaints and figure out which ones are worth investigating. The Nelson file was thin, but it seemed worthy of attention. Buyers were complaining about a seller who operated from a rented mailbox in Tyngsboro,

Massachusetts, a town near the New Hampshire line. The seller was offering hard drives and other computer components but not delivering — or occasionally sending broken products. He was also selling illegal copies of software such as Adobe PhotoShop, which buyers found they couldn't register.

It didn't take long for Higgins to connect the Tyngsboro mailbox to Krista Nelson, whose name was on the box-rental form. Higgins learned that Krista and Jay Nelson lived in a rented house on 32 acres on a mountain in Lyndeborough, New Hampshire, about a half hour's drive from Tyngsboro. He also discovered that a postal inspector based in New Hampshire had already visited the Nelsons earlier in 2000 to inquire about other complaints relating to auctions that traced back to them.

"This was someone who was ingenious at devising new ways to beat the system," says U.S. postal inspector Tom Higgins. "He did it for a living."

Nelson had claimed then that he'd simply fallen behind with his business. He promised that he would refund his customers' money, and he later supplied the New Hampshire postal inspector with a list of all of the customers who'd complained and how much he'd refunded to each. But the scams continued, under different screen names on Yahoo and eBay.

"I figured I'd better step back and consider the scope," says Higgins, explaining why he didn't visit the Nelson home right away. "When you interview someone, you want to know as much as you can. Clearly, this guy wasn't telling the whole story" to the New Hampshire postal inspector.

Higgins started tracking money transfers from Nelson's accounts on PayPal, an online payment service now owned by eBay, into accounts at the Bank of New Hampshire. (Auction bidders often send sellers money through PayPal.) At that point, Higgins was the only person on the Nelson investigation — and he was conducting it in parallel with seven or eight other investigations for which he was responsible.

Higgins had been on eBay once or twice, but he'd never bought or sold anything on the site. Working the Nelson case was "a fast learning process," he says. "It was like skipping 101 and going right to the master class."

By summer of 2000, Nelson had "left the realm of having dissatisfied customers and stepped over the line to conducting failure-to-render scams," Higgins says. "And everything he was doing involved fictitious information and false identities."

MORE INTERESTED IN BOOZE THAN BOOKS

Nelson grew up with adoptive parents in Rockford, Illinois. His father ran a property-management company that dealt with apartment buildings and shopping malls. Nelson studied criminal justice at a local community college and later attended Illinois State University in Bloomington, but he didn't graduate. "I was more interested in drinking," he says. By the time he reached his twenties, Nelson had amassed enough DUI convictions to qualify as a felon, and he had spent time in Cook County Jail.

He had been interested in computers since he was a kid, and when he got out of jail, Nelson managed to land an IT-support position at the Eureka Company in Bloomington. He wasn't beyond fudging the truth to get a better job, though. When he applied for a job as a Lotus Notes administrator at Caterpillar, for example, Nelson said that he had a degree in criminal justice and that he was familiar with Notes. "I got a copy of *Lotus Notes for Dummies* and learned enough of the buzzwords," he says. After three rounds of interviews, "they hired me on the spot," Nelson says. "I'd never even turned on the program." But he was a quick study, and he says that he was soon competent at creating and maintaining Notes databases.

Nelson's older brother had started selling computer equipment on a fledgling auction site called eBay. When Krista, who worked for State Farm at the time, found out that employees there could get deep discounts on surplus office equipment, she bought Hewlett-Packard inkjet printers from State Farm 10 at a time, and Nelson posted them for sale on eBay. Then his brother connected him with a man who had a large supply of computer software, and Nelson started selling that too.

By 1997, Nelson's auction income had surpassed his Caterpillar salary, and he quit to run his auction business full-time. "I would hire neighborhood kids to bubble-wrap modems for me or type up labels," he says. "I was working 16 hours a day, seven days a week." Several hundred pieces of mail came in every day, and several hundred packages went out, Nelson says.

At that point, at least some of the auctions Nelson ran were legitimate. One of his user names from that era, Diamondsoft, had 58 positive ratings in eBay's feedback system and only one negative rating. (Diamondsoft mostly sold copies of Microsoft Office.) But the negative rating offered a hint of what was to come: "I think they are thieves," the buyer wrote in March of 1999. "My bank paid my check 12/28/98 and I'm still waiting."

Other buyers began finding themselves in similar situations. "I sent money order, they sent nothing," another buyer wrote in May 1999. Eventually, a postal inspector knocked on the door of the house that Nelson rented from his brother and told Nelson that there had been complaints about his auctions. The sheriff and a representative from the Illinois attorney general's office also dropped by.

Nelson decided that it might be a good time to move to New Hampshire. "My wife hated the Midwest, and she'd lived in Nashua [New Hampshire] before," he says. Another motivating factor: The Illinois attorney general was building a case against the Nelsons for failing to deliver merchandise they'd sold, selling pirated software, and establishing new screen names with false information after their old screen names had been suspended. So Jay and Krista relocated to Lyndeborough. (They later reached a settlement with the Illinois attorney general, agreeing to pay $6,000 to their customers and $1,000 to the attorney general's Consumer Education Fund.)

Since most auction bidders look at a seller's feedback messages before they place a bid to determine whether the seller is trustworthy, Nelson devoted a lot of energy to creating positive feedback profiles for his various online identities. One identity of Nelson's would "sell" an item to another, and then the "buyer" would post positive feedback on the "seller." Nelson would also buy inexpensive items, like paperback books, from sellers who actually existed, hoping that they would add good feedback to his profile. He didn't care about actually receiving the books, and he regularly used a fake mailing address.

Once an identity had received enough positive feedback to be considered trustworthy, Nelson would set up a "Dutch auction," in which he claimed to have a large batch of a particular item to sell. Dutch auctions allow sellers to post quantities of identical merchandise all at once, rather than item by item, and bidders can buy as many as they want. By the time buyers started complaining to Yahoo or eBay that they'd paid but never received the product, causing that particular identity of Nelson's to be suspended from selling, Nelson would have collected most of the money. In June 2000, one identity, harddrives4sale, took $32,104 from would-be buyers on Yahoo; in September, another identity raked in $12,985 on eBay.

By the fall of 2000, when Higgins felt he had made enough progress to take the next step in his investigation, the Nelsons had moved again. They'd purchased a historic house on Main Street in Gilsum, New Hampshire, a town near the Vermont border. The house, built in 1883, had once been an inn, and Nelson converted the third floor, which had served as the inn's ballroom, into his office. Nelson hardly kept a low profile: He coached Little League, led a Boy Scout troop, and occasionally helped his neighbors with computer glitches.

Higgins first met Nelson on the morning of October 20, 2000, when Higgins arrived at the front door of his house with a search warrant, two New Hampshire state troopers, six fellow postal inspectors, and a battering ram. The last proved unnecessary: Nelson answered the door when Higgins knocked. "Mr. Nelson, we're federal agents from the U.S. Postal Inspection Service," Higgins told him. "We have a federal search warrant from a magistrate regarding your activity on Internet auctions."

Higgins and his team took five computers from Nelson's house, along with several boxes of documents. The search took about six hours, and afterward, the computers were sent to a crime lab in Virginia for analysis.

Nelson expected to be arrested that day. But Higgins first needed to comb through the evidence from the search and write up a formal complaint against Nelson. "I knew there was stuff on my computers that would screw me," Nelson says.

LEARNING OF HIS OWN INDICTMENT ON THE 11 O'CLOCK NEWS

After the search of his house in Gilsum, "we figured Nelson was on notice," Higgins says. But then Higgins got calls from Stoney Burke, a member of eBay's antifraud squad, and his contact at PayPal, who reported, incredulously, that Nelson still seemed to be at it. (Yahoo's auction service was much less cooperative with the investigation, Higgins says. A Yahoo spokeswoman issued a statement: "When we are contacted by the authorities, we work closely with them to provide the requested information in a timely manner.")

With a proud smile, Nelson says that shortly after his home was searched, he built three new computers. "They took the CPUs but left the keyboards and monitors," he says. "And we had a lot of extra parts sitting around."

With his new computers, Nelson continued vacuuming money via eBay and Yahoo auctions. In November and December of 2000, under the name Susancutey, he took bidders for more than $30,000 on Yahoo Auctions. As YoshiInc on eBay, he "sold" $7,600 worth of computer gear.

On the advice of Michael Gunnison, an assistant U.S. attorney in Concord, New Hampshire, Higgins decided to take a small slice out of the bigger pie and focus on one crime for which they could arrest Nelson. They didn't necessarily think that they could keep him in jail — but they wanted a judge to impose pretrial conditions that would stop him from running auctions.

The small slice that Higgins and Gunnison focused on was an auction from August 2000 in which Nelson interacted with a customer who'd won a Yahoo auction and expected to pay Nelson for a 32-megabyte RAM card for his laptop. Nelson took the customer's credit-card number to consummate the transaction. (He had no ability to process a credit-card payment, however.) Nelson never sent the RAM, but over the next two months, he used the customer's Visa number to establish an America Online account — which he later used to conduct other fraudulent auctions — and to set up monthly subscriptions to several porn Web sites.

The next time that Higgins knocked on Nelson's door, in January 2001, he didn't bring the whole posse. He arrived with just one other postal inspector in tow and a warrant for Nelson's arrest in connection with a single charge of wire fraud, for the unauthorized use of the credit card. Nelson answered the door in his bathrobe. Higgins allowed him to dress before packing him into a car for the hour-long trip to the federal courthouse in Concord. Though Nelson was cuffed in the back of the car, Higgins let him read the arrest warrant. They made small talk. "He seemed like an affable enough guy," Higgins says.

They arrived in Concord just before noon. The U.S. Marshal's Service took custody of Nelson, though Higgins did Nelson's fingerprints and mug shots. In the afternoon, Nelson made his appearance before the federal magistrate, James Muirhead. Muirhead listened to Gunnison describe the ongoing investigation Higgins was working on. Then he heard from Nelson, who sounded contrite, promised to get a job, and mentioned that his wife was pregnant. Muirhead released Nelson and told him to return to Concord for his arraignment in a few weeks. There were also pretrial conditions, as Higgins and Gunnison had hoped for: Nelson had to stay in New Hampshire and "refrain from any use of computers."

A grand jury indicted Nelson on one count of wire fraud on February 7. Nelson found out about the indictment by watching the 11 o'clock news. "We didn't sleep much that night," he says. Nelson was required to appear in Concord again for his arraignment on February 15. He feared that they'd keep him in jail until the trial — and he was convinced that he would wind up serving a long prison term.

On the 14th, Krista called her husband's pretrial service officer to inform him that Jay had disappeared in the Cherokee and had left a note. On the 15th, no one knew where Nelson had gone. "We were looking at a potential flight situation," Gunnison says. Few expected Nelson to show up in court.

And he didn't. He was now officially a fugitive, and it was the responsibility of the U.S. Marshals to find him. Higgins kept working the case too.

A COLD FEELING INSIDE

On the US Airways flight, Nelson brought his newest computer with him, a Toshiba laptop that he'd bought at a Best Buy in Concord on February 2, three days after agreeing in front of the magistrate to refrain from any use of computers.

Nelson connected through Pittsburgh and landed someplace warm. He took a taxi to the motel room he'd reserved, which turned out to be in a seedy neighborhood. "There were hookers and strip clubs and adult bookstores," Nelson says. "The first room I got had a mildewy smell to it. So I went back to the office to change rooms. As I was walking back from the office, I realized what I'd done. I'd just left my wife, walked away from everything. I got this cold feeling inside."

Nelson was paranoid about being caught. "I thought I saw a U.S. marshal behind every rock," he says. But after a while, Nelson convinced himself that he was "a really small fish in a really big pond." Higgins had no idea where Nelson was, and neither did the U.S. Marshals. Krista Nelson's Jeep Cherokee, parked at the airport parking garage, wasn't even found for several months.

Nelson's auctions continued to pop up on eBay and Yahoo, but at that point he seemed mostly focused on eBay. In March and April, he took in almost $8,000 on eBay, spread over 73 different transactions. Then came nearly $20,000 in April and May as "Biggerthanu." Then $27,000 as "Skunkker" in May and June. Nelson was a mass manufacturer of electronic identities.

Higgins decided that if he was going to catch Nelson, he would need to tap into the online-auction community. He began contacting buyers who'd lost money to all of the Nelson scams that he knew about. He asked them to complete a Web-based survey form that he'd designed especially for the case. As information poured in, Higgins sifted through it.

Bryan Small, a union electrician in Chicago, bought an Intel Pentium motherboard in May 2001 from an eBay seller called Biggerthanu. It was for a computer that Small was putting together. He paid $188.50 via PayPal but never got the merchandise. "I felt rather p.o.'ed," Small says. "I decided to do what I could." So, like Higgins, Small started to email other buyers who'd been burned by Nelson, asking for information.

Why did Small make the effort? "If you go and rip people off, you make the whole system look bad," he says. "And once the system looks like it's not trustworthy, then no one wants to be affiliated with it." Small forwarded all of the information that he had collected to Higgins.

Contained within Small's cache of emails was the case's first big break. One of the emails Small had received was from someone who hadn't bought anything from Nelson but had sold him a digital camera. Luckily for Higgins, that seller had kept a meticulous database of every transaction, and he supplied the shipping address where the camera had been delivered. It had been sent to "John Nelson" at a Howard Johnson Express Inn & Suites in Orlando, Florida.

A postal inspector from Orlando went to the Howard Johnson's and showed the manager a photo of Nelson. The manager recognized him but said that he wasn't staying there anymore. Yet Higgins was encouraged. He now had a rough sense of where Nelson was — or at least where he'd been recently.

Then he made what seemed like a huge mistake. In talking about the case to a reporter for MSNBC.com, Higgins mentioned that he thought that Nelson was in Florida. He intended to indicate that that information was off the record. But it ran in the MSNBC.com article on June 7, 2001.

"We were concerned that the MSNBC story had blown everything," Gunnison says. "Why wouldn't Nelson be Googling his own name [to see what was being said about him]? We were convinced that he'd leave Orlando."

SPREAD-EAGLED ON THE SIDEWALK

Nelson wasn't planning to leave Orlando, but he was laying the groundwork for creating a new identity in the real world, just as he'd been able to churn out new identities online. In libraries and on the Web, he researched how to obtain a fake set of ID documents. He didn't have a bank account in Orlando, so he had to be inventive about how he pulled money from his PayPal account. Proceeds from his auctions went into the account, and Nelson used that credit to buy other things on eBay, such as gold coins, CD burners, and other electronics.

Often, his purchases weren't mailed to him at hotels where he was currently staying. Instead, he'd have things sent to neighboring hotels. When he went to pick up the packages, he would tell the desk clerk that he was staying nearby and had made a mistake with the mailing address. Nelson took the electronics to pawn shops, where he sold them for cash; the coins went to a stamp-and-coin shop in Kissimmee, adjacent to Orlando.

One day at Disney World, Nelson met a Disney employee. She eventually moved into his motel room. He told her that his wife had been killed in a car accident and that he was a special agent with the Department of Justice. Nelson said that because of the types of cases he was working on, the agency had had to move him out of New Hampshire for his own safety — and that she shouldn't tell anyone that they were living together.

In Boston, Higgins thought that the MSNBC.com article had surely tipped Nelson off. Instead, it wound up being the key to finding him. An AM talk-radio station in Orlando, WDBO, broadcast a piece about Nelson, mentioning that the notorious scammer was thought to be in Florida. One person who happened to be listening to the show that day was Ann Fettig, the owner of A&R Stamp and Coin in Kissimmee. The name Jay Nelson rang a bell with her.

Fettig, 60, looked through the records in her shop and found a copy of Nelson's New Hampshire driver's license. (Fettig's policy is to photocopy the license of anyone she buys from.) "He came in about 12 times over a period of six weeks," Fettig says. "He'd have one or two gold coins at a time. He was very chatty, and he seemed to have plausible reasons for having the coins and selling them."

In her spare time, over the next two weeks, Fettig scouted for information about Nelson on the Internet and eventually found his wanted poster on the Postal Inspection Service's Web site. "I wanted him to stop so that he wouldn't keep scamming people," she says, although she doesn't buy or sell through online auctions herself. "After I found the photo, I realized it definitely was him." She contacted Higgins.

Higgins was overjoyed to hear from Fettig that Nelson was a regular visitor to her shop. He started putting together a plan for Nelson's arrest. And immediately found out that his managers wouldn't let him go to Orlando to do it himself.

"We were at the end of our fiscal year and under a budget directive. I was obviously a little disappointed," he says, with typical understatement. Higgins had to contact the postal inspectors in Florida and ask them to handle the arrest. He filled out the requisite paperwork, and the Orlando office put two inspectors on the case. The U.S. Marshals arranged to post an agent inside Fettig's shop to wait for Nelson to appear.

Nelson had last been to the shop on June 29. Fettig took a vacation in early July, and when she reopened the shop on July 10, deputy marshal Sam Maddox kept her company. Nelson showed up the next morning, before the shop was open, and waited outside. Fettig and Maddox were already inside, and Fettig was worried that Nelson had seen Maddox and been scared off, since she always ran the shop alone.

"Something didn't feel right," Nelson says. "I didn't go in. I lit a cigarette and walked away from the shop." Maddox came flying toward Nelson with his gun drawn. A second later, Nelson was spread-eagled on the sidewalk. Maddox put plastic handcuffs on him. Nelson wasn't armed. "He just had the coin he was trying to sell me," Fettig says.

"I was glad to be done with it," Nelson says. "I was tired of running." But he was surprised. "I knew I wasn't big enough to be on *America's Most Wanted*. But I never thought I'd be on the radio in Orlando." Nelson asked to be taken directly to jail; he didn't want to face his girlfriend back at the motel.

Gunnison and Higgins spent the next few months assembling the case against Nelson. (They investigated Krista as well, but ultimately decided not to file charges.) Last summer, Nelson pled guilty to mail fraud, wire fraud, identity fraud, and money laundering. It was one of the first times that PayPal transactions had been defined as money laundering, Gunnison says, although that definition wasn't tested in a trial.

Nelson told the judge at the U.S. district court in Concord that he was very sorry. "We said that his comments needed to be taken with a cargo container full of salt," Gunnison says. The judge brushed off Nelson's pleas for leniency and handed down the maximum term. This past March, Nelson was sentenced to spend six and a half years in federal prison.

Higgins was pleased to hear that Nelson would serve serious time, given that Nelson was a white-collar criminal. "This was someone who was ingenious at devising new ways to beat the system," he says. "He did it for a living."

DOING SERIOUS TIME IN JAIL

Today, Higgins still works as a postal inspector in the Boston office, and Gunnison has been promoted to chief of the criminal division at the U.S. Attorney's office in Concord. Nelson earns 17 cents an hour working on construction projects inside the medium-security federal prison at Otisville, New York. His face looks more worn than in his mug shot. He has lost most of his hair and buzzed the rest down. He is separated from Krista, who gave birth to their son while he was in Florida. She has filed divorce proceedings. He is pursuing a degree in business administration by taking courses offered at the prison.

"Until the day I got caught, I thought that no one had lost money," Nelson insists, explaining that he had thought that his buyers would be able to get their money back from PayPal or their credit-card companies. But he also says, in a prison interview, "I could've taken 20 times more than I did. I could go and create a fake identity on eBay the day I get out." A moment later, he says that of course he would not do that.

Nelson, now 35, will be at Otisville until 2007 — although it's possible that he could earn an early release. While there, he's not allowed to use the computers.

Murder by Internet

Wired Magazine, October 1998

On the afternoon of March 19, 1998, a UPS driver named Armand Gevry delivered a cardboard box to the pea-green house at 3 Washington Street in Fair Haven, Vermont. Gevry lives two blocks away, and when Sheila Rockwell opened the door, she recognized him as the deliveryman who often brought shipments of citizen's band radio equipment to her son.

It was a cold, gray day outside—light snow changing to sleet changing to rain—so she quickly took the package from Gevry, thanked him, and shut the door. Rockwell, a weathered woman of 52 with hard blue eyes and wispy brown hair, carried the box down the hallway of her modest home.

Chris Marquis was talking on his new Ranger RCI 2990 radio with his girlfriend, Cyndi McDonald, when his mother brought the package into his wood-paneled bedroom. His 6-foot frame was hunched over the microphone on his desk, his dirty-blond hair was swept forward across his forehead, and a thin mustache fuzzed his upper lip.

Rockwell handed the 2-foot-long box to her son. She didn't recognize the return address, so she sat down on Chris's bed, curious to see what was inside.

Chris continued chatting with Cyndi. The name and address on the box—Samantha Brown, 1863 South High Street, Bucyrus, Ohio—didn't ring any bells for him either.

"I got a package in the mail," Chris told Cyndi. He'd met her two years earlier as a quiet, sweet voice on Channel 1. Cyndi was now in the 11th grade, a year ahead of Chris, but she attended school in Whitehall, the next town over. Their favorite date was a meal at the McDonald's on the far edge of Fair Haven.

"What is it?" Cyndi asked. "Who's it from?"

"Hold on. I don't know," Chris answered, as he grabbed his jackknife from the holster on his belt and slit the box open. Inside was a slightly smaller box made of styrofoam.

"Well, it's probably a bomb, then," Cyndi joked.

The explosion knocked Chris and his mother to the floor.

To his acquaintances online, Chris Marquis wasn't a teenager living with his mother. He was 27 years old, a father, and the proprietor of a Vermont store called the CB Shack. That was the identity Mark Sischo encountered earlier this year on the RCI Federation Web site, where CBers post messages to buy or sell the well-regarded brand of radios—RCIs—made by Ranger Electronic Communications.

"Chris had a message up," Sischo, who lives in Michigan, recalls. "It said, 'Anybody looking to buy, sell, or trade radio equipment, email me.' I had some stuff that I couldn't sell around here, so I was gonna do a trade." After corresponding by email, Chris taught Sischo how to use Mirabilis's ICQ software so they could chat in real time. They discussed the relative merits of Rangers and Unidens and Cherokees and Cobras. Chris, who used "Psycho" as his email name and CB handle and dubbed himself "PhantomOp" on ICQ, revealed his real name to Sischo. He also griped about his wife, sent a digitized picture of his daughter by email, and pointed Sischo to a Web page he'd set up to advertise the CB Shack.

Eventually, the two began trying to work out a trade. They agreed that Chris would send Sischo a Galaxy Saturn Turbo worth about $700, a couple other radios, and a few microphones and accessories. In return, Sischo would send three radios and microphones to Chris. Since the gear that Sischo was sending Chris was of lesser value, he also included a check for $100.

After exchanging tracking numbers with Chris so each could verify that the other had, indeed, sent the equipment, Sischo shipped his box by UPS in early March. But when Sischo visited the UPS Web site and punched in the 18 digits Chris had given him, he got the message "Unable to track shipment." He checked the number and tried again. Same thing.

Certain that Chris had intended to con him, Sischo called UPS and stopped delivery. He spoke to a representative of the company's security department, who asked whether Sischo knew anyone else who'd been burned by Chris Marquis. Sischo said he didn't but promised to see whether he could find others.

Sischo began posting messages around the Web and on Usenet groups. "Everyone who has been ripped off by Chris Marquis Email me immediately!!" he wrote to the readers of rec.radio.cb on March 14. The responses came quickly. Sischo heard from three or four people who had lost radios and money to the "proprietor" of the nonexistent CB Shack. One of them was NCTomCat, an America Online user who reported that he'd sent $25 to Chris to cover the shipping costs of a radio that never arrived.

In addition to emailing Sischo, TomCat was posting threatening messages on rec.radio.cb. "He ripped me off too," TomCat wrote on March 16. "I am posting ads about that crook all over the internet... the address I have is Washington St. Fairhaven Vermont... DONT MAIL THIS LIAR ANY MONEY OR YOU WILL BE POORER BUT WISER!!!!!! If I can find someone to pay the 2 way airfare, I will go there and collect everyones money back, and give him some severe dental problems to deal with... Are You listening Chris?? When You see a 6 foot 5 inch dark haired man at Your door, You better duck 'cause I will be about to drop the maul... on You noggin dude......."

"I could feel the building and windows vibrate," says Raymond Viger, Fair Haven's chief of police. Viger was on the phone when he heard the boom, and he slammed down the handset and rushed out the front door of the town's red-brick Municipal Building. The Korean War veteran knew it had been a serious explosion—the force was too powerful to have been a car backfiring or some kid lighting an M-80.

Standing on the front steps of the Municipal Building, which contains Fair Haven's town offices, its volunteer fire department, and its three-man police force, Viger faced the town common. On the left side was the Fair Haven Library, the Merchant Bank, and a row of shops. On the far side was a gas station, the Mallory Funeral Home, and the First Baptist Church. The right side was lined with big houses built in the 1800s.

It took about three minutes for Viger and Sergeant Jeff Lusk, who was riding in a patrol car at the time, to determine that the noise had come from Sheila Rockwell's aluminum-sided house, at the back left corner of the Municipal Building, not 20 yards from Viger's office.

"I could see fire," Sheila Rockwell recalls. "I was trying to put out these fires. There were disks on fire, and a lot of plastic. I was trying to find the telephone. Chris got up and ran for the bedroom door, but he just fell on his face."

Chris had several holes in his abdomen and burns and shrapnel wounds all over his face and neck. Most of his upper left thigh had been blown away. "I tried crawling over toward Chris and I couldn't," Rockwell says. "Every time I'd try to get up on my right knee, I'd collapse." Rockwell noticed that her knee was bloody and that most of the fingers on her right hand had disappeared. She asked her son how badly he was hurt, but he didn't reply: "Chris was moaning. He wasn't answering me. Just moaning."

When Chief Viger and Sergeant Lusk stormed into the smoke-filled bedroom, they found Chris and his mother lying on the blood-soaked carpet. Chris was face down and unconscious. A cardboard box half-filled with styrofoam peanuts was nearby. Above Chris's computer station, a hole had been blown through the roof, and below it, a matching crater was carved into the floor. The plastic cover of his inkjet printer had been melted away.

Rockwell was coherent enough to tell Lusk that Chris had been standing right over the inner box when it exploded. While they waited for Fair Haven's volunteer rescue squad, Lusk asked Rockwell whether she or Chris was having problems with anyone. Rockwell told him that there was a guy in Indiana who was mad at her son, and who had been threatening to come to Vermont that weekend to collect some money Chris owed him.

There was silence on Cyndi's end after Chris keyed off his radio mike to open the package. She waited 20 minutes, but Chris never came back on.

She was distraught, because they'd been inseparable—on and off the air—since they'd met one day two years before, when Chris was asking for a radio check and Cyndi gave him one. He was Psycho, and she was Schoolgirl. They talked every day for a year. Then Chris asked when he'd be able to meet her. She said, "Whenever you come over," and he came over. Cyndi remembers the date: June 27, 1996.

"On the radio, he was laughing all the time, but he was quiet when I first met him in person. Shy, but nice," Cyndi says.

They'd set a different channel to meet on every night and chatted for hours about music, movies, school, parents. They talked about Chris's dream of opening up his own computer business. When Chris and his mother had to run errands, he and Cyndi would keep talking on a mobile radio in the van until he drove out of range and Cyndi's voice grew faint before disappearing.

Mark Cutsinger was the closest thing Chris had to a friend, aside from his mother and Cyndi. ("Everyone hated him," says Jeremy, a Fair Haven teen who knew Chris. "He was a punk. All he did was talk shit on the CB, just trashing people. He got beat up a lot.") But Cutsinger, who runs a radio/computer shop in Middlebury, a college town about 30 miles north of Fair Haven, shared Chris's passion for hardware. "Chris guided me through a lot of computer stuff, and I taught him about radios," says Cutsinger, a lanky, mustachioed biker who uses Gonzo as his CB handle. Gonzo would answer Chris's million and one questions— and Chris constantly hailed him on the air, by phone, by email, and over ICQ. He had grown up without a father figure, and he seemed to think Gonzo would do nicely. Occasionally, Chris's unending queries would grate on Gonzo's nerves, and he'd stop responding, but he had a soft spot for the kid.

In rural Vermont, people use CB sets in their cars and homes as a cheap alternative to cellular phones or pagers. In Fair Haven, you can get in touch with almost anybody—or at least his neighbor—by putting a call out on Channel 1. During long winters, conversations on the CB become a way of keeping in touch with friends, since it's usually too cold and snowy to go out to socialize. "It's just people hanging out, like in a chat room," Gonzo says. "People have their own little channels, and they'll talk about anything from the weather to the sex they had the night before. It's just your typical rag-chewing, most of the time."

Truckers navigating the highways of Vermont also use the CB, of course, to find out about road conditions, speed traps, and directions to their next stop. They're usually on Channel 19—what Gonzo calls "the workingman's channel." That's where they'd encounter Chris Marquis. Gonzo also first came to know Chris as a voice on the radio. Sometimes Chris called himself Psycho, and other times he went by Taz, for the tattoo of the Warner Bros. cartoon character he sported on his right bicep. "His whole goal was to get in there and destroy people verbally," Gonzo says of Chris.

Chris had one of the most powerful CB setups around. He ran a Cherokee CBS-1000 base station and Ranger RCI 2970 mobile rig that he bought from Gonzo, along with a 300-watt linear amplifier (illegal for unlicensed users like Chris) and a high-quality Antron 99 antenna mounted atop a 50-foot pole. Chris's voice was well known to CB users in Fair Haven, Castleton, Benson, and Poultney, as well as Whitehall, New York, the town just across the border, where Cyndi lives. His audio signature—a digital clip of the Napoleon XIV song lyric "They're coming to take me away, ha-haaa!"—could be heard at all hours of the day and night.

Chris would use "noise toys" that created obnoxious sound effects to drown out truckers seeking directions. He'd berate anyone who dared to challenge his dominance of the airwaves. "It went beyond teenage mischievousness," says Gary Cook, who runs the CB Connection, a shop on the outskirts of Fair Haven. "A lot of teenagers are on [the CB], but none are as abusive as he was. I would never dream of saying things like that—the language, the type of insults."

Like Sischo, Gonzo at first had no idea Chris was just a high schooler. But when Chris came up to visit Gonzo's shop sometime in 1996, he arrived in his mother's blue minivan, with her in the driver's seat.

"Chris got anything he wanted," Gonzo recalls. "If Chris walked in and said, 'I want this $4,000 radio,' Sheila would find a way to get it for him." From the start, the pair's carefree spending habits struck Gonzo as odd. Then, as Chris and his mother began to trust Gonzo more, they told him about frequent shoplifting sorties, and they bragged about doing all their Christmas shopping for free.

But Gonzo is not the type to rat on anyone—especially a customer—and so he kept their confessions to himself. Instead, he took precautions. The one time he visited their house, he kept his motorcycle gloves on to avoid getting his fingerprints on anything that might be hot. "I wouldn't touch anything, and they laughed about that," he says.

Indeed, based on a financial affidavit Rockwell filed in April, it's hard to understand how else she found the money to lavish her son with all the high-end CB gear, not to mention a brand-new Acer PC, a Nintendo, a Super Nintendo, a Sega, a fax machine, a professional DJ setup, and a TV and VCR for his room. On the affidavit, Rockwell states that she has been unemployed for nearly a year and that her main source of income is a monthly $548 disability payment.

The disability, though, was Chris's. He suffered from retinitis pigmentosa, a vision disorder that rendered him legally blind at night and had begun narrowing his field of vision during the day. He had a blind person's cane, which he was supposed to use after dark, but he hated the cane, so instead he'd either stay inside at night or have Cyndi walk with him.

To supplement the disability payment, Rockwell says, she cleaned houses and did odd jobs around Fair Haven. Her landlords, the Shermans, paid her $20 for mopping the kitchen and $15 for washing their dog, for example. There was also occasional income from parties where Chris and his mother would work as DJs.

With expenses that exceeded $1,000 a month, though, how does Rockwell explain all those extravagant accouterments? She says, simply, that she worked hard to give her son everything he wanted: "I did spoil him. He was the baby, and I didn't know how long his vision would last."

The reality may be more complicated. On January 3, Chris and his mother were arrested for shoplifting at the Ames department store in Rutland. Chris had stolen $49 worth of CDs, gum, and pens, and Rockwell had taken merchandise, including 33 paint brushes and a Black & Decker drill-bit set, valued at $91.

Rockwell contends that this was the only time she ever shoplifted and that neither she nor Chris knew what the other was doing: "We were in two different parts of the store. I didn't want him to know I was stealing." But Gonzo says that when he visited their house, Rockwell asked jovially whether he'd seen them in the papers and laughed about the low fine she'd received for the offense —only $42.

Eileen Lavigne, Rockwell's daughter and Chris's half-sister, says that petty crime had become a habit for the two. "There were times I would go shopping with my mother [and] she would not only directly steal, but she'd take the tags off one item and put them on another—and Chris was right there," Lavigne says. "She's got a serious problem. And I think [Chris] got the sense that if she was doing it and not getting caught, it was OK."

On March 19, Gonzo was listening to his ham radio when he heard there had been an explosion next to the Municipal Building in Fair Haven. At first, he laughed: "I figured Chris had probably just blown up a linear." When he learned it was a package that had exploded and that Chris and his mother had been sent to the hospital, Gonzo felt sure he knew who had sent it.

Chris Dean was well known at the Little Big Horn Golf Club in Pierceton, Indiana. The burly, 6-foot-tall, mustachioed 35-year-old trucker, competitive but good-humored, held the record at the nine-hole course. He played in the Saturday-morning men's league, and a few years back he'd worked for course owner Lee Webb, taking care of the grounds, helping out in the office, and giving lessons.

Dean was also a familiar face at CB shops around Pierceton. Like Chris Marquis, he'd been bitten by the radio bug. Unlike Marquis, though, Dean was a licensed ham operator, and he was never known to be anything but considerate on the air.

Dean had grown up in Michigan, earned his commercial driver's license in his late 20s, and landed a job hauling steel out of Las Vegas. A few years later, he moved to Pierceton with his second wife, Diane. For a time, he worked for Webb at Little Big Horn. By 1995, though, he had landed a position with a distribution outfit called Sprint North Supply Company, which paid better and offered benefits. He drove a flatbed out of the company warehouse in Warsaw, Indiana, usually loaded with huge wooden spools of black telephone cable, earning $2,300 a month.

Dean was obsessively neat. Neighbors remember him constantly washing his cars—a Corvette and a Blazer. Joe Stump, his landlord, recalls that Dean kept his lawn buzzed down practically to AstroTurf length. "And the house was always spotless inside," Stump adds.

He liked to hunt, according to Don Chilson, pastor at Pierceton's Bethel Baptist Church and a golfing buddy of Dean's, and he took tae kwan do lessons at an academy next to the grocery store in Pierceton. He'd also recently configured his computer to access the Net.

It was online that Dean first encountered Chris Marquis, according to Gonzo. Chris had confided in his friend about his dealings with Dean. He'd told Gonzo about a fantastic trade he'd negotiated with a guy in Indiana: a Ranger RCI 2990 in return for a Cobra 2000 CB radio. The RCI, a sleek, rack-mountable black box, was a 10-meter amateur radio that had been modified to handle CB transmissions. Another hack enabled the radio's user to "freeband"—go outside of the 40 channels the FCC allocates for CB transmissions. A compression board had been installed to boost speech levels. "It was the loudest thing on the air," says Gonzo, who estimates that all the enhancements bumped the radio's value up to nearly $800.

What was strange about the trade was that a Cobra 2000 is worth only about $400. It's an older radio—all brushed steel and simulated wood grain—an emblem of CB's 1970s heyday, when "Smokey and the Bandit" and C. W. McCall's populist trucker anthem "Convoy" made the once-obscure hobby suddenly hot. Gonzo was puzzled; why would someone trade a radio worth $800 for one worth half as much?

When he visited Chris, Gonzo saw the 2990 Dean had sent. Then Chris told him that instead of sending Dean the Cobra 2000 he'd promised, he had shipped a Realistic mobile radio that didn't even work just so Dean would have a tracking number as the two shipments crossed in the mail. (Apparently, Chris had learned a lesson from the deal with Sischo.) As soon as Dean had gotten the junk radio, he'd started making threatening calls and sending hostile email. In one message Dean said he was coming to Vermont to sort things out.

As Gonzo recalls it, as soon as he and Chris were alone, the teenager confessed to worrying that Dean would show up at his door. Dean had just called again, he told Gonzo, but his mother had covered for him. He asked what he should do; Gonzo advised him to give the radio back. But a short while later Chris was upbeat again. Gonzo noticed that the boy always felt sure his mother could protect him from any real harm.

Indeed, when Dean had called that day, Rockwell had blithely told him her son wasn't in Vermont—she said he had been thrown in jail in another state.

Vermont enjoys a crime rate among the lowest in the nation. The day before the explosion made news, the front page of the Rutland *Herald*, one of the state's biggest newspapers, featured these two stories: "Skier Cuts New Trails as Activist" and "State Has Trove of Documents on Civil War."

On Friday, in the Herald and The Burlington Free Press, the daily that serves the state's most populous city, the bombing moved center-stage, with huge black headlines, sidebars, and graphics explaining how to identify letter and package bombs. The broadcast media descended on Fair Haven; satellite trucks, with their noisy generators, lined the streets near Sheila Rockwell's house.

"It was quite a day for this little Mayberry town," says Bill Eaton, a retired schoolteacher who has lived in Fair Haven all his life. Eaton, who used to go on fishing trips with Armand Gevry, the UPS driver, had grabbed his camcorder to document the scene at 3 Washington Street. In addition to the media, agents from the FBI and the Bureau of Alcohol, Tobacco, and Firearms had arrived to join the Vermont State Police in the search for evidence. Scouring the wet ground, they found pieces of debris from the explosion as far as three lots away.

On the rec.radio.cb newsgroup, TomCat was beginning to feel the heat. In a message titled "Was mad but not a killer," he said he had been fielding numerous calls from newspaper reporters asking if he was the bomber. TomCat declared himself innocent.

"I do not know anything about that incident with Chris Marquis," wrote TomCat. "I only found out about it today, and immediately called the FBI, introduced myself, and told them about his bad business dealings, and that I did in fact say ugly things on the newsgroups about him...But that is where it stopped... Just my telling the readers about his shady business practices... As I said, I called the FBI and said I will GLADLY answer any or all questions about this tragedy."

When FBI agents searched Chris Marquis's room, they found a piece of notebook paper on his desk, next to the computer his mother had given him for Christmas. On the paper was written Chris Dean's name, along with Dean's address and phone number, according to an FBI affidavit.

Investigators also eventually turned up Chris's wallet, which had been in his pants pocket at the time of the explosion. Inside, according to the affidavit, was a UPS receipt dated March 5, 1998. It detailed the shipment of a CB radio from Chris Marquis to Chris Dean at the same Indiana address listed on the piece of notebook paper. The tracking number, the affidavit stated, was 1Z 019 X55 03 1232 566 3. If you visit the UPS Web site and enter that number, you can see that the package was sent from Rutland via UPS ground service on March 5 and delivered to Pierceton, Indiana, at 1:56 p.m. on March 11.

And the name and address on the bomb package, Samantha Brown of Bucyrus, Ohio? That was a dead end. The FBI discovered that neither the person nor the street address existed. UPS traced the path of the package, and, according to the affidavit, it had been dropped off at a counter facility in

Mansfield, Ohio, around noon on March 18. It was shipped next-day air.

A representative of Sprint North Supply, Dean's employer, told the Feds that the truck driver's route included Indiana, Ohio, and Michigan. The spokesperson also mentioned that Dean was making a delivery to a company warehouse in Mansfield, Ohio, at around noon on March 18. (Bucyrus, Ohio, coincidentally, is a town along Route 30, a major east-west artery. A trucker would likely pass through it on the way from Pierceton to Mansfield.)

On the night of March 19, Special Agent John Hersh of the Rutland FBI office interviewed a friend of Dean's. According to Hersh's affidavit, the anonymous cooperating witness (referred to as CW in the document) had known Dean for several years and shared his affinity for CB radios. CW said Dean had been having trouble with someone in Vermont after they'd exchanged radios.

CW also told the authorities he was the one who had helped Dean configure his computer to access the Net. And he added that Dean had recently searched the Net to find instructions on building a pipe bomb. Based on the ingredients mentioned in the FBI affidavit—thumbtacks, a clothespin, black powder, and a pipe—and, assuming the friend's statement is accurate, Dean probably found an online version of The Anarchist's Cookbook, a guide to homemade mayhem that existed in print long before it found its way into digital form.

On March 14, according to the affidavit, five days before the explosion in Fair Haven, Dean had told CW that he "was going to send the guy a package in the mail, and, boy, is he going to be surprised," but Dean seemed to be ambivalent about what he wanted to do, because he also talked about simply paying Chris Marquis an intimidating visit.

CW's assertions, and the Sprint log entry showing that Dean was in Mansfield on March 18, led the authorities to believe that they'd found their man. By Friday evening, the day after the explosion, an ATF agent had been dispatched along with members of the Kosciusko County Sheriff's Department to arrest Dean. They found him at a friend's house in Winona Lake, Indiana, a few miles west of Pierceton. The entire investigation and arrest took less than 30 hours.

On Saturday morning, the front page of The Burlington *Free Press* trumpeted, "Bombing Suspect Arrested." There was a color picture of Chief Viger standing next to the US attorney who had announced the arrest. The accompanying article noted that Dean, who had no prior criminal record, was being charged with the interstate transportation of an explosive device intended to kill and injure, and causing an explosive device to be placed aboard an aircraft, knowing that it could endanger the safety of people aboard. The article also pointed out that, if convicted, Dean could face the federal death penalty.

Suddenly, TomCat was silent. After his "Was mad but not a killer" message, posted the same day Dean was arrested, TomCat vanished from rec.radio.cb.

What did it mean? Was he a suspect, after all? Could he possibly be Dean—and silent now because he was in custody? (Several people who corresponded with TomCat insisted that was ridiculous. And, certainly, TomCat's posted description of himself as 6 foot 5 didn't jibe.) The authorities weren't commenting.

America Online, TomCat's ISP, didn't wait to find out. The company said he had violated its terms of service, which prohibit threatening Usenet messages, and voided his account. AOL also sent out 16 "cancel" messages to the operators of Usenet servers around the world. TomCat's venomous screeds disappeared into the ether.

After his arrest in Winona Lake, Dean was sent to the Allen County Jail in Fort Wayne, Indiana. A few days later, on March 25, a US magistrate in Fort Wayne ruled that there was enough evidence against Dean to extradite him to Vermont, where he would stand trial.

US marshals escorted Dean to Burlington on April 2, and he was remanded to the maximum-security Northwest State Correctional Facility in Saint Albans, just a few miles from the Canadian border. It was that same afternoon—exactly two weeks after the bombing—that a closed-casket funeral service for Chris Marquis was held in the Mallory Funeral Home.

After protracted legal wrangling, on June 22 at the US District Court in Burlington, Dean entered a plea of not guilty on all counts. His three attorneys steadfastly maintain their client's innocence. "He has a solid and rich employment history, the respect and support of his neighbors, and the love and support of his family," says attorney Bradley Stetler. "He has lived a very typical middle-class life."

Last summer, people in Pierceton were still trying to reconcile the government's charges with the Chris Dean they knew. Dean was "personable, fun to be around," according to his landlord. "He got along with everybody."

"He was very friendly and outgoing," says a man who owns a CB shop that Dean frequented. "[The charges against him] seemed real out of character."

But in the weeks leading up to Dean's arraignment, FBI and ATF agents had been gathering more evidence. According to court documents, agents searching Dean's house found a styrofoam container—with missing pieces—that seemed to match the material used to encase the bomb mechanism. They found hex nuts that appeared to be identical to the hardware used as extra shrapnel in the bomb. They found fishing line similar to that used as part of the bomb's trigger mechanism.

In Dean's backyard, agents found evidence of a blast hole where, they assert in court documents, Dean detonated a prototype bomb. "Indeed, agents found the test bomb's end cap, which appeared to be made by the same pipe manufacturer that made the end cap for the bomb that killed Marquis," wrote Charles Tetzlaff, the US attorney in Burlington. There was also evidence that Dean purchased Bullseye black powder on March 14, the same day he is alleged to have had the conversation with CW in which he seemed uncertain about whether he should go to Vermont in person or "send the guy a package in the mail."

The US Attorney's Office argued that Dean should be held without bail, pending trial. Judge William K. Sessions III agreed, and Dean was sent back up to Saint Albans.

When Sheila Rockwell wants to get some fresh air, she asks her home health aide to help her get into a wheelchair. She still has an external fixator attached to her right knee—a blue-and-silver device like a metallic Tinker Toy that penetrates the skin and holds the bones and pins in place. As a result, her right leg sticks straight out, supported by an extension attached to the wheelchair.

Once Rockwell is situated in the chair, the aide rolls her out the back door and down a newly constructed wood ramp at the back entrance of her rented house. They pass Chief Viger's window in the Municipal Building, cross North Park Place, and don't stop until they get to the far end of the town common.

It would seem to be a spot with sad associations for Rockwell. She's parked right in front of the Mallory Funeral Home, near the place where, in winter, Chris and Cyndi would lay down on the ground, sweep their arms and legs back and forth, and make snow angels. But perhaps in a town as small as Fair Haven, it's not possible to avoid all the painful places.

She and her son were very close. Not only did they DJ together at parties and dances, they also enrolled in a program to raise guide dogs for the blind and attended training classes together every two weeks in Rutland. Rockwell drove Chris everywhere because his retinitis prevented him from getting a license. And since Chris hadn't been going to school during the months leading up to the bombing, he was home with his mother most days.

She claims she knew very little about her son's Internet and CB dealings. She says she had no idea that anyone other than Dean was complaining about being cheated by Chris and that even when Dean began calling the house, she was unsure about "the severity" of the threats.

Chris's mother acknowledges she knew her son was buying and selling radios, and she says that profits from the transactions were one of the family's sources of income. She regularly drove Chris to CB shops and tag sales, where he'd purchase used gear and accessories.

She also drove her son to the UPS station in Rutland to mail a radio to Chris Dean on March 5. "I knew it wasn't the radio he was supposed to send this guy," she remembers, "but Chris said, 'If I don't get him a tracking number, he's gonna kick my ass.' He said he needed to buy some time." She says Chris told her he had actually ordered the Cobra 2000 he'd promised Dean from one of his suppliers, a Kentucky outfit called Copper Electronics; it just hadn't arrived in time, and Chris needed to send something. Rockwell adamantly insists, "I don't know where the scamming idea came from."

But Copper doesn't sell the Cobra 2000, a discontinued model. And her daughter Eileen Lavigne claims that Rockwell "was very aware of what was going on." (Lavigne and Rockwell weren't on speaking terms at the time of the explosion, but they reconciled briefly afterward. They were estranged again when I spoke with Lavigne in August.)

"She put up the money to buy the radios," Lavigne says, "and she knew he was getting on the Net trying to sell these radios."

The CB shop owner in Pierceton felt terrible when he ran into Diane Dean at Wal-Mart a few weeks after her husband's arrest. She seemed to need money, and she asked him—without her husband's knowledge—if he would come to their house and take a look at the equipment there.

When the man arrived to appraise the radios, he was astonished by what he saw. His shop had been burglarized in January, and the police had never found the culprits. As he evaluated Dean's collection of radios, trying not to betray his surprise to Diane Dean, he estimated that about half of the equipment that had been stolen from his shop was in Dean's house—roughly $5,000 worth of merchandise. (Eventually, this equipment was seized as evidence.)

The store owner also believes that the RCI 2990 Dean sent to Vermont was stolen from his shop. "If I'm guessing right," he says, "[Dean had] taken all this hot stuff and was laundering it through the Internet." So while the radio he hoped to receive from Chris Marquis was worth only about half as much as the 2990, "he'd be getting a Cobra 2000 that wasn't hot."

Gonzo says the Pierceton man's story makes sense to him. Not only does it explain the uneven trade, but it explains "why [Dean] didn't go through the proper channels, reporting the scam with Marquis to the police."

But despite the Pierceton shop owner's certainty that Dean was somehow involved with the burglary, he still can't believe that Dean built a pipe bomb and mailed it to Chris Marquis, as the government alleges. "Chris Dean is a fairly smart individual, and I can't see him doing it as it's portrayed, leaving such a clear trail," he says.

Maybe a fluid sense of identity made both Marquis and Dean feel invulnerable. Catch me if you can.

Maybe Chris Marquis never understood that his actions could have consequences. Perhaps he thought his online identities would somehow shield him from real-world harm. He was Psycho, or Taz, or PhantomOp. He was also proprietor of the CB Shack, 27 years old, married. If no one could figure out exactly who he was, then how could they get to him?

Even when people like Mark Sischo and Chris Dean began closing in on the real Chris Marquis, the teenager still felt he was in control. When Sischo began sounding the alarm on rec.radio.cb and the RCI Federation site after he'd been burned by Chris, the youth had countered with a message of his own. Sischo was simply upset, Chris explained, because the CB Shack wouldn't sell him a radio he wanted badly. Even when an angry Dean started calling, started threatening to come to Vermont, the teen never felt he was in serious danger. If all else failed, his mother would handle it for him.

And what of the man authorities say murdered him? If the criminal charges are true, Dean made and mailed a bomb, taking no other precaution than making up a name, Samantha Brown, the girl from Bucyrus, Ohio, from whom no one would expect to receive such a nasty surprise.

Maybe it was easier to imagine killing someone he had never met. He tangled with Chris on the phone, by email, and over ICQ. But he never saw the teenager's face.

Could he—would he—have done the thing the authorities say he did if he knew that the person who'd conned him was a 17-year-old kid with failing vision, a mama's boy who spent his days on the Net and his nights on the radio talking endlessly to his devoted girlfriend? You have to wonder when it was that Dean first fixed his eyes on a picture of Chris Marquis—perhaps on TV, or in a Fort Wayne newspaper. You have to wonder what he thought.

Of course, it's possible, as golf course owner Lee Webb puts it, that "they got the wrong guy." Webb and others in Pierceton point out that if the government's accusations are true, then Dean learned how to make the bomb, tested it, and sent it all within seven days of receiving the worthless Realistic from Chris Marquis—a pretty short span of time. They argue that the government's lightning-fast investigation and arrest—30 hours, remarkable for a bombing case—was slipshod and rushed. They want to know who doesn't have some thumbtacks, a clothespin, and fishing line around his house.

Dean's attorneys spent the better part of the summer trying to convince the US Attorney's Office in Burlington and the Department of the US Attorney General in Washington, DC, not to seek the federal death penalty for their client. They searched for every scrap of mitigating evidence they could find. The last execution in Vermont was in 1954 (the state has since abolished the death penalty), and Dean's legal team didn't want their client to be the state's first test of the 1994 federal death-penalty statute, which allows the federal government to seek execution in certain cases, regardless of state law.

On October 7, Dean's attorneys presented their findings before a Department of Justice committee in Washington; if it is the committee's judgment that the death penalty should be sought, then the recommendation is passed to Janet Reno, who makes the final decision.

"If the government seeks the death penalty, the likelihood of a trial is greater," says Greg Waples, an assistant US attorney in Burlington working on the case. But with or without the death penalty, he points out, a pretrial settlement could result, as happened in the Unabomber case.

It's September, and Cyndi McDonald is back in school, starting the 11th grade again. She dropped out last year after the explosion and barricaded herself in her room for three weeks. She's trying to put together enough money to buy Chris's DJ equipment from his mother. "I want to continue doing it, go on with the business," she says. Chris was her first real boyfriend. She doesn't think she's ready for another just now.

Diane Dean flies into Burlington once a month and then drives up to Saint Alban's to visit her husband, who, from all reports, is handling his ordeal as well as can be expected. When she visits, they can sit together in the same room and hold hands—there's no glass wall dividing them, no telephones they must use to communicate from either side of a partition. After the visit, though, Dean is strip-searched for contraband before he is returned to his cell.

The Reverend Don Chilson has been writing to Dean and encouraging his congregation to do the same. "I tell him man's gonna let him down and our government's gonna let him down," says Chilson. "They're out to hang him. But I keep encouraging him spiritually to place his hope in the Lord—even if they give him the death penalty—because I know where he's gonna go."

Gonzo has testified before the Burlington grand jury that indicted Dean, but he sounds annoyed about his role in the legal process. He says it has taken up his time and hurt his business. He wishes he wouldn't get called up to Burlington again to testify once the trial starts. But he knows it's inevitable, even though no trial date has been set.

Sheila Rockwell has enlisted an attorney to find out whether Chris Dean has any assets she might be able to seize in a civil trial. Before school started again this fall in Fair Haven, she helped organize a Teen Appreciation Celebration on the town green, in Chris's memory, to benefit the Vermont Youth Development Corps. She brought Chris's CD collection over, and the music boomed out as the town's teenagers—all those kids Chris had not gotten along with—played volleyball, bladed, skateboarded, and hung out. She hopes it will become an annual event.

Every few weeks, she has to visit a doctor in Rutland to have her knee checked out. To get there, you head east on Route 4. About halfway, you cross a set of double bridges near West Rutland. Rockwell remembers that when she would drive into Rutland with Chris on errands, he'd always lose radio contact with Cyndi on the bridges.

Now, another memory crowds in: A few days after the explosion, when she was still in the hospital, she asked someone on the Fair Haven Rescue Squad when it was, exactly, that Chris had died. And she was told that he'd been alive in the house, and alive in the ambulance, but that he only made it as far as the West Rutland double bridges before they lost him.

7. Robotics

Making Robots, with Dreams of Henry Ford

Published in the New York Times, December 26, 2002

One robot was tossed into an abandoned building in Afghanistan by soldiers from the 82nd Airborne Division. Another shimmied through a thin air shaft in the Great Pyramid of Giza. A third hunted dust bunnies under Helen Greiner's bed.

Field testing for products made by the iRobot Corporation takes place in settings both exotic and mundane. "When you put robots into situations where there haven't been robots before," said Ms. Greiner, the company's president, "you very quickly find out whether they're up to the job, and what design changes you might need to make."

Ms. Greiner and her co-founders, Colin Angle and Rodney Brooks, who met at the Massachusetts Institute of Technology, have spent 12 years introducing their robot prototypes into new environments and then working to make them better. Ms. Greiner envisions a world in which robots handle tasks that are too difficult, dangerous, or time-consuming for humans. She describes iRobot's goal as "doing for robots what Apple did for computers, making them available to anyone who wants to use one." (At right, co-founders Colin Angle, Helen Greiner, and Rodney Brooks. Photo courtesy iRobot.)

iRobot is perhaps the only company in the world that develops and sells robots to the military, researchers, large corporations, and consumers. Most robotics makers focus on just one segment, and 2002 has been a busy year for the company.

Four of its rugged PackBots were shipped to Bagram Air Base in Afghanistan to help soldiers clear caves and compounds that had been occupied by the Taliban; one of them discovered a buried antipersonnel mine. A custom-built robot called the Pyramid Rover starred in a National Geographic program called "Pyramids Live: Secret Chambers Revealed," poking its fiber-optic camera into long-forgotten spaces. And retailers report that the company's Roomba Intelligent FloorVac, the autonomous cleaning machine that was put through its paces beneath Ms. Greiner's bed, sold briskly during the holiday shopping season.

But as iRobot has tried to nudge robots out of the domain of tech-savvy hobbyists and into the mainstream, it has occasionally struggled as a business. Developing first-of-a-kind robots is expensive, and the executives at iRobot have long sought to put one of their inventions into profitable high-volume production, like the original Apple II computer. "When we left M.I.T., we wanted to create robotic products that would touch people's lives on a daily basis," said Mr. Angle, who studied at the university's Artificial Intelligence Laboratory with Ms. Greiner. "We were just profoundly naïve, and had no idea how hard it would be to get there."

As a child growing up in London, Ms. Greiner dreamed of building robot companions like R2-D2, the dome-headed droid from the "Star Wars" series. And indeed, on a visit to iRobot's headquarters in this city just north of Boston, the cluttered office resembled a prop warehouse for those films. (The company was about to move to more spacious quarters in Burlington, Mass.) Several small treaded tank-bots were parked in the reception area. A "No Pictures Allowed" sign shielded the company's sensitive development work for the military. Inside, a visitor often had to step over robots in various stages of construction or deconstruction.

The robots rely on human guidance by remote control, as the PackBot does, or have a low-level ability to respond to stimuli in their environment, as the Roomba does when its downward-facing infrared sensor notices a staircase and signals the device to steer away from it.

When the company was founded in 1990, "we didn't know what we were doing," said Mr. Brooks, who serves as iRobot's chairman and as co-director of the Artificial Intelligence Lab at M.I.T. "We just knew that robotics was interesting and exciting." Back then, the company was based in Mr. Angle's living room. Its first contract was to build a six-legged insectlike robot named Attila for NASA's Jet Propulsion Laboratory. NASA was trying to decide whether robots for Mars exploration should have wheels or legs. The agency eventually settled on wheels, but it still buys equipment from iRobot for research purposes.

The company took its name from an Isaac Asmiov science fiction book called *I, Robot*, and its early revenue came from research contracts with government agencies like the Defense Advanced Research Projects Agency, or Darpa, at the Pentagon. But more recently, iRobot began developing products with commercial partners, like a doll designed with Hasbro called My Real Baby that was able to convey through sounds and facial expressions whether its owner was providing adequate care. The company has also financed some projects on its own, like the Roomba, a $200 device that got its name from the dancelike circular movements it makes as it cleans.

As the year's end approached, the company's 100 employees were racing to build and test new add-on modules for the PackBot that would eventually be delivered to Darpa and the British Defense Ministry, while also ensuring that enough Roombas would be manufactured to meet the initial demand.

Tom Frost, the PackBot project manager, spent six weeks last summer in Afghanistan with the 82nd Airborne Division soldiers who deployed PackBot to help explore caves and buildings. In a rural village called Nazirah, the robot team "sent PackBot into a suspicious compound, and using the robot's cameras, they were able to sketch a map of the compound that the soldiers could use when they went in," Mr. Frost said. That led to a project to develop a laser scanner module that could be plugged into the PackBot, allowing more precise maps of rooms to be created automatically and sent to the laptop computer used to control PackBot.

A shorter-term project involves building an extendable neck and head module for the PackBot. "One thing we encountered often in Afghanistan was piles of ammo or explosives or junk," said Col. Bruce Jette, who directs the Army's Rapid Equipping Force and supervised the PackBot's use there. Because the PackBot's cameras are only about six inches from the ground, "you'd have to drive the robot up on a pile of explosives in order to see past it, which is not the greatest idea," Colonel Jette said.

The new module, dubbed Explorer, looks like a cigar box balanced atop a shortened signpost. It folds down into the PackBot's low body when not in use, then pops up to get a look around, with numerous cameras in front of and behind its square head. There is infrared illumination for improved vision in dark places, a laser pointer to indicate to people working with the PackBot what its operator is looking at, and a zoom camera capable of reading small text on packages.

The PackBot's designers are proud of its durability — it can be pitched over fences or out second-story windows — and its svelte body. At 42 pounds, it can be carried in a backpack. "When we looked at which robots to bring to Afghanistan," Colonel Jette said, "other candidates were either too heavy, or the lighter ones weren't robust enough."

The soldiers, he said, "were pretty successful driving the PackBot off cliffs and into ravines." It was only after a plunge down a 30-foot cliff that a PackBot suffered enough damage to put it out of service. "But it only stopped working two days after the fall," Colonel Jette said.

Another PackBot module, a multi-jointed vertical arm, will be sent to Britain early next year for a second round of demonstrations for the Defense Ministry. This module was designed to investigate, handle and help detonate explosive devices safely for bomb squads.

In early December, the military projects were put on a fast track after the Army approved the purchase of more PackBots. But other groups at iRobot were concentrating on development in other areas. One project, a partnership with the Halliburton Company and the Intelligent Inspection Corporation, aims to create robots that will descend into oil wells to find leaks or other problems and, eventually, perform repairs. Another project, for a corporate customer iRobot says it cannot name, involves outfitting a vehicle used for farming or landscaping so that it can be driven or operate on its own, guided by the Global Positioning System.

The company has not been unscathed by the downturn in the technology sector, however. An expensive effort to create a robotic dinosaur was killed last fall after toy companies decided that consumers' "appetite for cool $100 electronic toys was gone," Mr. Angle said. Last spring the company eliminated about a dozen jobs. "It felt like we were stalled," Mr. Angle said. (At right, Angle holds two robot components.)

But by late summer, the PackBots were stationed in Afghanistan and in September, on the same day the company unveiled the Roomba, the National Geographic special was shown. Twenty-five iRobot employees gathered at Mr. Angle's house to watch the Pyramid Rover perform live. "We were drinking heavily, hoping everything would go O.K.," Mr. Angle said. During commercial breaks, they called the iRobot employee who was at the site in Egypt to see if the robot was working properly. (The robot did its job, but nothing spectacular was discovered.)

Since September, Mr. Angle has been absorbed with identifying any incipient problems with the first batch of Roombas. The robotic vacuum cleaner has been marketed through a 30-minute infomercial and a spot on the Home Shopping Network (285 Roombas were sold in 15 minutes), and has received generally positive reviews. ("The only glitch is that it stops to watch soap operas all afternoon," Entertainment Weekly said.) Mr. Angle hopes that the Roomba will prove to be the first mass-market profitable product that iRobot has developed on its own.

"There have been prior attempts to have robots do things like cut the lawn, but this is truly the first practical one that solves an everyday problem and isn't difficult to set up," said Steve Schwartz, a divisional merchandise manager for Brookstone, which sells the Roomba and other gadgets. "Our problem in October and November was that we didn't have enough inventory."

IRobot's founders say that ever since they started the company, people have asked them when a robot would be able to help with housekeeping. Now, Mr. Brooks says, people ask when Roomba "will be able to mop or wax the floors."

That could come next. In the meantime, Roomba's warm reception in shopping malls and the PackBot's accomplishments in Afghanistan have helped restore iRobot's sense of momentum.

"Robots used to be things that were bolted to the floor in factories, and ordinary people didn't interact with them," Mr. Brooks said, "just like computers in the 1960's and 1970's were locked away behind glass walls. In 50 years, I think the world is going to be full of robots, and we want iRobot to be one of the companies that's building them."

. . .

[Author's note: iRobot went public in 2005, and in 2018 brought in about $1 billion in revenue, much of it from the Roomba line of vacuum cleaners.]

Before Robots Rise, They Have to Master the Stairs

Published in the Boston Globe, October 20, 2017

The robots may eventually come to take your job.

But first, they'll have to figure out how to take the elevator.

Boston is home to a growing number of companies that are building or selling robots intended to roam free in human environments — rolling along sidewalks, climbing the front steps to drop off a package, entering conference rooms, and inspecting the engine of a broken car in a repair bay. And every one of them is grappling with a maddening range of obstacles that we humans don't think twice about. How many different types of doorknobs will you encounter today, and how many of those doors will be locked? How many acorns will you crunch on the sidewalk?

It's tough out there for robots trying to make themselves useful. "Nobody has really made any progress on the difficult challenges of robots operating in human environments," says Tom Ryden, a robotics industry veteran who now runs Mass Robotics, a shared workspace for robotics startups in Boston. "Just look at a typical home – it's incredibly hard to grasp, physically turn, then push or pull all kinds of different doors that you'd find there."

In 2013, I witnessed the cutting-edge of robotic door opening at MIT, when a team of researchers used a million-dollar robot named Atlas to try to open a door with one of those lever-like handles that runs parallel to the floor. One person worked a rope-and-pulley system that kept the expensive robot from falling down. Hydraulics whined loudly, and a siren on the robot's head warned humans to keep a safe distance. After a few minutes, the bot successfully opened the door. A few more minutes passed as it maneuvered through the actual doorway — sideways, since Atlas was too large to fit through the regular way. Total elapsed time: about 10 minutes. (At right, Atlas at MIT with professor Seth Teller.)

Hurdler Motors, a startup based in the Mass Robotics space, is designing a robotic cart that would help deliver packages to your doorstep. Its robot would ride on a delivery truck, and then dismount to navigate streets and sidewalks while carrying a small load of cargo. The Hurdler device is even designed to climb stairs to get to a front porch or entryway. Initially, it would work alongside a delivery person to carry more stuff than they can with a handcart today; eventually, says Michael Goren, the company's founder, it would operate on its own.

The design involves six or eight wheels fixed to the end of post-like legs that can move up and down to ascend stairs or get around obstacles on the sidewalk. "If a kid lays down a bicycle on the sidewalk, that stops all those guys," says Goren, referring to competitors that are designing rolling robots that just have regular wheels. "We can surmount those obstacles where others can't." But Goren says his plan for opening doors or pushing elevator buttons is that other companies will design arms to do those tasks, which could be added onto the Hurdler system — or that everything will eventually have wireless communications built into it, so the robot can silently request to have a door opened. He's hoping to raise a few million dollars to turn the company's prototype robot into a marketable product.

One company that has cracked the riddle of building robots that can thrive in the home is Bedford-based iRobot. It manufactures small, disc-shaped robotic vacuum cleaners that can make it over most thresholds and onto most shaggy rugs — but if you leave the door to the den closed, it definitely won't get cleaned. Incredibly, the company's Roomba 650 model was the best-selling vacuum cleaner in the United States last year. (Not just among robotic floor cleaners, but of any vacuum cleaner.)

But the Roomba does a job most of us dread, and it's relatively cheap — about $375. A much more expensive product from the company, the Ava 500 videoconferencing robot, failed to take off. The Ava looked like a motorized column with a TV screen perched on top; it sold for $70,000, or could be leased for about $2,500 a month. (At right, an Ava 500 bot.)

So imagine you bought one, and put it on the executive floor so that the boss could "beam in" to meetings via robot, or amble around checking on underlings. If the robot wanted to get down to the accounting department or the warehouse, it couldn't. "It costs you something like $20,000 per elevator to create a wireless interface so that Ava could call an elevator," says iRobot CEO Colin Angle. "It was cheaper to buy two Avas for separate floors than getting it to ride the elevator." To get through a closed door, Ava would wait for a person to come along, with a message on the video screen asking for help. Angle recalls that when he was an MIT student, he worked on a robot named Seymour that was designed to carry candy on board to try to bribe humans to open doors and push elevator buttons for it.

But even the world's biggest companies didn't seem to want to invest in an Ava for every floor of the building. So starting in late 2016, iRobot decided to spin off the videoconferencing bot as an independent company, Ava Robotics of Cambridge. A new version of the robot will be unveiled next month, according to Marcio Macedo, a former iRobot executive who is a co-founder of Ava Robotics.

Macedo says they have been beta-testing the new version at the MIT Sloan School of Management, where participants in executive education programs can virtually come to class, even if they can't hop on a plane to be there in person. Sometimes, people "beaming in" to the robot do ride the elevators, but by asking humans to press the button for them. (MIT also has Wi-Fi in its elevators — a key requirement for maintaining a link to the roving bot.) But even Macedo admits that even if a robot was able to work in an environment where every door could be opened automatically by waving a security card, would we want to give it the security card? "Security teams might worry that someone would 'piggyback' behind the robot when the robot was opening the door" to sneak into a locked area, he says. Would the robot know?

Some of my favorite buildings in Boston are those with elevators ancient enough to require licensed human operators. I think if the robots want our jobs, they can work at those addresses, and politely ask the operators for a lift to the third floor.

But they may still want to bring some candy.

Can the World's Most Successful Maker of Robot Videos Go Mass Market?

Published in the Boston Globe, July 6, 2018

Boston is not home to many entertainment studios, but it can lay claim to one of the most successful makers of YouTube videos: Boston Dynamics, which has racked up more than 225 million views on the site. The company's biggest hit so far shows a humanoid robot named Atlas, a kind of 21st Century Tin Man, traipsing across a snowy landscape, picking up cardboard boxes, and being knocked down by a human — but determinedly getting back up again.

Boston Dynamics was founded in 1992 to build some of the world's most advanced walking robots, and at that, it has succeeded. But far more people have seen the company's bots on YouTube — or on the HBO show "Silicon Valley," where a deer-like robot was hit by a car — than in person. That's because for all of its history, Boston Dynamics has been a research-and-development shop building tiny quantities of extremely sophisticated robots, mostly as part of Pentagon research projects.

Everything has been crafted by hand at the company's Waltham facility, and affordability, given the military customer base, generally hasn't been a factor. When I asked founder and chief executive Marc Raibert about the cost of an earlier version of Atlas, all he would divulge is that it was north of $1 million, but not quite the $2 million reported by some media outlets. Raibert had become like Antonio Stradivari, but for ambulatory robots instead of violins.

But now, Raibert's company is under new ownership — Japanese tech conglomerate SoftBank — and suddenly he has a mass-market vision. Boston Dynamics, he said, wants to build "the Android" of the industry — a robot that other software and hardware companies will build add-ons for, as they do for Android mobile phones. At a trade show in Germany last month, Raibert told the audience that after 26 years of "working on the future, the advanced stuff, now we're trying to make some practical products."

Two questions that haven't yet been answered: What useful work will they do, and what will they cost?

Boston Dynamics has gone through three phases since its founding. First was life as a military contractor, often working for DARPA, the Defense Advanced Research Projects Agency. Then it was acquired in 2013 by Google. The Silicon Valley firm was buying up robotics companies as part of a new strategy overseen by Andy Rubin, a Google executive who helped created the company's Android operating system.

"At a high level, Google wanted to make a robot that could do anything," said Alex Broadbent, a former Boston Dynamics project manager. "You open the box, turn on the robot, and tell it to cut the grass, clean the house, or take care of grandma. If you look at Google's products, they are easy to use and extremely versatile." (At right, Boston Dynamics founder Marc Raibert.)

Andrew String, another former Boston Dynamics employee, said Google wanted a robot that could sell for under $1,000. "Of course, that's a pie-in-the-sky dream." (String's current employer, iRobot Corp. of Burlington, manages to do it, with its lowest-end Roomba floor cleaner selling for $300.)

Under Google's ownership, Boston Dynamics decided not to pursue further contracts with the military. That eliminated the company's major source of revenue. When Rubin left Google in 2014, the whole robotics initiative seemed to lose momentum.

The third phase began in 2017, when SoftBank acquired Boston Dynamics from Google. The Japanese company already sells a humanoid robot called Pepper, which functions largely as a greeter in retail environments (Pepper's price over three years, which includes data connectivity and insurance, is about $14,000, according to the Robot Report, a trade publication.)

The first product Boston Dynamics will try to produce in significant quantities is its battery-powered SpotMini bot. SpotMini is a 60-pound, four-legged animal-like robot with a box-shaped body that moves around with surprising spryness. It can carry a payload of about 30 pounds, which could be cargo, or an add-on like a robotic arm or special sensor, and run about 90 minutes on a charge. At the CEBIT trade show in Germany, Raibert said the company plans to build about 100 SpotMinis by the end of 2018, and 1,000 a year thereafter. He posited a few possible uses for them: security, emergency response, and parcel delivery (yes, SpotMini can easily climb your front steps to get to the porch.)

SpotMini got a few million bucks worth of free publicity in March when Amazon CEO Jeff Bezos tweeted a photo of himself walking next to the bot at a California conference: "Taking my new dog for a walk," Bezos wrote.

But while the demos and YouTube videos dazzle the rest of us, many in the robot business are deeply skeptical that there is a market for a general purpose walking robot.

"The videos are jaw-dropping, but when I start thinking about what is the business model, that's where it gets shaky," said Dan Kara, a longtime robotics analyst at WTWH Media.

"What do legged robot systems give you that wheeled systems don't — other than it uses more power and it's less robust?" Kara said. "These things fail more often because it's complex stuff."

Kara said Boston Dynamics' plan may be to sell the first batches of SpotMinis to university or corporate research labs "to let them play around with it, and see what they come up with."

"My guess is that it will be very hard for Boston Dynamics to make the leap from cool research demonstration to cost-effective product," added Joe Jones, one of the creators of the iRobot Roomba, and now cofounder of Franklin Robotics, a Lowell startup developing a robot to weed gardens. "Research is all about the biggest bang, but the imperative for products is bang-for-the-buck."

Raibert declined to be interviewed, but he did suggest the company will have more to say in the fall — perhaps more details about the launch of SpotMini.

The first time I ever interviewed Raibert, way back in 2001, he had already identified the challenge his company would face selling products.

Talking about the work he did when he was a professor running a lab at the Massachusetts Institute of Technology, he said, "When you work in a place like MIT, you try to do the most advanced thing — layer after layer of complex stuff. With a product, you don't want it to be that complex. You want it to be something you can ship around in a cardboard box and [customers] turn it on and it works."

Boston Dynamics has been successful at many things in its first quarter-century. But success in the "cardboard box" phase will be the biggest hill for SpotMini, Atlas, and the rest of the company's bots to climb.

[Author's note: Softbank sold Boston Dynamics to the automaker Hyundai Motor Group in December 2020 for $1.1 billion.]

Betting a Quarter-Billion Dollars on More Efficient Warehouses

Published in the Boston Globe, February 18, 2020

Inside a low-slung, cream-colored office building near Hanscom Air Force Base in Lexington, a stealthy startup company has been working for seven years to design the most efficient warehouse in the world.

Last month, the company, Berkshire Grey, announced that it had raised $263 million from a group of investors to fuel its ambitions. When I stopped by recently, there were tall blue barriers blocking certain parts of the warehouse that the company didn't want visitors to see. One key slide in a presentation I was shown had the photos blacked out.

Not surprisingly, Berkshire Grey's CEO, Tom Wagner, used to work for the Pentagon, as a robotics program manager. And he has hired several hundred people — he won't be specific about the number — from top robotics companies like Amazon Robotics, DEKA Research & Development, iRobot, and Rethink Robotics.

"We are recruiting people from Silicon Valley to come here," Wagner, right, says proudly. For the company's first few years, Wagner says, the company was trying to keep such a tight lid on its plans that it was hiring robotics experts without telling them exactly what they'd be working on.

The problem that Berkshire is trying to solve is one that you create every day. When you order a pair of ski goggles or a tube of suntan lotion on your phone, you set in motion a process that today involves a fair number of humans touching that item on its journey from where it is made to the warehouse it is stored in to a series of FedEx or postal facilities to your front door. And humans, from the logistics perspective, are problematic: they need training, they take lunch breaks, they belong to unions so can't work 24/7, and they get injured. Often, during crunch times

— like the holiday shopping period — you can't hire enough of them.

That's one reason that in 2012, Amazon paid $775 million to acquire a Massachusetts startup called Kiva Systems. It wanted to reduce the amount of time humans spent walking the aisles of its warehouses to track down individual items, and instead use robots to transport the items that you'd ordered to a human standing in one spot, who would put it in a box. Amazon rebranded the company as Amazon Robotics, and today it has supplied several hundred thousand robots to Amazon's warehouses.

Amazon has been working for several years on how to automate the "putting it in a box" task. But it's a big challenge for robots to both identify an item — ski goggles or suntan lotion? — and pick it up without damaging it. In 2015, Amazon started sponsoring a series of competitions that invited university teams and startups to build robots that were up to the task. Amazon dangled tens of thousands of dollars in prize money. Berkshire Grey opted not to participate. "We already had all kinds of answers that other people had not found," Wagner says, "and we still have answers others haven't found. There was no reason for us to share or show what we were developing."

Berkshire doesn't plan to manufacture its own robots, cameras, or conveyor belts; it is designing new warehouse automation systems, and will have contract manufacturing partners build the actual gear. Berkshire will then assemble, test, ship complete finished systems to customers, and install them on-site with its own teams of employees. The company's "secret sauce," Wagner says, is custom-crafted software, and a set of cameras and sensors on an industrial robotic arm, that enable it to identify and pick up a wide range of items, from jars of marshmallow fluff to t-shirts in plastic bags to mesh shower loofahs. At the end of the robotic arm is a vacuum-powered suction cup, rather than anything that resembles fingers. When it needs to, the robot can "auto-swap" one kind of suction cup for another, improving its ability to pick up a given item based on its weight or size, explains Kevin O'Brien, a senior program manager at Berkshire.

The system still isn't perfect: in watching a short demo, I noticed that Berkshire may have stacked the deck in its robot's favor by sticking an extra UPC bar code on the items the robot was trying to identify. And when it couldn't "see" one of the items sitting in a plastic bin, a human employee had to nudge the item into a different position; after that, the robot identified it and picked it up.

Wagner says that the company's technology can be installed in a modular way — just automate a segment of warehouse activity — or purchased as a complete soup-to-nuts system. Without announcing it, the company has deployed hundreds of robots in the US that have already touched millions of items on their way through the supply chain to your door. During my visit, three large black robotic modules sat in Berkshire's assembly and testing building, being prepared to ship to the company's first overseas customer facility. Wagner says Berkshire can't disclose any of its customers: installing this kind of technology "is about competitive advantage," he says, and customers don't want to tip their hand to rivals. Wagner says the company expects to be able to sell its technology to e-commerce companies, companies that operate retail stores and also sell online, and companies that handle packages and run warehouses for customers, like FedEx and UPS.

Wagner, characteristically tight-lipped, won't disclose the total amount of money that his company has raised. But the $263 million it brought in last month is more than twice as large as the largest venture capital round a company raised in Massachusetts last year, and it's likely the biggest venture capital round a New England robotics company has ever raised. The lead investor is SoftBank, a Japanese tech conglomerate that has also put money into the coworking firm WeWork, Uber, and Slack, which makes collaboration software. SoftBank also owns Boston Dynamics, the Waltham company best known for YouTube videos of humanoid and animal-inspired walking robots.

"It's a stunning amount of money to raise for such an unheard of group," says Charles Grinnell, CEO of the agricultural robotics company Harvest Automation in North Billerica.

"Kiva-Amazon Robotics has been such a big thing, in terms of quantity of robots deployed and impact on operations that everyone is hoping to fund the next similar success," says Bruce Welty, founder of Devens-based Quiet Logistics, which designs automated warehouses. While it's an open question how many customers will want to spend the money (and time) to install one of Berkshire's completely automated warehouse systems, Welty says that there remain "a lot of unautomated warehouses in the world, and the volume of goods is growing because of all these small e-commerce orders coming in from everywhere. No one in the industry feels like the potential is constrained in any way."

But $263 million is a rather substantial chip to plunk down on the roulette table, and the bettors expect a big return.

8. Looking Ahead

I Chucked It All and Became a Turker

Published in the Boston Globe, April 1, 2012

A few weeks ago, tired of the niggling questions of editors and the constant press of deadlines, I decided to chuck it all and become a Turker.

What is a Turker? It's someone who performs small tasks that can't be automated. Once you sign up on the Mechanical Turk website, operated by Amazon.com, you can choose from an array of jobs that might take a few seconds or a few hours: you can translate documents from Tibetan to English, fill out surveys for academic researchers, or transcribe a 71-minute lecture about gastroenterology. How's the pay? That last task offered $2.85 for work that would likely take several hours.

I was curious about Mechanical Turk because it is just one of many websites cropping up that allow work to be farmed out globally, often to the lowest bidder. The phenomenon is sometimes called "micro-labor." Looked at collectively, the sites — some with links to Boston — seem harbingers of a new wave of outsourcing that will allow companies and individuals to get things done more cheaply and efficiently than before. The flip side, however, is that they seem destined to delete some number of full-time jobs, while creating more freelancers forced to scramble for income while paying for their own health insurance and trying to save for retirement.

Launching my career as a micro-laborer involved no interviews or drug tests, and it took all of 10 minutes. I signed up for Amazon's payments service, so the money I earned could be funneled into my bank account. Then, I began sorting through jobs posted on the site. Two bucks to write an "interesting and well-written" 1,000-word article on an assigned topic? Too much like my job as a newspaper columnist, at radically reduced pay.

I quickly earned 4 cents for looking at five images and deciding whether some descriptive terms that had been applied to them were accurate. The images were fun to peruse: pictures of Fiats being shipped from Italy, and photos of Johnny Weismuller, who starred in the Tarzan movies of the 1930s. I earned 7 cents by looking at some people's LinkedIn profiles and determining which job category the person best fit, then earned a whopping $4 for filling out a survey about leisure activities I enjoy. But I also had to give my micro-employer, Hammerhead Labs, access to my

Facebook and Foursquare accounts, which made me a little nervous.

At the end of my first two hours as a Turker, I had earned $4.37. But I also completed several jobs that hadn't been approved by the people who posted them; assigners get to decide whether a task has been completed satisfactorily before releasing payment. (My LinkedIn categorization project was rejected, with an admonishment to "work more carefully in the future.")

Mechanical Turk is just one example of the new wave of outsourcing. If you are a cosmetics company that would like to set up a blog with a constant stream of beauty tips, you can use Boston-based Skyword to hire writers. Skyword chief executive Tom Gerace says that over the last month, 1,200 writers produced 13,500 articles and blog posts for clients. The per-article payment ranges from $13 on the low end to $200 on the high end. But Skyword sometimes asks writers to produce an article for free, and pays them based on how often it is viewed — for instance, $3.50 for every 500 views.

GrabCAD, a start-up with operations in Cambridge and Estonia, allows mechanical engineers to create online profiles that help companies find them, and potentially supply them with projects. The site also runs "challenges" where engineers can show off their best design solution for a given product or part, and potentially win anywhere from $50 to $5,000, as well as a contract for future work

TaskRabbit got its start in Cambridge, but is now headquartered in San Francisco. The company has assembled a network of errand-runners in nine cities to do things like pick up a desk at IKEA and assemble it in a company's office. Founder Leah Busque prefers to call what they do "micro-entrepreneurship," not "micro-labor." "With nearly 13 million Americans looking for work, we are providing an alternative to the traditional 9 to 5 job," she says. "Our TaskRabbits can make money and build their own business on their own terms."

I spoke with one Cambridge TaskRabbit last week, just after he finished a job in Wellesley, installing a sink drain. Marc Hedges said he could earn $500 in a "pretty good week" doing handyman jobs through TaskRabbit. "This gives me flexibility, and I like dealing one-on-one with customers," Hedges says. But he previously worked as a union mason until the 2008 recession and says his freelance lifestyle "is not at all comparable to working union construction. There, you had an annuity and health insurance."

For companies and individuals, getting more work done while spending less is always good. But I do think these services will inevitably erode full-time jobs.

Ofer Sharone, a professor at MIT's Sloan School of Management, says the sites can be beneficial "for a small percent of workers with rare skills who now have access to a global pool of employers," or workers living in very low cost places. But the overall impact, he predicts, will create "a global race for the bottom, in which companies can have a global labor pool of professionals competing against each other on the basis of wages."

So far, I've earned $8.06 for almost four hours of Turking. That would explain why I'm back writing this column. I'm holding tight to this gig — at least until my editor figures out how to use Mechanical Turk to assign it to someone who'll do it better and cheaper.

. . .

[Author's note: GrabCAD was acquired by the 3D printing company Stratasys in 2014, for a reported $100 million. IKEA bought TaskRabbit in 2017 for an undisclosed amount.]

Microbes that Can Do the Dirty Work

Published in the Boston Globe, January 29, 2012

On the edge of Boston harbor, just a short walk from where Harpoon harnesses the power of yeast to produce tasty beverages, researchers are designing new kinds of microorganisms that might one day scrub wastewater clean, crank out fuel for our cars, or keep hospital equipment perfectly sterile. While making beer can be traced back to ancient Mesopotamia, this new field —often called "synthetic biology" or "engineered biology" — definitely belongs to the 21st century.

With government grants, and in some cases venture capital funding, the cluster of companies are trying to "build new microbes that can do things," in the words of Jason Kelly, a co-founder of one of the start-ups, Ginkgo BioWorks. He notes that the tools for reading and writing in DNA — understanding how organisms work and custom-crafting new ones — are getting cheaper and more powerful by the month.

"In the 1980s and 1990s, it took biotech companies ten or fifteen years to develop a new biological drug," says Christopher Pirie, a co-founder of Manus Biosynthesis, an MIT spin-out that is still in "stealth mode." "The tools we have now are enabling the designers of new microorganisms at a much more accelerated pace."

Three of the companies, including Cambrian Innovation, are neighbors in the Marine Industrial Park, a hulking collection of buildings on the harbor originally built for Army & Navy logistics and ship repair. (At right, scientists work in the lab at Cambrian Innovation.)

Cambrian is cultivating colonies of bacteria found in nature that, when charged with electricity, can serve as "living catalysts" in a chemical reaction. "These kind of electrically-active microbes were only discovered in 1999," says chief executive Matthew Silver. Packed together into modules, the microbes can perform tasks like converting carbon dioxide into methane gas — useful if you want to keep the CO2 from escaping into the atmosphere — or extracting pollutants from wastewater while generating electricity. (At right, Matthew Silver.)

One project, called Exogen, has received about $2 million in funding from the National Science Foundation and private investors, Silver says. It seeks to use bacteria for wastewater treatment. This is already done in places like the giant egg-shaped "digesters" on Deer Island, but Cambrian says its process would require much less energy.

Right next door, a start-up called Novophage is working with bacteriophages, a kind of virus that is a natural predator of bacteria. Explains chief executive Micah Rosenbloom, "We're engineering phages that find a specific kind of bacteria" — like the kind you wouldn't want hanging around a hospital or food-processing plant — "and can degrade it, or just find it and detect it and let you know that it's there," perhaps by changing color or emitting a radio signal. The phages might also be useful in combatting the bacteria that can gum up the machinery used in oil production or papermaking, Rosenbloom says.

The company has been sequencing the genome of different species of bacteria, like E. coli or listeria, and then building phages to detect or destroy them. To do that, Novophage takes phages that are found in nature and attaches a "payload" of custom-made DNA to give them new instructions. The company plans to start pilot tests this year, seeing how its phages perform in the real world.

The plan at Ginkgo is essentially to be a bacterial job shop, "building organisms and licensing them to other companies, in the pharmaceutical industry and energy and chemicals," says Kelly. One contract the company has with DARPA, the Pentagon's research agency, involves developing organisms that would have anti-copying technology built into them. "If you design an organism for a particular purpose, you may not want it to be able to be copied by everybody," Kelly says. And like Cambrian, Ginkgo is also working on the Department of Energy's electrofuels program, designing bacteria that can make a fuel that could replace gasoline using only electricity and carbon dioxide as inputs.

The company is preparing to move into a new 11,000-square foot office and lab space next month. Lots of technology has been designed into the new space to enable the company to speedily produce new strains of organisms. "It looks more like a chip fabrication factory, with robotic automation and barcoding, than a bench-top biology lab," Kelly says. "About a quarter of our team are software developers," working to write the programs that will control all the new machinery. Ginkgo has twenty employees.

Pirie, the Manus Biosynthesis co-founder, says his start-up has not yet received any grants or funding — and they're still hunting for office space. But the company has been talking to executives in different industries, including fragrances and cosmetics, about using microbes to produce "clean replacements for the chemicals they currently use," many of which come from petroleum. "Sometimes the issue is the price, and there are other examples where there's just scarcity," he says.

Any time you start talking about the genetic modification of living things, of course, some people are going to have concerns. At Novophage, they're sensitive to not making phages sound "scary." (They don't infect humans, only bacteria.) Kelly at Ginkgo acknowledges that "people have a visceral response to living organisms. But historically, we've done a lot of organism engineering in the past. If you have a dog, you have a genetically-modified wolf living in your house, and while you didn't do the genetic engineering yourself, you still trust it around your kids." (At right, Gingko co-founders Jason Kelly and Tom Knight.)

The biotech industry, which regularly relies on genetically-modified cells from hamster ovaries to produce its protein-based drugs, may serve as a positive poster child for synthetic biology companies. "Biotech has been a clean and safe industry, especially when you compare it to the chemical or oil industries," Kelly says.

In the 1980s, young people who wanted to be in the center of the action learned how to build spreadsheets. In the 1990s, they crafted Web sites. Today, they're designing and customizing microorganisms and phages, with an eye toward solving unsolved problems. In the labs of these new companies, it feels like the future.

...

[Author's note: Of these synthetic biology startups, Gingko has grown the fastest, attracting partners like Bayer and Cargill. It has also raised the most funding: $429 million as of 2019, including some of it from Bill Gates.]

Printing the Future

Published in the Boston Globe, July 30, 2015

Michael Perrone is standing at a workbench next to one of the world's most advanced 3D printers, trying to figure out what is going wrong. The printer, not yet on the market, can produce small objects out of plastic, and it is also capable of adding circuitry to them as it goes.

But just as your inkjet printer sometimes misbehaves, the Voxel8 prototype today doesn't seem to want to spit out the conductive silver "ink" that will form an antenna. The issue seemed to be that the power and Internet had been switched off and then on again, messing with the printer's electronics.

You've likely heard all the hype about our 3D printed: it's amazing, and by Christmas we'll have our very own "Star Trek" replicators down in the basement, spewing out thermoplastic so Santa doesn't have to show up with the sleigh.

Reality is rougher. A mutual fund of publicly-traded companies that produce 3D printers is down almost one-third over the last year, and MakerBot, a Brooklyn company that makes machines priced as low as $1,375, laid off 100 people in April and shuttered its three retail outlets, including one on Newbury Street in Boston.

"The so-called mass market for 3D printing is still pretty early and unproven," says Marina Hatsopoulos, the former CEO of Z Corp., an MIT spin-out that helped pioneer the industry. Hatsopoulos quips that "people who shop on Newbury Street do not have 3D CAD files in their wallets," referring to the complex digital models that must first be created before an object can be produced. And the cost of producing something on a 3D printer is still far more expensive than buying something mass-produced from the shelves of a Wal-Mart, Hatsopoulos says.

Lots of people draw a parallel to the first personal computers in the 1970s, which required lots of care and feeding, plus some programming knowledge. "The PC experience was oversold, too," says Ric Fulop, a Waltham venture capitalist who owns three different 3D printers. He expects that the market for 3D printers "will be ten times bigger in ten years than it is today."

If you wave away the smoke surrounding consumers buying 3D printers, there's still a very significant revolution happening in businesses and educational institutions. Analyst Terry Wohlers of the firm Wohlers Associates says he expects sales 3D printing products and services worldwide to nearly double between 2015 and 2016, from $4.1 billion to $7.3 billion.

In the Boston area, there are a number of companies that hope to capture some of that growth. Woburn-based Viridis3D uses a robotic arm to precisely sprinkle layers of sand that is then hardened with a fixative, creating a mold for casting large parts. MarkForged has a desktop printer that can make ultra-rigid parts out of Kevlar and carbon fiber. Somerville-based Formlabs used a dozen of its printers to create several hundred wearable digital bracelets at a conference in June. The bracelets featured several different designs, and they lit up to indicate commonalities between two conference attendees. (Above, 3D printed dragon pieces made by the startup Matter.io click into a Lego car.)

In July, Voxel8, a spin-out from a Harvard University research lab, announced that it had raised $12 million, its first significant round of venture capital funding. (The company was only founded last September.) Co-founder Dan Oliver says that rather than producing flat circuit boards that now must be wedged into a finished product, in the not-too-distant future designers will be able to incorporate circuitry into the product itself. One example he cites is a smartphone where the antenna is integrated into the outer shell, providing better reception and taking up less space.

"We think the next big jump is using printers to create finished devices, not just prototypes, with multiple materials in them working together," says Oliver. The company plans to start shipping its first devices later this year, at about $9,000 each.

But perhaps the most significant local player in this revolution is not a for-profit company, but a non-profit born at MIT called the Fab Foundation ("fab" being short for fabrication.) It supports the creation and operation of a network of more than 500 Fab Labs in 67 countries, outfitted not just with 3D printers but an array of other tools that enable students and community members to "make anything they can imagine," says Lass, the director of the Fab Foundation. (Lass is in the photo below, with 3D-printed earrings. Yes, she goes by just one name — though her given name is Sherry Lassiter.) The first one opened in 2003, at the South End Technology Center.

Neil Gershenfeld, the MIT professor who helped open that first Fab Lab, says that "innovation is a very chaotic messy process. It doesn't work in sterile boxes. Globally, these Fab Labs bring bright, inventive people out of the woodwork." He and Lass see Fab Labs as a key part of a city's infrastructure — a place for citizens to not just design products and make art, but to build things that solve urban problems.

This week, several thousand people will participate in the 11th annual Fab Lab Conference & Symposium in Boston. Among the sessions: executives from Google and Amazon.com will talk about making things with robots, and Beno Juarez of Peru will talk about setting up a floating Fab Lab on the actual Amazon.

Gershenfeld is already thinking ahead to the next few decades: "Today, we buy machines to put into a Fab Lab, but we're working very quickly to get to a next stage, where you will go to a Fab Lab to make the machines you need. You'll use a Fab Lab to make a Fab Lab."

Kind of mind-blowing, no?

The Hottest Class at MIT

Published in the Boston Globe, April 9, 2017

MIT loves numbers, so let me drop a few to illustrate the popularity of a course called 6.036. It is overseen by four instructors and 15 teaching assistants. Lectures are held in 26-100, the school's largest auditorium, with 566 seats.

But this semester, about 700 students signed up for the course — also known as Introduction to Machine Learning — according to Tommi Jaakkola, the computer science professor who created it. So at the first lecture, more than 100 students watched on a video screen in an overflow room.

Not enough students voluntarily dropped the course, so Jaakkola came up with some "preliminary homework" to weed more out, by giving them a sense of the level of linear algebra and probability that'd be required of them.

Why is something called "machine learning" so hot? And what is it? I dropped by Building 32 (also known as the Computer Science and Artificial Intelligence Lab) last week to find out.

Machine learning, first off, isn't about building smarter robots for the factory floor, or harvesters that work the farm more efficiently. The machine we're talking about here usually is a computer. It's ingesting a set of data, analyzing it, and identifying patterns. That might entail examining thousands of paintings to categorize some as Cubist and others as Impressionist, or looking at millions of mammograms to separate worrisome spots that lead to cancer from those that don't.

Radiology today, notes Regina Barzilay, another of the professors who teaches the course, is largely based on an individual radiologist's experience. With software, she says, "You can make the machine learn about the properties of a breast that will develop cancer versus one that won't."

The term "machine learning" is closely tied to artificial intelligence. "I don't actually make a distinction between machine learning and artificial intelligence," Jaakkola says. "They are both trying to solve the same thing — how automated systems can learn." (Both machine learning and AI have deep roots at MIT, going back to the 1960s.)

If you've ever shopped at Amazon, relied on Google Translate, or let Netflix suggest a show to watch based on what you've enjoyed in the past, you've taken advantage of machine learning. In Amazon's case, software looks at what you've bought in the past, what you've browsed on the site — as well as other factors — to put products on the page that are most likely to tempt you to click "buy."

It's a field that is advancing quickly. "For a while, I would select an article from an Israeli newspaper and use Google to translate it," says Barzilay, a native Hebrew speaker. "Every year it became better. Now, it's almost like turning on electricity. It does a great job. This happened within the last 10 years." Building software to decipher lost languages is one of Barzilay's big interests in computer science; a replica of the Rosetta Stone rests on the windowsill of her office.

Intro to Machine Learning involves three projects, which "connect the more theoretical, algorithmic stuff students are learning to actual data and problems," Jaakkola says. For instance, that can entail looking at a set of movie reviews and writing software to sort the raves from the pans.

But the techniques learned in the course can also be applied to higher purposes, like predicting whether a molecule being designed by a chemist on the hunt for a disease cure will prove toxic to humans, says Connor Coley, a graduate student at MIT who took the machine learning course.

When you don't have to focus as much on the issues of toxicity, or whether the molecule you're designing can be manufactured, that lets you spend more time focusing on the end goal, Coley explains.

One reason that Intro to Machine Learning is so popular in 2017 is that there are so many companies recruiting for employees or interns who understand it. In Boston, companies like Facebook, Amazon, TripAdvisor, Spotify, and the chipmaker ARM are hiring people with machine learning skills.

"There's a crazy demand for it right now," says Kat Bailey, an engineering executive at Acquia, a Boston company that makes digital publishing software. "There are more and more people coming out of school with some kind of training, but the demand is not being met." For Acquia, machine learning might be used to automatically put a blog post into a particular category on a website, or connect it with posts on similar topics.

At Wayfair, the Boston-based seller of home furnishings, machine learning is used to help the company send e-mails about a particular promotion — on patio furniture, for example — to those most likely to make a purchase. To attract future and recent graduates, Wayfair has been hosting university visits to its Back Bay offices, as well as evening talks focused on analytics and data. (One gathering that Bailey has hosted at Acquia is called the Boston Bayesians, for people interested in the use of Bayesian statistics in machine learning — among other things.)

Wayfair analytics director Dave Drollette says the company has also been participating in curriculum advisory boards at local universities "so they know the kinds of roles they should be prepping their students for."

While there are plenty of jobs for people who grok, or intuitively understand, machine learning, what about jobs held by people who, for instance, evaluate X-rays all day or scour legal documents? Machine learning does hold the potential to render large swaths of knowledge work obsolete.

Jaakkola and Barzilay are optimists. "I don't believe we should be crying about the time when more people were digging ditches manually," Barzilay says. "Now that we have excavators, it enables people to do more exciting things." Jaakkola acknowledges that machine learning and artificial intelligence will have an effect on existing jobs "that are easily automatable," but that the twin technologies will also have benefits that we don't yet understand. For instance, he says, "you can have a blind person who can be told what is around them automatically," without needing a guide or seeing-eye dog.

"Don't worry," Barzilay tells me, "we're not even close to having machines writing stories." Sure, there's already software that can package up a company's quarterly earnings report into something readable, but they can't craft "a beautiful Boston *Globe* story."

I hope she is right, because I couldn't answer a single one of the questions included in the preliminary homework.

9. The Pandemic Year

How One Layoff Played Out, from Two Perspectives

Published in the Boston Globe, April 23, 2020

On Tuesday, April 7, employees of the Boston company ezCater woke up to an e-mail from their chief executive, Stefania Mallett: Be available this morning for a call from your manager. All 945 employees who received the e-mail knew what it meant. This was the day they would find out who was being laid off, and who would still have a job.

This is how the layoffs played out for Mallett, a 64-year-old who traces her career back to the Massachusetts tech "miracle" of the 1980s, and Lily Cohen, a 24-year-old marketing staffer who joined ezCater last year — her first job after college.

The company was founded in 2007, with a mission of making it easier to get reliable catering for business meals. In recent years, it had become one of Boston's fastest-growing companies. The ezCater website features a roster of menus from restaurants that will deliver a big order for a company meeting. Schedule the date and time you want, and the food appears, with ezCater taking a 15 percent commission on every transaction.

Last April, the privately held company raised $150 million in a funding round that brought its valuation to more than $1 billion — making ezCater what's known in startup circles as a unicorn. To celebrate, there were unicorn cupcakes all around.

But precisely a year after all that sweetness, the company was watching as office closings and shelter-in-place policies brought its fast-growing business to a crawl. It had just launched a national marketing campaign, with highway billboards and mass transit ads bearing the slogan "Food has to work for work." Suddenly, almost no one was at work, and the idea of eating from communal salad bowls and pans of lasagna had lost all appeal.

Mallett says the declining orders were hardly a secret; she prides herself on having created a "radically transparent" company culture. "People could see the business results," Mallett says. "They knew bad things were happening."

The company was hustling to get its network of caterers to shift to individually packaged meals, rather than family-style ones, so that it could effectively sell to the essential businesses — such as factories and hospitals — that were still operating. On several all-hands videoconferences that Mallett led, there was talk of cutting costs on software spending and marketing, and the possibility of furloughs or layoffs.

As business deteriorated in March, several outside advisers suggested that Mallett move quickly to eliminate jobs, she says. But she didn't want to be rushed, especially since there was so little information about when people might return to work. May? September? "What if it comes back in pockets around the country," she wondered. Mallett says she and other company leaders created a financial model to think through "the best assumptions you can make about what you don't know."

Mallett says two things guided her decision-making. The first was her own experience being laid off earlier in her career. "I was asking people, 'Are we going to do layoffs?' And the management of that company lied about it until the day it happened," she recalls.

She also wanted to try to avoid a series of layoffs throughout 2020. "The second layoff is the really bad one," she says, "because everybody looks over their shoulder all the time," worrying about what will come next. "We tried very hard to make this one painful and deep, so that we wouldn't have another one. We cut as deep as we could work up the courage to do."

By the time April arrived, Mallett was telling employees on a Zoom videoconference that a decision on layoffs was coming soon. She recommended they take any personal photos or files off of their company laptops. It seemed like she was struggling to hold back tears, according to several former ezCater employees.

Lily Cohen had started working at ezCater in February 2019 as an intern, just after graduating from Northeastern University. The internship turned into a job in June. Cohen worked as a brand marketing associate, helping ezCater manage its trade show appearances, marketing events, and the annual company holiday party.

The job was the reason she stayed in Boston. Cohen felt it was designed especially for her skills and interests: "They hired me for me," she says. "I loved the company so much. It was a place that made me really happy." In January, she helped plan an offsite meeting for the marketing team: There was brainstorming and talk about big goals for 2020. At the end of the day, everyone went to Flight Club in the Seaport to have drinks and play darts.

On April 7, when Cohen checked her e-mail around 9 a.m., the note from Mallett was already in her inbox: The layoffs were happening.

"You are always hoping that it's not going to be you," Cohen says. "I was picturing all the reasons why it wouldn't be me. I was a lot cheaper than a lot of the more senior people there."

Cohen knew she'd need to be on Zoom, and she "wanted to look presentable," so she took a quick shower and put on a favorite sweatshirt.

Cohen then got a message from her manager's boss, asking her to join a Zoom meeting around 9:45. Before it took place, she got a text from a colleague who had already been laid off and had her access to the company's computer systems shut off. At that point, Cohen says, "I kind of knew — I just had a feeling."

The videoconference was led by her manager's boss, and another executive. Cohen was being laid off, as was her manager. All told, 420 employees would lose their jobs.

"We spoke to every single employee," Mallett says. "You did not get laid off by e-mail or a Slack message. You had a face-to-face conversation" over Zoom.

Yet it was tough to do layoffs remotely, she acknowledges. "There's a dimension of warmth that you could only project through your voice." There were no hugs and no handshakes to thank people for the work they had put in. "I couldn't have been as warm as I would've liked to be," Mallett says, choking up a bit.

In the span of about a month, she says, "We went from being this tremendously fast-growing company to having to lay off half our people."

Mallett writes via e-mail that she and the rest of the leadership team at ezCater took pay cuts: "It feels right for the execs to kick something in, even though what has happened is in no way the fault of anyone in the company." (People at other levels of seniority didn't have their pay cut, she adds.)

Employees couldn't go out at the end of the day to have a last drink together at a favorite bar, as often happens at companies when there are job cuts. But there were alumni chat groups set up quickly on the messaging system Slack, and former colleagues made dates to connect for coffee or wine over Zoom.

The layoffs affected almost everyone at the company that Cohen interacted with daily, so it was "a little bit comforting that it happened to so many other people," she says. And it was "maybe less embarrassing" for having happened over Zoom, rather than in a conference room.

But the hardest part, Cohen says, is that she was by herself. After the Zoom call, she was alone. There was no one to hug, that day or since. Cohen, who like others is sheltering in place because, occasionally goes on walks with her sister, who lives nearby, but she has not been near the rest of her family.

Cohen got about four weeks' pay as severance, and she has applied for unemployment compensation. She has some savings and is not too worried about how soon she will find her next job. "I want to wait for something I know I'm going to really enjoy," she says. "I'm trying not to put a ton of pressure on myself."

None of the colleagues she worked most closely have yet found new jobs.

Shortly after she was laid off, ezCater shut off her company laptop, but it hasn't sent instructions about how to return it. "I put it up in my closet, so I don't have to look at it every day," Cohen says.

And everything she left at her desk is still there — the photos, the string of holiday lights, the certificates she received at company events — right where she left them on March 10, the last day most employees went into ezCater's office.

The plan is that when it's safe to be back in the office, there will be a day when everyone who lost their job can go in and pick up their belongings. No one can guess when that will be.

. . .

[Author's note: It took several months, but Lily Cohen eventually found a new job in September 2020, with a healthcare technology company.]

She Bought an RV and Hit the Road to Raise Money

Published in the Boston Globe, October 4, 2020

For Robin Liss, Thursdays are for staying put somewhere there's a good wireless connection.

Liss has been living — and running her startup company — out of a recreational vehicle for the past month. She schedules most of her internal calls and videoconferences with colleagues on Thursdays, so she makes sure she and her boyfriend, David Simpson, are not driving down a remote highway that day. "Or at least we keep the drive to early morning or late night," she explains.

Liss jokingly refers to the 24-foot vehicle as Delta II, since in her peripatetic pre-pandemic life, she had attained Diamond status as a frequent flier on the airline.

Liss still owns a condo in Cambridge, and her company, Suvie, still has an office there — though it is mostly unused. (The company sells a $900 countertop appliance that can both refrigerate and cook food, using the sous-vide method of heating bags of ingredients in warm water.) As she looked toward the fall, she knew she'd need to raise another round of funding to keep the company going. While other entrepreneurs might line up a slate of Zoom meetings with prospective investors, Liss came up with a different plan. She bought a used RV at a Vermont dealership for $34,000 and hit the road.

After all, if Suvie's 30 employees were interacting with Liss primarily as a face on a screen, what difference did it make if she was in her Harvard Square home office or at the Hollywood RV Park in Los Angeles?

Liss says the ongoing road trip, which started Aug. 29, is about two things: visiting friends and family and meeting with current and prospective investors.

"We haven't seen a lot of national parks or roadside attractions on the trip," she says. Instead, Liss and Simpson have sought out urgent care clinics when moving from one state to another, to get COVID-19 tests. And they've avoided public restrooms and dine-in restaurants.

"We take health precautions very seriously," she says, adding that the main reason they chose to travel by RV "was so we could travel in a socially isolated way, and see family who are socially isolating."

She has also had meetings with current investors in her company and with others to who, she wanted to make a pitch on investing — some in backyards, others in public parks, separated by six feet and with masks on.

Why does Liss feel so strongly about meeting face-to-face?

"Business is built on trust and relationships, and it's very hard as human beings to build that trust and those relationships remotely, for whatever reason," she says.

Prior to the trip, the company had raised $12 million, primarily from individual investors, as opposed to venture capital firms. "The people who've invested in us are those who have connected with my passion, the team's passion, and our hard work and grit. It's hard to get that sense over a Zoom call," she says.

One of Suvie's local backers is Andy Palmer, chief executive of Tamr, a Cambridge data-management startup. "She's a role-model entrepreneur," he says of Liss. "When things aren't working for her, she basically changes and mixes it up. This trip was definitely that. And it worked — she got her financing done." (Pictured at right, the Suvie appliance.)

Liss says she had always been curious about RVs, but her fast-paced lifestyle never seemed to offer the opportunity for much ground-based travel. A year or two ago, it wasn't unusual for her to sleep two dozen nights a year aboard a plane, traveling for work to China, California, and other places. (The Suvie appliance is manufactured in China.) "Compared to sleeping on a plane, the RV is luxury," she says, though she and Simpson do occasionally bump up against the extremely limited square footage. When she needs to make a 3 a.m. or 4 a.m. call to China, there's no other room to escape to.

"That has probably been the hardest part of working from the RV," she says. Liss pays for a Verizon portable hot spot, a subscription to public Wi-Fi hotspots offered by Skype, and, as a backup, she can link her laptop to her AT&T smartphone.

Liss is currently in Texas and plans to stop in St. Louis to see relatives on the way back to Cambridge. She expects to arrive home sometime in October. But Harvard Square is not known for its RV-sized parking spots, so she thinks she will need a place to store the Gulf Stream B Touring Cruiser.

Plans beyond that are hazy. She'd been thinking of driving to Las Vegas in January for the Consumer Electronics Show, which she normally attends, but it's going to be held online. She may visit family in Michigan over the holidays.

Running a business from the dinette of an RV is not exactly a trend — but at least one other local founder is doing it. Brent Grinna is chief executive of EverTrue, a Boston company that helps schools and colleges raise money from alumni. He bought a 36-foot Winnebago in June and set out for Iowa so that he and his wife, with their three children in tow, could visit their families.

"We greatly value Wi-Fi and laundry facilities," Grinna says from West Glacier, Mont. During meetings with colleagues and customers, "My Zoom box looks the same, but we are all much happier." His itinerary has him heading to Seattle, Sonoma Valley, New Orleans, and Key  West, Fla., before returning to New England next spring.

And Palmer, the investor in Suvie, acknowledges he has started to look at RVs himself and to think about planning his own trip out West. He's considering visiting his daughter in Los Angeles and seeing his company's customers around the rest of California, over a few weeks.

"There was a thing that we got addicted to in our tech lifestyle: You're always popping on a plane to go somewhere else, do something else, meet someone new," he says. "Maybe that modality doesn't work anymore."

Business used to involve jetting here and there at 650 miles per hour. But perhaps 65 miles per hour is the ideal speed for the corona era.

(Photos courtesy Robin Liss, Suvie, and Brent Grinna.)

Will COVID Kill Cities?

Published in the Boston Globe, September 8, 2020

There is a debate brewing about the future of cities, fueled by the coronavirus pandemic. On one side is the "quick rebound" crew, and on the other, the "rise of the rest" adherents.

The first group suggests we are going to see a temporary dip in urban vitality, followed by a rebound once the pandemic abates. The second believes that business shutdowns and the growing prevalence of work-from-home policies could gut cities like Boston, New York, and San Francisco, giving people an opportunity to decamp for places that are cheaper, cleaner, quieter — and perhaps with better schools, to boot.

That could spur what investor Steve Case, the cofounder of AOL, has dubbed the "rise of the rest," a reinvigoration of smaller cities that haven't seen spinning studios, latte dispensaries, and Google campuses spring up over the last decade.

And the anecdotes are starting to accumulate: People who have become unmoored from their urban offices are opting to relocate. They're trading Bay Village in Boston for woodsy Norfolk; Hoboken, N.J., for Cape Cod; San Francisco for Denver.

But Richard Florida, a professor at the University of Toronto, and author of the book *The New Urban Crisis*, says there isn't yet data that shows any sort of "mass abandonment" of cities like Boston and New York. A small percentage of New Yorkers started forwarding their mail this spring, Florida notes — but many were wealthy folks relocating to their second homes upstate, in Miami, or in the Hamptons. And the real estate site Zillow observed that New Yorkers and Bostonians were about 5 percent more likely than last year to be searching for new homes outside of their cities — but cities like San Jose and Detroit saw far bigger jumps (10 percent and 15 percent, respectively).

Florida says that the anecdotes about pandemic-triggered moves among your social circle "are 100 percent correct," but that they may largely be an acceleration of the kind of city-to-suburb relocations that often happen when young people start to have families.

"There's nothing new about this," he says. "It's as age-old as post-war America. People in the family-formation years are very nervous right now — and for good reason. The pandemic may be sending people to buy houses in the suburbs, just like it sent people to buy cars because they were scared of public transit."

And Florida points out that many of the people with the ability to consider relocating are white-collar workers whose jobs can be done via Zoom and Google Docs. "The front-line workers and the middle class can't go anywhere," he says.

Mark Muro, a senior fellow at the Brookings Institution, says that over the last decade, he has tracked the data about where innovation and startup activity happens across the United States. His research group noted that five cities — Boston, San Francisco, San Jose, Seattle, and San Diego — were where most of the innovation-related jobs were being created. They called these cities the "superstar hubs." In contrast, 90 percent of the rest of the country was actually declining, when you looked at the concentration of industries driven by scientific and technological breakthroughs, and the jobs they generated.

"The COVID moment," Muro says, coupled with an increased adoption of videoconferencing, could lead to some decentralization. Still, he writes via e-mail, "I don't see any dire depopulation of the Hub, nor do I see an explosive 'rise of the rest.' But I think you could see tech workers relocating to the Berkshires or Maine, and some modest moving to places in the Heartland."

That might be a good thing for everyone, to the extent that real estate prices in those superstar hubs "calm down a little," he adds. Florida agrees that an "affordability reset" would be a good thing for many US cities. He predicts that some empty office space will get converted to residential housing, and that cities could become younger as older people move out because of health concerns.

And if the pandemic stretches on for another year or more, cities that are warmer — and support meetings and lunches in outdoor settings — could see an influx, Florida suggests.

When it comes to housing prices, Boston isn't yet seeing a slump that would suggest people are abandoning the city en masse. In fact, median sale prices for single-family homes in Greater Boston increased by 6.9 percent in July compared to last year, while condo prices rose 2.2 percent, according to the most recent report from the Greater Boston Association of Realtors. But rents for September are down about 3 percent compared to last year, according to data from Apartment List.

Over time, housing prices and rents in big cities will be a key indicator of whether we're seeing a true sea change. So will the kind of migration data that LinkedIn collects when a member of the social network changes the location on their profile. The latest data LinkedIn has released on migration shows that people have been leaving college towns like State College, Penn.; College Station, Texas; and Champaign-Urbana, Ill. Warmer and less-expensive places like Austin, Texas; Charlotte, N.C.; and Tampa, Florida have been gaining workers.

Another data point to watch: Are venture capitalists becoming more willing to fund startup companies outside of the superstar hubs? Again, there's anecdotal evidence over the spring and summer of VCs getting more comfortable making investments in companies via videoconference, without having met the founders in person. Brad Feld, a Boulder, Colo.-based venture capitalist, is a fervent believer that the "local bias" that VCs have long had, about investing in startups located in the cities where they are based, is rapidly ending.

But data from the National Venture Capital Association, at the mid-point of 2020, shows that Boston and San Francisco's share of overall VC dollars being invested has been growing this year. And the share of "other" places getting venture capital — outside of big cities like Seattle, Chicago, and Philadelphia — is down so far in 2020 compared with 2019. Still, it's early.

Florida points out that "this is the third time just in the past couple of decades that people have predicted the death of New York and the end of cities. The first was after 9/11. The second was after the financial crisis." Each time, he says, "cities came back stronger than anyone — including me — expected." (Though metropolitan budget deficits, he concedes, will be a big challenge going forward.)

As the late business theorist Clayton Christensen often pointed out, data is only available about the past, not the future. And we're all living through an intense experiment in working from home, schooling our kids from home, and trying to care for elderly family members from a distance, that could spark some major decisions about where we want to live come winter — or later, if we're still trundling through 2021 without major changes in the public health situation.

The impact of those decisions on the future of cities will be tracked over years, not the five-and-a-half months of pandemic times we've lived through so far.

Muro, for one, says he hasn't seen enough data to convince him that anything truly dramatic will happen as a result of COVID: "We just don't really know how this is fully going to play out."

A Tweet That Paved a New Path for Blacks in Tech

Published in the Boston Globe, July 8, 2020

On a Saturday morning in December 2018, Pariss Chandler posted a short message on Twitter — and followed it up with a photo of herself in the driver's seat of her car. She had just started a new job as a software developer at Genuine, a Boston digital marketing agency.

"What does Black Twitter in Tech look like?" Chandler asked. "Here, I'll go first." Her photo followed, along with her new title.

That single tweet drew reaction from around the world: Kentucky, Michigan, California, Brazil, Ghana, Nigeria. Some of those responding had been working in the technology industry for decades; others were asking questions about the best schools for learning how to code, or how to find a mentor.

The original tweet has more than 5,000 comments and shares, and it led Chandler, who lives in Cambridge, into an unexpected role as a catalyst helping to elevate the profile of Black people working in the tech industry, and to draw more of them into it.

In many smaller tech companies, it can be tough to find a single Black employee, but at larger companies that have more developed human resources departments, and more established diversity initiatives, the numbers seem to be trending upward — slowly.

A report published by the Massachusetts Tech Leadership Council earlier this year said Black employment in technology roles had risen from about 3,942 people in 2015 (or 3 percent of the industry's employee base in the state) to 7,541 in 2018 (5 percent).

A similarly slow rise is happening nationally — from 7 percent in 2010 to 9 percent in 2019 — and at individual companies that voluntarily release diversity data. At Boston-based ezCater, which operates a food-ordering website for group meals, Black employees accounted for 2 percent of the workforce in 2016 and 4 percent in 2018.

Chandler says her initial objective was simply to spotlight Black people already working in the tech industry. She had only recently entered it herself, having been through a four-month Web development boot camp organized by Resilient Coders, a Cambridge nonprofit. But shining a spotlight on Black people in tech quickly turned into helping employers attract and retain them.

"I started getting lots of direct messages on Twitter from people who wanted to know, 'Can you recruit for us, because we have a diversity problem,'" Chandler says. "Even though I didn't have experience, I just said yes, because it seemed like an amazing opportunity to get more people who look like me into this industry."

After she started doing some informal matchmaking between workers and employers, she noticed there was sometimes a retention problem. Some new hires didn't find the culture of the hiring company welcoming. So Chandler began to offer diversity, equity, and inclusion consultations to employers.

"I'm the middle-woman outside the company," she says. "I'm working in the candidate's interest, not to protect the company."

She can relay feedback from new hires to company HR reps to help them understand "how do we solve problems and resolve biases," she says. "Some companies love the feedback, and they want to work to get better. Others are difficult, and there are excuses why they can't fix current processes."

Chandler says she often opts to stop working with companies in the latter category.

Chandler's 2018 tweet developed into a website (blacktechpipeline.com), an e-mail newsletter, and a business called #BlackTechPipeline. (She was initially working with companies pro bono, but later started charging fees.) The newsletter generously gives visibility and links to other diversity, equity, and inclusion consultants. Chandler has balanced #BlackTechPipeline with a full-time job, and it hasn't always been easy. In April 2019, she quit the job at Genuine after five months "because of how overwhelming it became." She now works for a Florida company, G2i.

"I'm working all the time, pretty much," Chandler says, in addition to home-schooling her 7-year old son. But "this has always been my passion," she says, noting that she grew up in a Cambridge household in which issues of bias and racial equity were always part of the conversation.

The next stage for #BlackTechPipeline is a job-postings board, which Chandler hopes to launch sometime in July. In addition to job listings, each employer will have a profile page that can showcase "an in-depth, transparent description of what it's like to work at that company, with photos of the team," Chandler says, and details on the company's diversity, equity, and inclusion initiatives.

David Delmar Senties, executive director of Resilient Coders, calls Chandler "a huge presence in our alumni community." One of the central accomplishments of her Twitter activity, he says, is that "it's tearing away the idea that Black tech talent just doesn't exist out there, which is a prevailing sentiment that we have to contend with."

Chandler says the work she has been doing has been focused on Black workers in tech nationally and internationally, and that she has only just begun to get connected to local organizations such as the New England Venture Capital Association, which runs a coaching and internship program for minorities called Hack Diversity.

Both Tom Hopcroft, CEO of the Mass Technology Leadership Council, and Chris Anderson, president of the Massachusetts High Technology Council, say they haven't yet met Chandler or heard about her efforts.

"I am like this lone little planet out there — with friends," Chandler says.

It's a positive sign that Boston has a cluster of nonprofits, for-profits, and trade groups working to gather data, create opportunities, and ultimately increase the percentage of Black workers in the tech industry's workforce.

Chandler's #BlackTechPipeline is one of the newer entrants in that cluster; the Massachusetts High Technology Council, founded in 1977, plans to introduce a new diversity initiative Thursday. But we need more connections and collaboration between these entities, so that they're amplifying — rather than duplicating — each others' efforts, and sustaining the focus on this issue over time.

Moderna: 'When the Spotlight Found Them, They Were Ready'

Published in the Boston Globe, December 18, 2020

When people in the Cambridge biotech community talked about Moderna Therapeutics a year ago, it was not as a company that was Most Likely to Succeed.

Moderna was approaching its tenth birthday, and had successfully gotten zero products approved by government regulators for sale anywhere in the world. It had gone public in December 2018, but its stock price hadn't risen much over the course of 2019. There was lots of skepticism that the company's approach — trying to use an injected type of custom-crafted RNA to instruct the body's cells to battle a disease or virus — could work. And some of the company's clinical trials involved making vaccines, a dim corner of the biotech landscape considered "neither sexy nor lucrative," in the words of Michael Gilman, a serial biotech entrepreneur and former Biogen research executive.

"Everybody was scratching their heads about how much this company was worth" — about $6.5 billion at the end of 2019, says John LaMattina, a former head of research and development at Pfizer. The company also hadn't disclosed much data about how its RNA technology worked, which contributed to the perception that Moderna was all hat and no cattle.

Then came the COVID pandemic. Moderna had already been testing vaccines for MERS, another respiratory ailment, and Zika, a mosquito-borne disease. When the company received the genetic sequence of COVID on January 11th from China, it was like a cook who had already prepped the ingredients, pre-heated the oven, and set the table. Moderna had the tools to design new vaccines, and it already had good relationships with the National Institutes of Health, which help Moderna quickly kick-start a clinical trial.

Think about this: Governor Charlie Baker declared a state of emergency in Massachusetts on March 10th, and most of us stopped going into our offices sometime that week. The next week, the very first person got injected with Moderna's experimental vaccine as part of the Phase I trial, which included 45 healthy participants. The federal government rolled out its

Operation Warp Speed initiative in mid-May, to accelerate the development of tests, treatments, and vaccines for COVID. The initiative helped funnel about $4 billion in government funding to Moderna, in exchange for 200 million doses of the vaccine. Moderna is planning to produce vaccines at its production plant in Norwood, as well as at plants owned by partners.

Moderna found itself in "the right place at the right time," says Satish Tadikonda, a managing partner of Avigo Solutions, which consults to the biotech industry. The company was having a hard time using RNA molecules to spur the body to battle diseases, he explains, because they could be toxic at too high a dose, and ineffective at too low a dose. But for a vaccine, a small dose could trigger the production of sufficient antibodies to neutralize any COVID virus they encountered.

Over the summer, Anthony Fauci of the NIH was suggesting that he'd be satisfied if a COVID vaccine was 70 or 75 percent effective at preventing the recipient from getting infected. The results from Moderna and Pfizer, both in the mid-90s, "knocked the socks off everybody," says LaMattina, the ex-Pfizer executive. "For a place like Moderna, this gave them all the credibility they needed for their platform. A year ago, you never would've expected anything this profound or rapid."

Noubar Afeyan is a co-founder of Moderna and the company's chairman; Afeyan also runs Cambridge-based Flagship Pioneering, an incubator for new biotech ventures.

Afefan says that he is used to people expressing skepticism about the companies that Flagship creates. (In the case of Moderna, Afeyan collaborated with a trio of professors from Harvard Medical School and MIT.) "Most breakthrough innovations are descendants of unreasonable starting premises," Afeyan says. "We should not work on things that start life at a proven, understandable, relatable starting point, where some expert tells you it's a good idea."

Moderna's "unreasonable starting premise" was that you could program an RNA molecule, inject it, and spur the body to make its own medicine — in Afeyan's words, "have the patient be their own bioreactor." (A bioreactor is a big, metal vat typically used to produce protein-based drugs.)

Once COVID began spreading, and Moderna decided to develop a vaccine, Afeyan says the company's atmosphere was transformed into "almost a war-like environment. You see these movies where the military moves in, and sets up tents and bridges — it was like that. I've been involved in lots of fairly significant undertakings. This was completely incomparable." As an example, he cites the fact that Moderna's production plant in Norwood was designed to make personalized vaccines to treat cancer "in tiny quantities for a handful of people, which is a totally different infrastructure than making hundreds of millions of doses of a vaccine." Manufacturing staffers worked around the clock to adapt it, Afeyan says.

The company viewed COVID as an opportunity to show the world that technology it had labored over for nearly a decade could do something important. "It didn't hurt that all day long, they heard about people dying, and lives that could be saved," Afeyan says. "That propels people. It gives them a sense of purpose. We were given a big opportunity. Everybody's suffering, and we have a chance to do something about it." (Afeyan is second from the left in the photo; second from the right is Moderna chief executive Stéphane Bancel.)

The Operation Warp Speed initiative certainly put gas in Moderna's tank, and it was run by Moncef Slaoui, a former GlaxoSmithKline executive who had served on Moderna's board. (Slaoui resigned from the board, and later divested of his Moderna stock, after pressure about potential conflicts of interest.) Without Warp Speed, Afeyan says, developing a vaccine "wouldn't have taken five years, like [President] Trump talks about it, but it wouldn't have happened as fast as it did. I don't give credit to the politicians, but to the people who did the work."

Moderna's trajectory over the last year "is truly unbelievable," says Bruce Booth, a partner at the Cambridge venture capital firm Atlas Venture. A company that stock markets valued at $6.5 billion last December is today valued at $56 billion. And it will crank out hundreds of millions of doses of vaccine over the next year. That, Booth says, has "probably never before been seen in our industry."

While vaccines were once considered a backwater, "now we know that rapid vaccine development can literally save civilization," says Gilman. "When the spotlight found [Moderna], they were ready."

· · ·

[Author's Note: This piece originally ran in slightly different form on the *Globe*'s front page, the day after Moderna's vaccine received emergency use authorization from the FDA.]

10. Fun Stuff

Tin Toy

Published in the Boston Globe, December 19, 2010

For many children, the story of a toy begins the moment it is pried from its plastic-and-cardboard prison on Christmas morning. For those who work in the toy industry, though, the story usually starts more than a year earlier.

Take the $15 tin truck made by Schylling Associates Inc. of Rowley, the state's biggest toy company. It's a rolling piggy bank, emblazoned with colorful characters and artwork, and its life began in New York City the February before last. The path it traveled from there to China to Massachusetts to toy stores around the world offers a glimpse into the way today's globalized toy business works. (Photo at right courtesy of Schylling Associates.)

Schylling was founded in 1975 by Jack Schylling, a recent Harvard grad who felt he wasn't cut out for office work. He began selling toys as a street vendor at Quincy Market, and grew Schylling into a 60-person company that includes two of his brothers, David (the chief executive) and Tom (the chief financial officer).

Revenues of the privately held company are in the double-digit millions, Jack Schylling says, and David Schylling says that even through the recent recession they grew, albeit slightly. Schylling's annual product catalog contains 1,000 items from Olivia the pig tea sets to pedal-powered firetrucks to handmade-looking sock monkeys.

Schylling specializes in the kinds of toys that parents and grandparents remember from their own childhoods that didn't require batteries, or come with online instruction manuals.

"They're really the only company that is actively keeping timeless toys available for current and future generations," says Stevanne Auerbach, an author and toy industry specialist known as "Dr. Toy."

In February, nearly every toymaker treks to Manhattan for the American International Toy Fair, which has been held annually for more than a century. More than 10,000 toy buyers from mom-and-pop stores and major chains show up to see what's new. At the 2009 edition, David Horvath and Sun-Min Kim, who created the series of malformed-but-lovable dolls known as Uglydolls, happened to stop by Schylling's booth at the massive trade show.

"We started talking about a line of Uglydoll tin toy products," says Paul Weingard, Schylling's vice president of product development. "Later that summer, we started working on actual product designs."

What attracted Schylling to working with Horvath and Kim, a husband-and-wife duo from California, was that Uglydolls were sold in the same kind of independent toy, book, and clothing stores with which Schylling already had relationships. And Uglydolls, introduced in 2001 as plush toys, hadn't flooded the market with spinoff products.

When toymakers produce toys featuring characters like the Uglydolls, Elmo, or Darth Vader, they typically pay a licensing fee to the creator of the characters that's usually 10 to 12 percent of the wholesale price of each item. With the Uglydoll trucks, Horvath got involved in creating the art for each of the six trucks Schylling would produce. A delivery truck dubbed the Jeero Express, for example, features a snaggle-toothed green driver waving from the cab, and the slogan, "So fast, your package will burst into flames!"

Once the trucks were designed, Schylling put them into its 2010 catalog and showed some early prototypes at this year's toy fair. "It was easy for people to add some Uglydoll items onto an order with us," Jack Schylling says. "They knew that the dolls had been selling well, and they didn't feel it was a big risk to spend $45 to try six trucks."

Schylling sells its products to about 3,000 independent or specialty toy stores, and another 3,000 stores that primarily sell books, clothing, or other products. During the recent recession, company representatives said, about 30 percent of their retail customer base vanished.

Even before this year's toy fair, Schylling had placed an order for about 12,000 tin trucks with a factory near Shanghai. The manufacturing process starts with sheets of tin — containing about 60 percent recycled metal — from Finland. Colorful artwork is printed on the sheets in China. Workers then fold the trucks together using an

array of tools and their hands, sliding tabs into appropriate slots. (Photo courtesy of Schylling Associates.)

"It's more like a traditional workshop, as opposed to a mass-production factory with lots of machinery," says Weingard. "There's no easy way to mechanize it."

Once the first batch of trucks was assembled and packaged in China, it was loaded onto a ship called River Wisdom in Shanghai; sent through the Panama Canal to the Port of Boston; then trucked to Schylling's vast warehouse in Rowley, on the North Shore. When orders from retailers come in, Schylling workers roam the aisles with carts, pulling individual toys from large cardboard boxes stamped "More Fun from Schylling." The orders then go into FedEx trucks.

Sally Lesser, owner of Henry Bear's Park, a three-store local chain, says the tin trucks first showed up in her stores in October. "They're cute little things, and they appeal both to kids and to collectors," she says. When the $15 tin toy is sold at a store like Henry Bear's, the retailer keeps $7.50.

Of Schylling's $7.50, nearly half — about $3.50 — goes to making the toy. Then, you add in shipping costs, marketing materials and trade show travel, warehousing, the sales force, and the possibility that Schylling will be left with unsold merchandise.

"Our net profit could get down into the low single digits," Jack Schylling says. "Toys are a very competitive industry."

Why bother with it? For Weingard, it's about the creative process of coming up with a new idea; shepherding it through design and manufacturing and into toy stores; and ultimately seeing his toys under Christmas trees.

"The process can be really technical, and there are a lot of complex issues that don't have anything to do with play," Weingard says. "But what really makes it exciting is when you remember that these toys are going into kids' hands, and they're going to think of ways to play with them that you've never dreamed of."

DNA-Testing Louie, the Mystery Mutt

Published in the Boston Globe, October 12, 2019

My wife was the first to cave and buy a DNA test to figure out what kind of dog we'd adopted.

Louie came from a shelter in Rhode Island, and every time we'd bring him to the neighborhood dog park, people would ask — or hypothesize — about what breed the little white fluffer might be. Havanese? Malti-poo? Bichon Frise?

"No idea," we'd say. "He's a mutt."

The first canine genome was decoded in 2005, led by researchers at the Broad Institute in Cambridge. (They read the DNA strands of a female boxer named Tasha.) In 2009, Wisdom Health, part of the food and pet care giant Mars Inc., launched the first dog DNA tests for consumers.

A descendant of that product, the Wisdom Panel 4.0, was the one my wife bought, for $85. You collect a saliva sample from the pet, ship it to Wisdom, and wait two to three weeks to get the results by e-mail.

The verdict on Louie, according to Wisdom? 62.5 percent Chihuahua. The remaining 37.5 percent was an even split between miniature poodle, cocker spaniel, and English springer spaniel, Wisdom's website informed us.

After that, when the dog was getting a bath, we might squint a bit and say, "Yeah, his eyes are kind of bulge-y, like a Chihuahua's."

The Wisdom test predicted that Louie's adult weight would be 13 to 24 pounds. Currently, he clocks in at a little more than 14 pounds. Not bad. (Photo at right by Paul Vanecko.)

Then, earlier this year, I bumped into Zenobia Moochhala, who mentioned that she'd recently taken a job as the chief operating officer of a Boston startup called Embark Veterinary. Moochhala was a cofounder of Care.com, the Waltham company that operates a marketplace for nannies and other caregivers.

My first question was, how was Embark different from Wisdom? More accurate, Moochhala told me. While Wisdom analyzes about 1,800 genetic markers, or DNA sequences that we know something about, Embark says it looks at more than 230,000. The company raised $10 million from investors in April, and it pays to be the official dog DNA test of the annual Westminster Kennel Club Show.

A while after our conversation, Embark sent me a complimentary test kit (it retails for $199), and I was again collecting spit from Louie's mouth. His Chihuahua eyes bulged at me skeptically. "This time, it's for work," I explained.

After the sample was sent, I soon started receiving regular updates from Embark via e-mail. The sample was en route to the lab. The sample had been received. DNA processing was about to begin.

In mid-September, the results came in. Embark and Wisdom agreed about some aspects of Louie's heritage, like ancestors that were probably miniature poodles and cocker spaniels. But Embark pegged him at just about one-third Chihuahua, and 36 percent rat terrier. Rat terriers, I learned from the site, were often kept as farm dogs in the early 20th century, "bred for catching barn rats in haystacks."

What was I supposed to tell strangers? Did I have a dog that was mostly rat terrier? Mostly Chihuahua?

It was time to consult the experts. First, I rang up Elinor Karlsson, director of the vertebrate genomics group at the Broad Institute. She told me that "we don't have a way, or haven't agreed on a way, to measure the accuracy of the different tests."

And if the providers of DNA testing haven't (yet) published scientific papers about their analytical processes, "you have to take it with a grain of salt," Karlsson says. "It could be 100 percent right, or not, and you'd have no way of knowing it." (Karlsson confesses that she is a cat person: "Dogs are a fantastic genetic model," she says. "But a cat's purr — you can't really beat that.")

Next, I consulted Jerold Bell, an adjunct professor of genetics at Tufts University's Cummings School of Veterinary Medicine.

"A mixed-breed dog that has been a mixed-breed dog for generations doesn't necessarily have pedigreed parents behind it," Bell says. For that reason, the testing could just say that a portion of a dog's heritage is unknown — but "the consumer wants them to make a call on it," he says.

Even Moochhala at Embark acknowledges that dog DNA testing is "a new enough space" that there isn't yet an objective third-party authority that assesses whose results are the most accurate: "The answer is no, or potentially, not yet," she says.

The other aspect of canine DNA testing is about health issues. Embark's test told me that Louie was free from 14 genetic conditions that were "common in his breed mix" — everything from eye problems to seizure disorders to exercise-induced collapse. There were also more than 100 other health conditions that the test said he is free from, but many of them only afflict specific breeds.

That was good news...

... Until I talked to Karlsson at the Broad, who notes that "there is only a tiny percent of diseases, many very rare, that we can test for."

She and Bell told me that it isn't yet possible to flag dogs that are likely to develop conditions such as heart disease, diabetes, or cancer. Karlsson says that in her conversations with pet owners, when tests came back clear, as mine did, "I discovered that people thought their dog wasn't going to get sick, that they were genetically fine."

Not the case. And Bell worries about DNA tests raising alerts on some serious health conditions, such as a spinal cord disease called degenerative myelopathy, that will cause distress for pet owners — "but in most dogs, [having the gene] does not cause the disease at all," he says.

Bell is a practicing veterinarian in Enfield, Conn., so I asked him what he tells his clients about DNA testing. "There's still a large novelty component to it," he says.

As people in the United States spend increasingly more on their pets — about $75 billion this year, according to the American Pet Products Association, a trade group — the dog DNA testing market seems likely to keep growing. Embark now employs 58 people, Moochhala says, up from 35 at the start of the year.

What am I telling people at the dog park about Louie's background?

"It's complicated. He may be mostly Chihuahua, or mostly rat terrier. But if you get a dog DNA test done, I'd recommend you do just one."

Four Centuries of Massachusetts Innovation: The Quiz

Published in the Boston Globe, May 26, 2016

When visitors to Boston arrive on a flight from Shanghai, Dubai, or Rome, they aren't all coming here to visit Cheers or Old Ironsides. Rather, Massachusetts Port Authority chief executive Tom Glynn says, many of them are bringing kids to college, attending robotics conferences, or meeting with biotech firms.

So in addition to being known for the Shot Heard 'Round the World, Glynn wants to make sure Boston burnishes its rep as a place that regularly produces societal, scientific, and technical breakthroughs that change the world.

This summer, Logan will debut a new link between Terminal E, where all those international flights pull in, with the busy Terminal C, home to JetBlue. And part of the link is a major display on four centuries of innovation in Massachusetts. Says Glynn, "We have tons of posters about the past at the airport. This is a chance to try something different." (The exhibit was created by Bob Krim of Framingham State University and Janey Bishoff of Bishoff Communications.)

I went to see the exhibit, took lots of notes, and came up with this quiz based on some of the innovations it highlights. Easier questions first; answer key at the end.

1. When Robin Chase and Antje Danielsen started _____ in Cambridge in 2000, it marked the start of the "sharing economy" trend that led to companies like Lyft and Airbnb. In 2013, the company was acquired by Avis for $500 million.

2. Few people know that _____ University was publicly funded for the first 200 years of its existence. Its faculty have won more Nobel prizes than any other single school.

3. Percy Spencer, the inventor of the _____ ____, now a common appliance, developed it after noticing that a magnetron device had melted a chocolate bar in his pocket. His next experiment entailed seeing what happened when popcorn was placed near the magnetron.

4. When James Naismith invented the game of "Basket Ball" in Springfield, players tried to toss a _____ ball into hoops made from peach baskets.

5. A _____ built in East Boston, the Flying Cloud, made it from New York to San Francisco in a speedy 89 days. Its record stood for more than 100 years.

6. Sales of the $300 _____ machine invented by Elias Howe of Cambridge didn't immediately take off — even after Howe challenged five seamstresses to a competition and finished more work than all of them.

7. Launched in 2004, _____ attracted 1,200 college students as users in its first 24 hours.

8. A Belmont dentist (and Harvard University prof) named George Franklin Grant patented the golf ___ in 1899 because he didn't like getting his hands dirty.

9. In 1919, one of the country's first female industrial chemists, Louise Giblin of Dorchester, contributed to the development of _____ as a breast milk substitute for infants. It can still be found on store shelves today.

10. Harvey Ball created what you might call the original emoji, the _____ ____, in 1963 to help raise employee morale at the State Mutual Life Assurance Co. in Worcester, following a series of difficult mergers and acquisitions. He was paid $45 for his icon, which was never copyrighted.

11. Ronald Herrick gave his identical twin, Richard, a _____ in 1954, marking the first successful human organ transplant. The operation was done by a team led by Joseph Murray at the Brigham.

12. The first liquid-fuel rocket was launched from an Auburn farm in 1926, reaching 141 feet in height. Its inventor, _____ _____, had studied at Worcester Polytechnic Institute before becoming a physics professor at Clark University.

13. William Morton and John Collins Warren performed the first operation on a patient who'd been anesthetized in 1846, using a surgical amphitheater atop _____ _____ _____.

14. Rugged robots made by MIT spin-out _____ have gathered images and data from caves in Afghanistan, the wreckage of Ground Zero, and the earthquake-damaged Fukushima Daiichi nuclear reactor in Japan.

15. After being asked by his young daughter why she couldn't see the photographs he'd just taken, _____ ____ invented instant photography.

16. Inventor _____ _____ sold his children's textbooks and spent time in debtor's prison to fund his research into rubber, eventually developing the vulcanization process that made the material more durable and better able to withstand temperature extremes.

17. A Harvard Business School student named Dan Bricklin came up with the idea to digitize the paper spreadsheets he had to use in classes. The end result was an Excel predecessor called _____, which helped persuade thousands of businesses to purchase personal computers.

18. When someone suggests, "Give away the razor, but sell the blades," they're referring to a business model created by ____ ____ _____. He sold 51 razors and 168 blades in 1903, his first year of production. By 1915, razor sales had hit 450,000, and blade sales had surpassed 70 million.

19. Massachusetts was the first state in the United States to educate students in a public _____ (1635), establish a public ____ (1643), abolish _____ (1783), build a _____ to reduce downtown gridlock (1897), and legalize ___ _____ (2003).

20. The telephone was invented in an "incubator" building owned by Charles Williams Jr. near Government Center in Boston. The first telephone line ran from Williams' office in that building to his residence in nearby _____. His phone numbers? 1 and 2.

Answers: 1. Zipcar 2. Harvard 3. Microwave 4. Soccer 5. Clipper Ship 6. Sewing 7. Facebook 8. tee 9. Similac 10. Smiley face 11. kidney 12. Robert Goddard 13. Massachusetts General Hospital 14. iRobot 15. Edwin Land 16. Charles Goodyear 17. VisiCalc 18. King Camp Gillette 19. school, park, slavery, subway, gay marriage 20. Somerville.

A Freedom Trail for Innovators

Published in the Boston Globe, July 7, 2013

If you live in Greater Boston, one thing is certain: You have walked the Freedom Trail a few too many times.

So I'm proposing a different kind of walk through Boston and Cambridge: an Innovation Trail that focuses on the past, present, and future of innovation here. We'll always have Paul Revere's place and Old Ironsides, but what about the incubator where Thomas Edison and Alexander Graham Bell tinkered or the world's only "Walk of Fame" for entrepreneurs?

The Innovation Trail picks up just a few years after the Freedom Trail leaves off: The newest spot on the old trail is the Bunker Hill Monument, built in 1842. The oldest stop on this new trail is the Ether Dome at Massachusetts General Hospital, where surgical anesthesia was first demonstrated successfully in 1846.

The Freedom Trail was essentially invented by a newspaper columnist in 1951, who said it could be rolled out with just "a few dollars and a bucket of paint." In 2013, the paint isn't necessary. I created a digital map of this new trail (https://bit.ly/inno-trail), and shot several videos with people like Bob Krim of Framingham State University; Steve Vinter, who runs Google's Cambridge office; and Doug Williams, head of research and development at Biogen Idec. You can see the videos at https://vimeo.com/showcase/6669001.

1. 30 School Street, Boston African-American draftsman and inventor Lewis Latimer once worked here. He helped Alexander Graham Bell create the drawings used for the telephone's patent filing and later worked with Thomas Edison to extend the useful life of the light bulb.

2. Corner of Court and Washington streets, Boston, near the Old State House Boston's most historic sewer. Few people remember that Edison began his career in Boston. He used a sewer at this intersection to dispose of explosive chemicals used in his lab, pouring them into sarsaparilla bottles and lowering them down.

3. Outside the JFK Federal Building, Cambridge Street, Boston Edison and Graham Bell once rented lab space in the same building here, where inventors cultivated ideas related to the new field of telecommunications. (The building no longer stands, but look for a pedestal commemorating it.)

4. 55 Fruit Street, Boston Inside the Bulfinch Building at Massachusetts General Hospital is a top-floor operating theater known as the Ether Dome. In 1846, surgeon John Collins Warren excised a tumor from the neck of a patient who had been knocked out using ether — the first successful demonstration of anesthesia. (You can go in as long there's not a lecture.)

5. 2 North Grove Street, Boston Showcasing the evolution of medicine, Mass General's Museum of Medical History and Innovation opened in 2012. It's free, open weekdays only, 9 a.m. to 5 p.m.

6. 12 Lime Street, Boston The former home of Harvard Business School professor Georges Doriot. Doriot started what is regarded as the first venture capital firm, Boston-based American Research and Development. Among its investments: Digital Equipment Corp., which turned the firm's $70,000 investment into more than $350 million. (This is a private home now owned by the founder of Plymouth Rock Assurance; it's not open to the public.)

7. One Broadway and 101 Main Street, Cambridge The two buildings known as the Cambridge Innovation Center may be home to a denser collection of start-up and venture capital firms than anywhere on the planet. The center, founded in 1999, also served as the first Massachusetts home for tech giants Google and Amazon. (At right, one of Amazon's early offices in Cambridge.)

8. One Memorial Drive, Cambridge This is one of two large Microsoft facilities in Kendall Square, housing a research team as well as product development and regional sales.

9. 50 Memorial Drive, Cambridge, MIT Sloan School of Management Founded in 1914, the Massachusetts Institute of Technology business school was recently ranked in the top five in the country, just behind the Wharton School at the University of Pennsylvania. Its alumni have started or run companies like Ford, Zipcar, Hewlett-Packard, Boeing, and Genentech.

10. 1 Amherst Street, Cambridge MIT's Trust Center for Entrepreneurship is where student entrepreneurs learn startup skills and work on their own ventures, using free office space. MIT's living alumni have founded more than 25,000 companies that employ more than three million people.

11. 75 Amherst Street, Cambridge The Media Lab at MIT has spawned products like Lego's Mindstorms robotics kit, the iWalk prosthetic foot, and the video game "Rock Band." A first-floor exhibition space, showcasing the work of professors and students, is open to the public. (At right, Media Lab student Natan Linder demonstrates an augmented reality projector in 2011. Linder was later a founder of two companies: Formlabs and Tulip.)

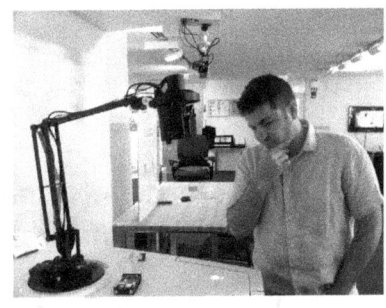

12. 500 Kendall Street, Cambridge Founded in 1981 with a focus on treating extremely rare diseases, Genzyme was part of the first wave of biotechnology companies. It was acquired by France's Sanofi in 2011. This was the first LEED platinum-certified office buildings of its size in the US.

13. Outside the Kendall Square Marriott, Cambridge (Main Street side, near the Kendall T stop) Created in 2011, the Entrepreneur Walk of Fame recognizes founders like Steve Jobs of Apple and Mitch Kapor of Lotus Development Corp.

14. **5 Cambridge Center, Cambridge** Google's Cambridge office. Google developed key parts of its Android mobile operating system in Kendall Square. In 2011 the company paid $700 million for ITA Software, a Cambridge start-up specializing in airfare search.  (The publicly-accessible Kendall Square Rooftop Garden, reopening in 2022, gives you a glimpse into the Google offices, if you don't have a friend who works there and can get you in to sample the high-quality free cafeteria food. At right, a library-like workspace inside the Google office.)

15. **145 Broadway, Cambridge** Founded in 1998 by MIT students and a professor, Akamai Technologies uses 127,000 servers around the world to help customers speed delivery of digital content like Web pages and videos.

16. **225 Binney Street, Cambridge** Biogen Idec's major products treat multiple sclerosis. The company was started in 1978, and two of its founders, Walter Gilbert and Phillip Sharp, have won Nobel Prizes.

17. **415 Main Street, Cambridge** The DNAtrium at the Broad Institute offers free, interactive exhibits exploring insights into human biology, and how they lead to treatments.

18. **500 Main Street Cambridge** MIT's Koch Institute for Integrative Cancer Research works on new approaches to treating cancer, like nanoscale "smart bombs" that can find and destroy tumors with fewer side effects.

19. **32 Vassar Street, Cambridge** Inside the Stata Center at MIT are labs focused on computer science, artificial intelligence, and robotics (they gave birth to iRobot Corp.), and a small, ground-floor exhibit about student "hacks," or pranks, through the years. The creator of the World Wide Web, Tim Berners-Lee, works here. The building is located on the site of what had been known as the Rad Lab, where half of the radar systems deployed by the US military during World War II were designed.

20. 700 Main Street, Cambridge This building was once the site of the first plant making passenger railroad cars in the US, Kimball & Davenport. (Note the railroad tracks embedded above some of the windows.) Later, it was used as part of the first "long distance" phone call, from Boston to Cambridge, and as Edwin Land's private research lab when he ran Polaroid. It's now an incubator for biotech startups called LabCentral.

21. 250 Massachusetts Ave., Cambridge One of Cambridge's best examples of architectural reuse: The former NECCO candy factory is now the Novartis Institutes for Biomedical Research, the main research operation for the Swiss pharmaceutical company. (Note the Wonka-esque glass elevators. A water tower atop the building was once painted to resemble a roll of Necco wafers; it now features a DNA design.) For bonus points, drop by the last still-operating candy factory in Cambridge, owned by Tootsie Roll Industries, at 810 Main Street — take a sniff to see if they're working, but don't expect to see much.

22. 265 Massachusetts Ave., Cambridge Open daily, The MIT Museum showcases technologies from the slide rule to expressive robots, as well as archives from Polaroid Corp., founded a few blocks away. It's also home to the world's biggest collection of holograms. (Note: the MIT Museum is planning a move to Kendall Square in 2022.)

The Freedom Trail peters out in Charlestown, far from an MBTA stop. The Innovation Trail is more considerate: You end up just about three blocks from the Central Square T station. And even closer are two popular hangouts for MIT smarties and the startup set: Miracle of Science, for those who'd like a beer, or Flour Bakery, if you'd like cookies, meringues, and coffee.

About the Author

Scott Kirsner was part of the team that created Boston.com, the Boston *Globe*'s first website, in 1995. He has spent more than two decades as a business journalist writing for the Boston *Globe*, *Wired*, *Fast Company*, *Variety*, *The New York Times*, *BusinessWeek* and other publications.

His focus on how innovations that matter get introduced to the world has taken him to the White House, the Sundance Film Festival, the United Nations, and the headquarters of Google, Amazon, Disney, iRobot, General Motors, and many other companies. Scott is the author of several books, including *Fans, Friends, and Followers*, about the revolution in how artists and creators can use digital tools to further their careers, and *Inventing the Movies*, which explores the challenge of bringing new ideas to a century-old, change-resistant industry: Hollywood.

Scott was among the founders of the Nantucket Conference and the Convergence Forum, two annual events that bring together investors and entrepreneurs in tech and biotech, respectively. In 2013, he co-founded a media and events company, Innovation Leader, which focuses on how new products and services are created inside Global 1000-scale organizations.

He lives in Brookline, Mass. with his wife, Amy Traverso, two cats, one dog who has been DNA-tested twice, and one teenager. You can follow him on Twitter: @ScottKirsner.

. . .

[**P.S.** If you enjoyed *Innovation Economy*, please add your rating or review to the book's page on Amazon.com: http://bit.ly/innoeco-amazon.]

www.ingramcontent.com/pod-product-compliance
Lightning Source LLC
Chambersburg PA
CBHW060829220526
45466CB00003B/1035